Cosmopolitan Sexuality

Cosmopolitan Sexuality articulates the ethnographic and anthropological studies of varied embodied projects in Indian metropolises. With particular reference to the city of Bombay, the book draws evidences of gendered representations – their desires, appeal and aspirations to be and to express their sense of self. The book attempts to establish arguments to a deconstructive notion of any fixation of identity categories and build a robust and complex understanding of sexual experiences, love, emotions and interpersonal relationships – an unusual way of local as well as global patterns that are culturally scathed in the contemporary new India.

The book is relevant to contemporary embodiment studies – the invasive means of desiring corporeal reconstruction on one hand, and dress, ornamentation and makeup on the other. Transgressive politics are discursively and materially constructed to their everydayness and their unique ways of re-representation. Adding to ethnographies on civil society, non-governmental organizations (NGOs) and participatory research, 'health' is viewed in new dynamics of shared knowledges and communicative practices. This has enabled the building of fresh arguments around community and public health, with new visions of the anthropologies of empowerment.

Ahonaa Roy is Associate Professor of Sociology and Social Anthropology at the Indian Institute of Technology, Bombay, India, and Research Associate at the University of Pretoria, South Africa. She is also a Tata Fellow at the Centre of South Asian Studies, University of Cambridge (2022). She has published widely on sexuality and sexual health, social medicine, sexuality studies, masculinity studies, embodiment and body studies, and gender and subaltern studies. She edited the volume *Gender, Sexuality Decolonization: South Asia in the World Perspective* (2020).

Cosmopolitan Sexuality

Gender, Embodiments, Biopolitics in India

Ahonaa Roy

CAMBRIDGE
UNIVERSITY PRESS

University Printing House, Cambridge CB2 8BS, United Kingdom

One Liberty Plaza, 20th Floor, New York, NY 10006, USA

477 Williamstown Road, Port Melbourne, vic 3207, Australia

314 to 321, 3rd Floor, Plot No.3, Splendor Forum, Jasola District Centre, New Delhi 110025, India

103 Penang Road, #05–06/07, Visioncrest Commercial, Singapore 238467

Cambridge University Press is part of the University of Cambridge.

It furthers the University's mission by disseminating knowledge in the pursuit of education, learning and research at the highest international levels of excellence.

www.cambridge.org
Information on this title: www.cambridge.org/9781108490443

First published 2022

Printed in India by Thomson Press India Ltd.

A catalogue record for this publication is available from the British Library

ISBN 978-1-108-49044-3 Hardback

To my parents, Pronab Roy and Dipa Neogy-Roy

Contents

Figures

Abbreviations

ART	antiretroviral therapy
BAS	Bombay Alternative Sexualities
CBO	community-based organization
GID	gender identity disorder
GRS	gender reassignment surgery
HIV/AIDS	human immunodeficiency virus/acquired immunodeficiency syndrome
HRT	hormone replacement therapy
INGO	international non-governmental organization
LFW	Lakmé Fashion Week
LGBT	lesbian, gay, bisexual, transgender
MCGM	Municipal Corporation of Greater Mumbai
MDACS	Mumbai Districts AIDS Control Society
NGO	non-governmental organization
PFLAG	Parents, Families and Friends of Lesbians and Gays
STI	sexually transmitted infection

Acknowledgements

I have accrued many debts over the course of writing this book from unfailing love and intellectual and inspirational support. I am grateful for it all. Three individuals for whom I have the deepest appreciation are my doctoral supervisor, Andrea Cornwall, and Ashok Alexander and Arnab Gupta from Bill & Melinda Gates Foundation, New Delhi, for the doctoral grant. This project is more than a book; it is an intellectual and personal journey deeply entrenched in livability and personal and political engagements, and in my geographical (dis)location from Calcutta to London, leading to an exhilarating experience. I evolved through many periods of self-doubt and apprehensions that provoked me to walk the long, unending crossroads to muster self-belief.

This book is the culmination of my doctoral research. Many people have generously invested their time and effort in reading, editing or discussing the work in various capacities. Filippo Osella, Geert de Neve, Paul Boyce, Katy Gardner, Vinita Damodaran, Susan Jolly, Caroline Osella, Mark Johnson, Margaret Sleeboom-Faulkner, Atreyee Sen and Ann Whitehead – their anthropological conversations and teachings at the University of Sussex, Brighton, and beyond and their acute insights stoked the flames of my love for anthropology. Also, not to forget, my formative years in academic training under the wing of Sujata Patel, R. Raj Rao and late Sharmila Rege in Pune are some of the best times that I am supremely indebted to.

I am also deeply grateful to Raewyn Connell for her critical appreciation for this work. Her intellectual vivacity has shepherded the meticulous re-reading and rewriting of a few parts of this work.

My editors at Cambridge University Press – Qudsiya Ahmed, Sohini Ghosh and Priyanka Das – have been a delight to work with. They heroically marshalled a horde of unruly passages into readability with meticulous editing and proofreading.

This book would not have been possible without the Tata Trusts' fellowship grant to the University of Cambridge for seven months. Thus, I am profoundly indebted to T. Ravishankar, Ruksana Savaksha, Percis Elavia, Vanajakshi Gowda and Srinath Narasimhan. Special thanks also go to Thomas Phillip at the Partners in Development Initiative, New Delhi, for my doctoral fieldwork grant.

I am further grateful for the generous intellectual community in Cambridge and the South Asia Centre there which helped cultivate valuable intellectual support and encouragement to finish this work. My thanks are due to Shailaja Fennell, Sujit Sivasundaram, Joya Chatterjee, Samita Sen, Jaideep Prabhu, Minna and Malini Desai.

The blend of academic and political engagement at Sussex, London, Cambridge, Bombay, Pretoria and beyond are courtesy of Anna Porroche Escudero, Vasu Reddy, Sudeshan Reddy, Rohee Dasgupta, Surya Monro, Caroline Wilson, Samantha Syiem-Clark, Shannon Phillip, Michael Edwards, Rubina Jesani, Apratim Choudhary, Jawad Quereshi, Cory Walia, Vaneesh Bharija and Kiran Umap. I acknowledge their warmth and kindness with special thanks.

This note of acknowledgement would be incomplete without expressing my deepest gratitude to my research respondents whose lived experiences strengthened my resolve to do justice to their life-narratives through this book.

In addition, I extend my heartfelt gratitude to my colleagues at the Indian Institute of Technology (IIT), Bombay – N. C, Narayanan, Siby George, K. N. Narayanan, C. Sebastian, Kushal Deb, Shishir K. Jha, Satish Agniotri, Surajit Bhattacharyya, D. Parthasarathy and Suddhaseel Sen. I thank my students in Delhi and at the IIT Bombay, who shaped my thoughts and accompanied me on the path of teaching–learning and critical thinking. I cannot overstate the value of the intellectual buoyance, enthusiasm and support of Devang Khakkar and Subasis Chaudhuri, the directors at the IIT Bombay. I received immense encouragement from them during their respective tenures to complete this work.

Warm thanks are due to colleagues and friends across the United States, Europe and Australia – John Schneider, Sanjay Srivastava, Ahmed Afjal, Sara Shroff, Kuntala Lahiri-Dutt, Laura Merla, Nilanjan Sarkar, Srimati Basu, Svati P. Shah, Abhijit Das, Venkatesh Srinivasan, Noor Abu Asab and

Gayatri Gopinath. Unforgettably rewarding insights and generosity from Asis Nandy, Shiv Visvanathan, Nandini Sundar, Nivedita Menon, Shohini Ghosh and Satish Deshpande have contributed to my work during the days of my teaching stint in Delhi.

My marvelous and ever-so-loving cousins, Madhumita Gupta, Durba Roy-Gupta and Nandini Neogy, and my aunts Alo Pal and Mridula Choudhury, will always have a special place in my heart for their affection. My uncles Deb Roy and Manas M. Neogy and my aunt Sati Roy taught me to love books. My late grandmothers, Gauri Dasgupta and Pratibha Neogy, whose feminism in principle and praxis as first-generation feminists from Calcutta and as educators whetted my appetite for learning.

Finally, I extended my thanks to my parents, Pronab Roy and Dipa Neogy-Roy, to whom I owe immense debt now and always.

1

Introduction

میں نے مرد کی عائد کردہ پابندیوں کو قبول نہیں کیا، لیکن
اُن پابندیوں کو قبول کیا جو میرے ذہن نے مجھ پہ عائد کی ہیں ...
میں سمجھتی ہوں کہ بہتر ہے کہ اِسے بین السطور کہا جائے زیادہ مناسب ہے
کیونکہ رمز و کنایہ بھی تو شاعری کا حُسن ہے۔

I did not accept the restrictions imposed by men but accepted the
restrictions that my mind imposed on me.

I think it is more appropriate to call it interlinear because symbolism
is also the beauty of poetry.

—Ada Jafri (from Mahmood 2008)

OPENING SCENE

One afternoon, as I walked down the lanes of Malvani slum, Bombay, I
noticed that inside the Sakhiyani office (a community-based organization
[CBO] for *hijras*) there were *hijras* shrieking with laughter. When I peeped
in, I saw a group of ten *hijras* sitting inside. They had taken off their upper
garments, and they were comparing the size of their breasts and teasing each
other by recalling incidents when their *panthis* (boyfriends or clients) had
complimented them on their breasts. They had developed their breasts by
consuming or injecting female hormones in their body. Some had undergone

silicone breast implant surgery. And some elderly *hijra*s had worn tight-fitted brassieres and enhanced and accentuated the shape of their breasts by placing something inside or on the sides.

Geeta, who is a *hijra* in her late thirties had undergone silicone implant surgery at a state-owned hospital in Bombay. That afternoon she showed her breasts to the other *hijra*s and claimed that her breasts were the biggest amongst those of her fellow *hijra*s. She also claimed that she had consumed hormone tablets as well as undergone breast implant surgery. According to her, she was blessed with a 'double effect'. Her boyfriend 'Michael' was happy with her breasts and told her he would marry her. In response, she clapped her hands (in the *hijra* way, a sign of *hijra*-authentication to mark their identity and evoke a sense of *hijra* masculinity) and mocked him for the marriage proposal. She then laughed heartily.

Geeta is the head of the Sakhiyani office, the CBO in the slum that works on promoting the sexual health of *hijra*s. She has rented a small room in the slum, and appointed staff to manage her book-keeping and conduct outreach work (such as sexual-health awareness) in the slum. Unlike other young *hijra*s who go for sex-work in the evenings or elderly *hijra*s who go to *badhai* events (offering blessings at people's homes on occasions of marriage or child birth), Geeta earns her living quite satisfactorily from the revenue generated at the Sakhiyani office. According to Geeta, she developed her breasts to look good, to enhance the femininity of her body. But sometimes, unknown to her boyfriend, she engages in sexual relationships with other men. She says that *hijra*s cannot remain happy with just one man.

Dhamni ('breasts' in the *hijra* language) is a popular topic for discourse amongst all the *hijra*s in Bombay. They are obsessed with the development of their breasts. And their fixation with developing big breasts is so strong that to save money they sometimes cut back on other expenses like food and house rent. Not only young *hijra*s, but elderly *hijra*s also sometimes desire to develop their breasts. According to them, they do not want to develop breasts to attract men, but 'breasts' would make their body more feminine and help them feel 'like a woman'. The *hijra*s are not women, and they do not want to 'become' women. In fact, they laughed at and mocked some young *hijra*s who behaved like women, in the sense of not clapping their hands in a *hijra*-like manner, and wanted to get married to a man. But for the young *hijra*s the development of breasts is exciting. They go to each other's homes in Malvani slum or elsewhere in Bombay to gather knowledge about how they can enhance their breasts.

Geeta discouraged her *hijra-chela*s (disciples) from undergoing these sorts of breast development. She told them that these processes may prove to threaten their lives. Some of the *hijra*s believed what she said, but others did not. Among those who did not believe her were her office accountants, Chappi and Priya. These *hijra*s were high-school graduates and had joined the *hijra* community after completing their studies. Unlike other *hijra*s who have little or no education, Chappi and Priya challenged Geeta's claims about the impact of breast development and consulted the local doctor. When they found that Geeta's statement was incorrect, they informed the other *hijra*s in the slum. In fact, Geeta had made this statement to discourage other *hijra*s in the slum from breast enhancement. She felt that if her peers started developing their breasts, then men, women and other *hijra*s in the slum would give her less attention. Moreover, she feared that Michael, her boyfriend, might also transfer his attentions onto other *hijra*s who might develop bigger breasts than her. Her emotional insecurity was so strong that she asked clinics and drug stores in the slum not to release any female hormone tablets or injections to any *hijra*s. This caused confusion and disagreements between Geeta and other *hijra*s in the slum.

Geeta has never gone out for *pan*, or sex work. But on some evenings, she has assisted her *hijra-chela*s to get dressed. Some of them who have developed breasts through hormonal supplements feel a sense of insecurity about the size of their breasts. But those *hijra*s who have undergone silicone implants do not have to shape their breasts before going out for sex work. It is important to note that every *hijra* house has a long mirror which is regarded as an essential object for daily survival. A mirror in the front room of one's house, beside which are laid out accessories like bangles, necklaces, jewellery and other ornaments, marks a fundamental part of their life. The mirror for them symbolizes a deity which is adorned with dazzling lights, small and big. Whenever they dress, or even when they critically appraise themselves in the mirror, the lights around it are switched on. They look at their reflections countless times – at their appearance, improvements in their looks and the development of their breasts. The focus of their dressing is to highlight their breasts. According to them, men are obsessed with large breasts; the more they enhance them, the more they can entice men. Also, around their mirror, they usually stick poster-photographs of Bollywood actresses whom they find most attractive. When asked about these, they reply that they aspire to be as feminine and beautiful as these actresses.

When dressing themselves, *hijra*s stand in front of their mirror naked. They first put on their brassiere, consciously choosing a size smaller than their own, to help make their breasts appear larger and their cleavage look 'sexy'. After putting on their brassiere, they insert pieces of cloth under their breasts so as to create a rounded shape. Thereafter they put on 'cup-shaped concave pads' to make their breasts look larger and well-shaped. They then dress in Western clothes like tops, denim pants and high-heeled shoes. Sometimes, if they have shaved their legs, they prefer to wear a skirt. They believe that their *panthi*s would prefer to see their 'saaxy' (sexy) legs which would add to their income, and that exposing the body and skin in addition to enhancing their breasts is very 'Western', symbolizing high-value *hijra* prostitutes. They prefer to keep their hair long and wear a ribbon shaped like a rose or sunflower. Their application of cosmetics is heavy and bold, including red glossy lipstick, thick foundation and thickly applied eye make-up. This flamboyant clothing and style creates an image in the public eye of flashy '*hijra* prostitutes'. After dressing, they look in the mirror from different angles – front, side and back – which brings them a sense of satisfaction and a smirk on their face, indicating perhaps their thoughts of how beautiful they look and how many *panthi*s or men they would be able to entice.

THE ANTHROPOLOGY OF BELONGING

The account narrated previously features an extensive mobility, curiosity and a reflexive ability to locate a sense of embodying sentiments of the contemporary *hijra* subculture in the city of Bombay, which evokes a bio-political interplay and embodied practices of breast development and consumption of hormonal supplements that firmly anchor to an expression of corporeal aesthetics strongly desired by the *hijra*s. This emerging cosmopolitan consciousness creates a feeling of excitement and a desire of being 'feminine' with an implicit gendering. It attests to the way in which commodity and consumption infuse in prefixing the legitimacy of art and gendered contouring. Michel Foucault's (1976 [2008]) reflection on bio-politics mediates the strange way that 'life' and 'law' interrelate in modern politics. On further reckoning, Foucault's 'biopower' in the context of modernity observes the body through new regimes of power–knowledge, eluding norms and demands by judicial forms to protect life. In fact, the operation of 'law' and 'governmentality' crosses the boundaries of politics – inciting social hierarchization of the body's regulation (Campbell and Sitze 2013: 49).[1]

Hormones and the development of breasts in *hijra*s further reinforce a corporeal indication of a new concept of race that tends to revitalize the biologism of the body in a controlled and hierarchized political re-fixation. In other words, sexualization has been able to develop an artificial unity of the specific anatomical elements: the breasts that function to conduct gendered symbolism on the one hand and an erotic zone of pleasure on the other. Further, the body's intelligibility formulates a radical expenditure of the boundaries of the body's surface that qualifies the constitution of 'anatomo-politics' (Lemke 2010). Addressing these new forms of social life within the *hijra* subculture creates the condition for a new recognition that deeply delves into the intersection of body and agency, politics and resistance. Further, the erotic comprehension of their body as seen as an experience of desire figures a strong logic of their feminine being. Upon reinterpreting *hijra* embodiment, gendered meanings offer a socially specific representation of their localized sexuality. That being said, the multiple positions of the *hijra*s in city-spaces mark their lived-experience, material conditions and their economic and political status so as to assert their subjectivity which is beyond cultural specificity.

The *hijra*s in Bombay move literally and symbolically beyond their traditional way of life (kinship-centric), involving themselves with the commodity world of consumption and beautification. Fashion therefore becomes a cosmopolitan legitimacy and a democratic ideal that arguably develops within a specific nexus of the sexed condition of the primordial unity of the material body to that of the social perceptibility that is attuned to desire. Desire is transcendental. It can break open history, politics and meaning to a state of 'becoming' (Biehl and Locke 2017: 16–17). The Deleuzian inscription (Smith 2007) helps here to unveil the ways in which the *hijra*s struggle to articulate desire, suffering and their own sense of knowledge to immerse themselves in a particular configuration and embody cultural representation to build their individual subjectivity (Biehl, Good and Kleinman 2007). Saba Mahmood's (2005) interpretation of 'desire', as not opposed to resistance, conceives desire as a capacity for action made possible by concrete historically specific relations. 'Desire' linked to 'intentionality' brings forth different modalities of agency (see also Ortner 2006). What makes this a different analytical perspective on agency is that it escapes the binary of resistance–subordination, further raising questions of resignification of norms and having implications on the possibilities of narratives and new experiences. In this sense, the analytics of feminization within the *hijra*s crafts the endeavour of anthropology to understand the emergent, the open, the polysemic and the uncertain. The dynamic narrative processes are derived from the embodied encounters in one's lived experience. Desire therefore is an enunciated effect of the subjects' position that could expand and challenge the dominant theories of (bio)power and structural violence. Stating this from a subaltern position – 'desire' is inseparable from 'becoming'. It is *not* an agency or determination as restricting a structuration, if social and subjective. Instead, it is an articulation of lives, the voices of individuals, which awakens with a dimension of experience.

In this book, the reality reference to the body and its embodied project critiques foundationalism and addresses gender as a discursive construct or an effect produced at the level of the body (Balsamo 1996). The system of differentiation considers an openness that moves beyond the sterile debate of the external, that is, the social perception of gender. Instead, this embodiment is sensed with a subjective experience of desire that further involves an ontological condition. Borrowing from James Mensch (2020), my claim to embodiment grasps the Kantian refutation of 'idealism': the openness of our 'selfhood' involving the ecstatic quality of feeling that makes the dimensions of experience relate how consciousness is shaped. In other words, Kantian transcendence and 'selfhood' is a 'sense', a subject of experience that involves the 'space' in which the body is situated – a relation in its own consciousness of the body's self-affirmation with spatial relations. Thus, the book also talks about, in addition to *hijra*s, the varied gendered embodiments of gender transgressors which is not just 'the flesh'. Embodiment as evoked is the frame of consciousness building a gender(ed) customization of the body's aesthetics – the feminine value but not female, but of course one that mediates through the intersection of the socially available gender-meaning. Additionally, the re-signification is portrayed in a multitude of embodied forms which further conveys the non-boundaries of the already-given embodied strategies.

To note further, the embodiment is not only a belonging, but a sense of 'becoming'. In sum, it is a cultural and corporeal dialogue that the gendering of bodies is related to a fantasy of being feminine, or 'becoming' a woman. The gendered discursivity conceives an account of a transgressive process to a state of a 'metaphysical rebel' (Jenks 2003). Relating further, 'rebel' to the pure negation of the rule limits boundaries of the already existing subcultural tradition, to a dynamic force of cultural reproduction, breaking through and reaffirming a new cultural order. The point to investigate is the real presence of these corporeal transgressions, which rest on the features of modernity accelerating desire. Modernity's self-determination of the will and unconstrained acts act on their desires. These transgressive modes account for an internally determined willing that questions the institutionalized authority of the gender structure – a clandestine attack claiming democratic social change. Charles Tilly's 'dispersed resistance' orchestrates 'transgression' as a distinct form of resistance that performs politics and life with new analytics of efficacy (Scott 1992: 8–9).

Translating the meaning of transgression in this book inspires two important debates. First, transgressions in the form of resistance that co-opt identity play by various means of protest by gendered representations; or, in other words, the varied ritualistic performances, both social and political, to violate hierarchies, like the Urs carnival in Ajmer, queer pride rallies, World AIDS Day in Bombay – emphasizing the spatiality or the reification of space to a development of networks and spatial dynamics, creating discursively generated culture-specific ideas. This can be further related to Saskia Sassen's (2008) idea of 'global mobility and the new organization of space', showing alliances in a peculiar involvement with the regional, national and global manner of regulation (see also Sassen 2012). Such transcendences further break the dualist thought with a critical attention to how the material reference to spaces and human acts is 'relationally ordered' to an integrating matrix of 'action' (Linklater and Mennell 2010). In other words, transgressions and space-making are organized around the performance of action. In the words of Dieter Lapple (2001), transgression categorically relates to the meaning of 'action', prefiguring the organized ways to create an epistemological idea of space within the purview of freedom that further creates spatial indeterminacy. This can be taken further to the immanent relationship of space and action, demonstrating an integrated sense of belonging as composing a relational arrangement of material properties within relational mobility of corporeal belonging (Merriman 2012). Again, these sorts of 'play or inversion', or a sort of carnivalesque resistance with either fun or protests, motivates a grotesque discourse violating the dominant one. These sorts of representation also enact the power of transgression to critique the dominant ideological content and to challenge the interpretive frames.[2]

Second, transcendence is an intersubjective experience that struggles to negotiate the subjective capacity of the desiring subject within a discursive position. This determining autonomous self in terms of the Kantian strategic move is truly 'free' only by virtue of 'an activity'. Therefore, philosophy's deeper determination is to arrive at an insight that Georg Wilhelm Friedrich Hegel and Friedrich Wilhelm Nietzsche call 'internally determined by her own willing' (Gemes and Janaway 2009). The 'will' in fact is the rational state that vitalizes the varied performative, phenomenological and conscious experiences (Dudley 2002). This critical self-reflexivity that tries to understand the intersubjective dialogue refers to the discursivity of the inner differentiation. Further to this sense of 'experience' is how consciousness is shaped. Attuned to these larger debates of corporeal transcendence, the political standpoint of identity in difference-politics has shifted to micro-narratives from the concept of 'subject' to the vision of 'agency' (Benhabib 1986). More broadly, the paradigm shift is a signal to the materialization of social thought in the context of vitalized and dynamic biological experiences. The varied performative metaphor, as stated in this book, decentres the intellectualist and discursive subject to a point of affective experiences. It rethinks the agentic potential to a point of critical empiricism. My attempt is to cross the epistemic threshold of a state-led management of biological life. I adopt an organic approach to re-read ethnographic (re)configurations of gender(ed) minorities that are already racialized, classed and biologically determined. But my anthropological insight refutes a universalizing model or any sort of interrogated operations of power. Rather, my approach attempts to reflect the history of inquiry. In other words, it conceptualizes the aesthetics of gender(ed) significance that are coupled with their lived experiences, embodiment, their personhood, self-making and the preconditions of intersubjectivity. And that adds to the strength of the ethnographic content of the book as detailed in the embodying subjective mark – focusing the senses, emotions and the essential and affectual fluid materiality and sociality.[3]

CONCEIVING MODERNITY, OTHERWISE

The era of reflexive modernity understands the implication of remapping of inequalities and social vulnerabilities as an expression of power relations in the national and global contexts (Beck 1992). This cosmopolitan remapping of inequality has to take into account the parameters of social inequality that no longer rely on the premise of the distinction between the national and the international. Territorial, political, economic, social and cultural boundaries are mutually reinforcing within a transnational frame of reference. Capitalist convergence and homogeneity point to the fundamental role of difference in mobilizing capital, labour and other resources. To reckon, Paul Gilroy's *The Black Atlantic* (1993) convincingly argues that the idea of nation, nationality and national belonging does not hold any fixed entity. Instead, it is a symbolic principle of organizing a new transnational process. Anna Tsing (2009), writing on 'transnational supply chain capitalism', focuses on labour mobilization in supply chains and the performance of gender, ethnicity, nationality, religion and citizenship. The configuration and political functions of border zones allow an analytical distinction between processes of nation-formation and territorialization. Crucial here are the diverse territorial regimes as embedded in new transnational systems of regulation. But the specific importance of the nation state in this context is evident in the frames of reference of transnationalism that the globalization process derives from the transformation within dynamic ambivalences and opportunities that cut across national boundaries (Sassen 2005; Levy 2016; Sznaider and Beck 2010; see also Levy and Sznaider 2005).

John Urry's (1995: 167) 'aesthetic cosmopolitanism' models a reflexive subject who delights in desire of consumer discernment – featuring extensive mobility, curiosity about other cultures and broadening sentiments for cultural embodiment. Again, aesthetic cosmopolitanism is firmly anchored within 'consumer culture' and the cultural symptoms of 'consumer citizenship' that define modern experience as cultivating feelings and excitement for modern urban life such as fashion, design and culture. These affective and desirous elements of feelings, fantasies and lifestyle consumption outline the complex articulation of difference within the cultural production of cosmopolitanism and consumption (Nava 2002; Jones and Leshkowich 2003). The 'aesthetic' of cosmopolitan-making has deeper implications, such as creating new forms of engagement with the logic of cross-cultural differences and the commodification and capital investment of spaces – establishing a mode of marketing cultural difference within consumer logic (see also Binnie and Skeggs 2004: 39; Beck 2005. Sznaider and Beck (2006) evoke cosmopolitanism as a transgressive potential of hybridity, relating to a kind of 'benign multiculturalism' that allows a democratic consumption based on material artefacts. To elaborate further, the modern cosmopolitan self thus formed relies on the hierarchies of race, class and gender that further transcend these differences (Vertovec and Cohen 2002: 16–18; see also Calhoun 2002; Featherstone 2002). But primarily, consumption depends upon ethico-political orientations concerned with the de-territorialization of modes of membership and affiliation. That is to say, citizenship culturally traverses the nation state, imagining shared identity interests, exposures, inclusivity as well as exclusivity.

A Radical Embodiment

The subjective meaning of this cultural difference is a discrete form of consciousness and a structure of feeling, precisely a political site of consumption practices based on collective engagement. And in the light of this, collective representation in the form of national identity is open to diverse solidarities through interlocking and interdependent relations across borders (Brunkhorst 2005: 47–48; Held 2005). And further, adding greater hope is the new material condition of 'global cities' with a new international division of labour managing global production networks, new geographical formations and complex border-zone facilitation (Sassen 2001 [1991]: 327). Again, cross-territoriality and the sovereign social and political agency allows us to focus on what Arjun Appadurai (2000) calls 'post-national social formations', arguing further about a global order exhibiting 'grassroots globalization' or 'globalization from below' – instancing pluralized world political communities.

In order to explain these deliberations as opposed to economic supra-global tenets, cosmopolitan sensibilities also address self-determination with respect to cultural pluralism (Aboulafia 2010: 84). Also, to consider here is Jacques Derrida's *The Monolingualism of the Other* (1998) that reflects the gendered representations in this book (see also Chow 2008). Decentring the '(inter) national' particularity of minority groups, I have tried to avoid geopolitical determinations and any stable discursive structure. As Derrida suggests, 'monolingualism' motivates 'nationalist aggressions' or 'monoculturalist homogenized-hegemony'. In line with Derridean understanding, this book reflects a critique of any particular linguistic specificity or a condition of cultural belonging. To undertake this deconstructive challenge is to advocate disarticulation – a reconceptualization of 'language' and nationality (cultural) – and to avoid traps of gendered nationalism within cultural-linguistic singularity. Against the differentiated and essentially alienated conditions of these marginalities, this book attempts to offer intrinsic multiplicity or plurality as voiced by the disempowered. Following this understanding as implicit in this project allows us to rethink the particular community and the subculture with a resonance of rejection of national identity and beyond any nationalist determination – iterating a cogent method of non-systemic boundless flows of people, information, capital, representation, and so on. This methodological proposition conceives of continuous movement and absolute flows to understand the chaotic, indeterminate horizons across spaces that fundamentally form the conviction of this piece of work.

Establishing this reasoning, this book uniquely positions a provincial approach to facilitate a re-inscription of modernity from the hidden logic of coloniality. Contesting this level of content is a focus on de-Westernization, engaging with the question of difference to problematize interconnected and interdependent worlds of unity within 'otherness' (Gupta and Ferguson 1992: 14). In this localized perspective of cosmopolitanism, Pollock (2000) reflects that indigenous and native narratives could be part of national identity as a further inclusive strategy. Participation of the 'provincial', which was earlier unacknowledged, sees vehement objection by global politics of power and a closer emphasis on geopolitics and internal coherence within national borders. This decentring and provincial cosmopolitan lens brings new understandings in harmony, consensus, cohabitation and multiculturalism as echoed in the post-colonial writings of Homi Bhabha (1994), Edward Said (1994), Martha Nussbaum (1996) and Ania Loomba (1998). This particular multiculturalism is not devoid of globalism and bourgeois cosmopolitanism. On the contrary, an intrinsic advocacy of world citizenship asks for corroborative reference of mapping cartographies of cohabitation to a point of 'alternate globalization' (Sassatelli 2012) – in other words, Negri and Hardt's (2004) 'multitude' whose global interests would converge against the privileges and established power of 'imperialism' and the 'Empire'.

Thus, the thrust of this work is to pose questions on 'local', parochial, rooted representations that may coexist with trans-local, transnational and modernist worldviews of the cultural hegemony of identity construction. Homi Bhabha, who possibly coined the term 'vernacular cosmopolitanism', writes of the impact of the historical–colonial situation in post-colonial times, where an absolutist conception of culture and identity caused by globalization emerges as a post-colonial and cosmopolitan synthesis of the intrinsic civilizing mission of one economic–cultural state (Knowles 2007). Social theories in this legacy have built upon critical and radical plurality standpoints of non-unitary decolonial dialogues. Stuart Hall's (Werbner 2009) 'cosmopolitanism from below' echoes similar critiques of fascist history as Gilroy's (1993) 'crisis of identity' by imperial and opportunist governments and globalization and cultural anxieties.

This book therefore anthropologically describes ordinary people's imaginative and discursive interactions – the varied means of gender(ed) transgressions within the cosmopolitan spaces of Bombay. The sociability of the city's space can be seen as a global phenomenon on the one hand, and as new forms of mobility, borders and transitions enforced by the hybridization of culture and lifestyles, on the other. The varied gendered representations and cultural displacement imply the bio-political economy of the bodies, desires and performativity – a process of sexualization that is embodied along axes of difference. As a whole, 'capital' introduces a cosmopolitan complexity. That being said, the body's perceptibility inhabits a site of one's own subject position which is further politically informed. It takes into account the embodied and the embedded notion of one's location in terms of space (geopolitics) and changing time (from the past to the present). This transcendence and the methodological move attune to the complexity and diversity of cosmopolitanism in a renewed global condition, resulting in the proliferation of locally situated micro-universalist claims that Genevieve Lloyd (1996: 74) calls 'a collaborative morality'.

The conditions for this renewed political agency call for a radical resignification of multiple ecologies of belonging. The embedded representation recasts non-essentialist lived and embodied experiences as providing an active object of desire. The very liveable present that is rooted in the ordinary micro-practices of everyday life motivates a profound sense of hope. Hope is a way of dreaming possible futures; the varied gendered representations aim at reconstructing the social imaginary of their embedded or conscious desires – proposing a rubric of lifestyles, intimacies, romance, corporeal enhancement, solidarity and citizenship, and radical corporeal transformation.

METHODOLOGICAL STANDPOINT

I conducted my ethnographic research in the city of Bombay for a period of sixteen months (Figure 1.1). Most of my ethnographic observations were made in the city of Bombay and nearby urban fringes. Much of this fieldwork was conducted between 2008 and 2009 as part of my doctoral field research.

Subsequently, I conducted further research from January to June 2013 which, along with the period spent on my doctoral field research, totalled to sixteen months. The research for this book is further based on multi-sited ethnography: travelling to the city of Ajmer (Rajasthan) in Western India, the city of Pune (Maharashtra) and other smaller towns and villages in the state (province) of Maharashtra.

For the duration of my fieldwork, I had rented an apartment in the city's suburbs and travelled to various sites – Malvani slum, multiple hospitals, meetings with activists, various rallies and parades, religious gatherings, meetings with government and international non-governmental organization (INGO) officials, funeral processions and so on. The usual destination was Malvani slum. More precisely, it was Geeta's office; in the slum's narrow lanes and alleyways, I got to know vendors, garment shops, country-wine (*desi daru*) shops, meat shops, vegetable vendors and elderly residents, and even befriended the station house officer (SHO) just in case I had to seek their help. Based on varied locations for my research in Bombay, and to navigate spaces and places, I was associated with different strands of gender minorities, female sex workers inhabiting the slum, regular families living there, doctors, beauty parlours, fashion designers, activists, academics and many more. Significantly, every gendered representation did relate to a discrete class and social status. And often times, their politics and gender-based activism had different meanings related to their class-based claims.

In my study, I have also tried to understand, deconstruct and interrogate 'participation' and 'observation' as two distinctive yet analogous research methods. Based on the dialectics between 'observation' and 'participation' in ethnographic research, there is a tacit way to enrich the research data. The participation of the researcher in the field allows them to undertake the innovative mechanism of objective observation. This new mechanism of 'participating' and 'observing' highlights different ways of 'participating' in the field. The method of participation reveals the intricacies of the performances, lives and interactions of the research participants. This provides the researcher with a vivid understanding of 'how, 'what' and 'where' as well as a detailed description of the phenomenology of life, embodied practices, emotions, feelings, and so on (Rainbow quoted in Aull-Davies 2004: 83; see also Rock 2001: 32; Gillham 2008: 41–42; Emerson 2001: 22).

I have tried to 'step-in' vigilantly as an 'observer' or/and as a 'participant', or sometimes 'participant observer', in the research field. I do not relate my politics and ideology to mainstream feminism. To explain, my critical standpoint actively transgresses popular political programmes of gender that essentially affirm the material repudiation of the feminine or the female. My political stance emphasizes the deconstruction of gender as a stable category.

It yields a deconstructive philosophy that particularly sketches a position demystifying presence or identity. 'Gender' in the contemporary urban milieu, in particular reference to the non-West, validates the task of undoing the construction of loaded languages, practices and popular rhetoric, shifting attention to dislocation, difference and depoliticization. In other words, my standpoint is not to build an heuristic and epistemic ordering. Rather, it is to consider relations and intersections that disrupt the dualist mode, foregrounding arenas of critical gender pedagogies. Potentially, this act of de(gendering) offers a transcendental experience – a negotiation of the 'self', suggesting the properties of 'desire', which is relatable to a gender-heterodox.

At the initial stage of my fieldwork, I self-interrogated (both intellectually and personally) and realized that as an 'outsider' there is a need to maintain a balance between the researcher (myself) and the research participants. Besides, I found it more meaningful to engage in 'deep immersion' to be able to see from the inside how the research participants live and how they carry out their daily routines. My intent was to dissolve the baggage of pre-existing impressions. This approach, at least for me, with my absolute love for anthropology and more so as an ethnographer, aided in fostering insights into others' lives over an extended period. Malinowski's (1978) gauge of 'immersion' to reflect the perspectives of the ethnographer's constant negotiation and to harmonize 'the native' and the researcher's own sensations in the world she or he inhabits, was perhaps the most suitable approach, which I tried to inculcate. However, there were challenges in conducting research on a subculture which is quite strict in terms of an outsider's admittance – a closed network and more so a popular social unit which is significantly disparaged in 'mainstream' society, and one that perhaps required an anthropological study in the contemporary context. Navigating this particular cultural and social obscurity was not an easy task, and especially as a researcher, the 'insider–outsider' syndrome was a genuine challenge that I had to grapple with whilst also witnessing severe loathing, avarice, envy as well as astonishment. There were instances when my research required me to withdraw from the banter, but at others, foster camaraderie. I was fearful of the unpredictable temperaments of the research participants, but I somehow managed to not let these factors affect my research.

My association with the research participants did not involve any categorization or building of acquaintanceships based on social class. Perhaps my training as an anthropologist in the British university system, and the stark transition from youth to adulthood and from India to the United Kingdom, developed in me an understanding of the nuanced meaning and philosophy of human rights, citizenship claims-making and social movement at a time of cultural globalization. I suppose I acquired and embodied the ability to appreciate and advocate social justice with compassion. Also, I embodied certain elements of the suffragette to negotiate and engage with policy issues with the local and regional governments, in instances like forums and university-led symposiums during my stay in Bombay.

My immersive participation allowed me to understand the community intimately, which would never have been possible by means of secondary sources like books, journals or articles. This helped demystify existing myths, comprehend the nuances of the respondents' lives and contextualize the ethnography whilst making an attempt to build a fresh anthropological text.

My methodological approach significantly builds on the rhetorical task of altering the mundane perspectives and practices of the gendered participants I have studied. Instead, I have tried to situate narratives within a social context of 'telling'. 'The social' is the cultural manifestations of the social interactions in which people actively participate (Frisby 1997: 8–9). The emergent possibilities of new forms of narrativity by individuals in the gender-liminal space lay emphasis on subverting the universalization of 'calling'. Kate Drabinski (2014) displaces the category of the gendered self in calling, further suggesting complicity in identarian politics. Instead, her deconstructive mode proposes individual stories and narratives, aiding in a critical way to understand the productive possibility of how 'being' of the individual creates the fundamental meaning.

My thoughts in this piece of work conceptualize the lived experiences of individuals from the *hijra* community, the fluidity of gender and the plurality of their gender(ed) expression. The fluid embodiment moves away from the essentialist and the social constructionist idea of gender, and transgresses the social naturalization of sexual differences. The transgression is a political stance, quite radically democratic, to understand sex and gender that constitute the dominant binary. The transgression further conceptualizes the role of self-construction as a narrative process interacting with society and the environment. This becomes the point of departure for my political standpoint, highlighting the emergent possibilities of narrativity that derive the embodied experiences enforcing seemingly objective ways of self-construction. Anthropologists have accounted for the importance of narratives in social science research – emphasizing how narratives build an inter-subjective space that echoes the complex dynamics of cultural values, communication processes, subjective life and personal pain (Shohet 2007; Buchbinder 2010). Narratives further, in the form of storytelling, set out an account of one's own suffering, which is culturally not sanctioned, and provide a crucial window as a cultural process, opening a form of power enabling the construction of agency.

Quite significantly, the self-representations of femaleness, as narrated in this book, frequently call attention to existing texts and particular scholarship on the care of the body. Dress, ornaments, western clothing, the irreversible processes of beautification and body enhancement and related consumption practices mark the gendered bodily meanings that earn more physical capital (Bourdieu 1986), becoming the culturally acceptable (feminine) body and attempting to approximate feminine semiotic signs to reclaim gender through various processes of sexed embodiment. To bring it into context, anthropological studies of the body and its material context of embodiment posit a critical role for the complex and interactive network between the 'body' and the 'city' which further builds coded meanings and significations that the city produces on the body. To put it differently, the city and its spatiality organize a specific conception of sexual and social relationships, which nonetheless structure and form the constitution of its corporeality (Deleuze and Guattari 1975 [1986]: 198). Moreover, the 'biopolitical strategy' of the body – its spatial politics that is linked to the ideological representation of consumer capitalism – provides the site of the socially constituting feature of the modern erotic world. 'The body' and body parts provide a logic of two political meanings of feminine (gendered) transgressiveness: first, the symbolic representation of mapping the body and its physical marker that reinforces the sexing of the body; second, the meaning of gender(ed) ambivalence (un)acquiring the 'female body' as opposed to 'the feminine body' – the particular grotesque sphere and the physical mark, or the boundary dividing multiple 'trans' identifications.

Further, on a methodological note, I have consciously used the terms such as 'participants', 'respondents', 'individual' and 'person' instead of 'subject'. In my understanding, and with my personal experience in the field, I have realized that the respondents have narrated their specific desires and their inherent ways of representing themselves. Also, in many cases, respondents have expressed intense dislike as well as anger if they are addressed with a category-led identity. Addressing people as 'individuals' rests on the malleability, unfixity and fluidity of how an 'individual' wants to represent themselves, which is again a constant act of 'becoming' based on their inherent desires. Further, my research tries to establish a philosophy of decoloniality and therefore to disavow identity category, believing in the indefiniteness of multiple axes of representation. The non-fixedness is based on acts to re-represent their own self. In addition, to my understanding, subjective-driven representation limits further understanding of the desirous self, while a reductionist approach leads to a power-driven scholarship building a hierarchy of the researcher and those being researched. De-subjectification calls for subversion to uniquely locate the research respondents with dignity. Perhaps, writing from the non-West, for the non-West and the global audience, that subaltern methodology is a mutual knowledge-sharing and recognizes occupational nobility.

This argument links further to Adriana Cavarero (2000), who in her book, *Relating Narratives: Storytelling and Selfhood*, adds to Hannah Arendt's philosophy, viewing 'narration' as immanently 'political' and 'embodied'. Cavarero writes: 'narration' opens up to understand the political aspect of vulnerability by which the process of narration dismantles and disperses the strangeness being hidden. Further remarking on the 'narratable self', she notes, stating the uniqueness of the desires of the self in the act of 'saying' brings the speakers to an understanding of an embodied practice which is framed within their life stories (Cavarero 2000). This unique process of narration via means of storytelling does indeed enable the creation of a strong political argument that brings forth the possibility of an agency – to see beyond the social – but the story in itself holds such powerful political values of 'saying' as a rhetorical process that it eventually emerges as an integral scene of the free-willing self.

To critique, claiming an identity category might have a sociopolitical horizon of a popular location which is mediated by a socially perceived self, denoting the modality of the power structure (Alcoff 2006: 335). Thus, 'subjectivity' is the reflection of a collective identity, imagined and constructed by culturally and historically situated discourses and practices (Polletta and Jasper 2001: 298; Ortner 2006). Alcoff's claim is to locate 'subjectivity' beyond cultural specificity – representing multiple systems of gender, interweaving with differences, discourses and physical markers on the body that is embodied. This leads to an understanding of the subversion of 'subjectivity' as an individual's relation to the non-dominant position and instead to the embodied processes of bodily (re)presentation that are perceived and experienced by means of desires. Katrina Roen (2001) expresses the rage of her political standpoint with the racialized interplay of gender liminal bodies, the discourses that amount to complicity with colonial culture coupled with medical discourses. Her post-colonial analysis of gender transgression inspires critical thinking and the 'gender liminal ways of being'. Claiming 'trans' with the discursive pathways of the medicalized understanding of gender may seem to be 'dangerous'. The Western academic hegemony of the popular 'queer theorists' jeopardizes the complexity of gender and sexual embodiment and describes the levels of desires and embodied processes of the 'sexed body' (Prosser 1998; Elliot 2001).[4]

I am also aware that the ethnography has been severely challenging though I braved my way through it. There were instances with severe threats. But I also realized, anthropological research on sensitive topics can never be smooth. Hurdles are inevitable. And in those instances when a researcher 'immerses' herself in the field, she cuts across the threshold of safety and peril. Both as an 'observer' and while participating as a researcher, I recorded the menace present when the respondents were out for sex work, especially in the motorways connecting cities. When conducting my ethnography at roadside bars and food stalls, the respondents' sudden disappearances for sex work left me in a situation where I was subjected to unwanted attention and attempts at harassment. There were drunken men halting at the food stalls on the motorways for food, cigarettes or toilet breaks – usually truck drivers or local goons or other visitors, evoking a sense of toxic masculinity. Those situations were noxious and, with police complicity, created an atmosphere of extreme peril.

In another instance, when researching the underworld and the sex workers' alliance with them, I was hounded by the underworld gang to my home and places I travelled to. In addition, Malvani slum posed another unique set of challenges. There were meat shops, country-wine shops and local adult film theatres in the shanty slum-based locality in almost every lane. Ruffians from the slums gathered at these shops and especially at the theatres which broadcast four shows a day, starting from noon. Their gazes were disconcerting and appraising. Often times the goons followed me; on several occasions they passed lewd remarks and pulled at my *dupatta* and dress. Later, after I built an association with the local CBOs in the slum (besides Sakhiyani), I was introduced to some other local heavyweights who happened to be political leaders. This helped immensely in building a counter-threat to my stalkers.

COSMOPOLITAN ETHOS AND THE MAKING OF BOMBAY

The city's name was officially changed from Bombay to Mumbai in the year 1995, under pressure from the regional political party, the Shiv Sena, which ruled the state from 1995 to 1999. But in this book, I have steadfastly addressed the city as 'Bombay' rather than Mumbai. The reason I have done so is that 'Bombay' signifies its inherent cosmopolitanism, shared history, philosophy and a sense of belonging. The place and the space in the city's making indicate its nativity – my reference to 'Bombay' describes its 'experiences' of migration, multiculturalism, economy, the harbour, the film industry, colonial architecture and the city's diverse forms of art that together build the cultural landscape of contemporary Bombay. Therefore, building any argument on the representational space of the city with its cosmopolitan fervour signals an enactment and recognition of reclaiming cultural citizenship, further reinstating the history and the meaning of this particular global city with an equitable representation as 'Bombay'.

The recent theorization of cosmopolitanism aims to build ideas responding to neoliberal globalization that proposes a framework of market-driven regulation on a global level. Cosmopolitan theory (Appadurai 2002a, 2002b; Appadurai and Breckenridge 1995; Beck 2005; Leahy 2013) by anthropologists and sociologists reminds us to reimagine a political community which is not bound by borders but adopts discrete democratic ideals articulating a 'cosmopolitan order'. Immanuel Kant acknowledges a 'cosmopolitan community' that supports a form of 'law' and 'order', enabling the legitimate participation of human beings across societies, erasing cultural differences and creating liberal democratic ideals. Kant's 'cosmopolitan order' adheres to the elements of state sovereignty as a basic moral principle of universal human dignity that would allow an 'order' rising above particularities constructed to the logic of the complex multidimensional relationship between global and local forces. This further implies a unique condition of understanding territoriality in which different locales are interconnected with the intensification of interaction.[5] David Held et al. (1999) discuss the idea of 'territoriality' in a cosmopolitan cultural climate that conflates the various projects of global interconnectedness with varied globalized perspectives in the understanding of ethnicity, technology, finance, media, ideology, and so on. This kind of imaginative landscape relates to Arjun Appadurai's (1996) framework of 'disjuncture', shaping a condition of modernity that transcends the very spatiality of the 'local' with the interplay of varied globalized perspectives.

Appadurai cites the characterization of 'disjuncture', relating it to Bombay, providing the city's images of globalization coupled with its elusive histories and evolving finance, crafting the shifting economies to a global scale of rising financial capital (2002a: 55). His argument further relates 'hypermodernization' with the cosmopolitan ethos that Bombay was instilled with after World War II. Appadurai recalls the 1970s as a period of 'sudden' economic regulation and new mobility of labour with growing migration bringing in white- and blue-collar workers who eventually built the commercial and political core of the city, with its employability in the Fort area of South Bombay (2002a: 50). This slowly created the 'circulation of cash and work' with growing impetus for 'business', further addressing 'new markets' operating on the entrepreneurial energy of the city. Appadurai relates the 'new market' syndrome to the complex capitalist niches of the transnational space, whereas in other contexts he evokes his theorization of multiple 'scapes' (Appadurai 1996, 2001), conflating the incorporation of the disjunction with its economic and cultural specificities, situating the newness of the global epoch that moves out of local situations to global circulation (see also Tsing 2004: 455–456).

Appadurai's analytical trope of 'disjuncture' (1996: 32) constantly tells us of the 'new global cultural economy' with special emphasis on his concept of 'deterritorialization' (1996: 37); this refers to the interplay of the semblance and difference of new visions of culture that challenges bounded imaginaries. This further speaks of the formation of new geographical spaces, the erasure of fixed nation-state units and a new form of political project which is highly contingent with new forms of political participation and new ways of creating citizenship.[6]

Arjun Appadurai and James Holston (1999: 17) have sought to mark the core meaning of modern citizenship that expands the political meaning of modern public life and erodes the understanding of citizenship which is historically situated in the primacy of the nation and its national boundaries. As they suggest, citizenship repudiates the constitution of many distinguished representations with a culture of difference and appropriates an urban space that evokes a new notion of membership and solidarity. This creates a new social condition that contributes significantly to changed conditions of work, living and sustenance as concerns new claims of civic components. Thus, it is possible to observe the complexities of governance and law that build the context of new relations of urban governmentality. In saying so, modern citizenship entails the intensification of the city's space rendering the politics of democracy and further articulating the political economy of mass migration, globalization of the economy, rights-based discourses and many more – evoking an ideology of universal equality.

Figure 1.1 Glimpses of Bombay from the Arabian Sea. Picture taken from a boat on the way to an island near Bombay.

Source: Photograph by the author.

Social History of Bombay since the 1970s

Appadurai characterizes the city of Bombay like other cities such as Bangkok, Hong Kong, Sao Paulo and Mexico City – cities particularly 'seduced' by global capital. The city's character is conceptualized as a 'disjuncture', with economies shifting from manufacture and industry to those of trade, tourism and finance, and yet retaining its histories and temporalities. Bombay as a city with its interesting history of having been a fisherman's village, and named after a local goddess, eventually turned into a seat of the colonial government oriented with a bourgeois ethos which led to it being referred to as a 'Fordist city', dominated by trade, commerce and manufacturing. The 1950s marked the emergence of the cosmopolitan spirit of the city, with its economic expansion. Appadurai points to the port's significance to the city as a longstanding site for commerce, imperial trade and colonial power, shaping industrial capitalism and the role of communities, like the Parsis, Muslims, Hindus, Baghdadi Jews, Syrian Christians, Armenians and many more. After World War II, the importance of commerce led to the creation of the manufacturing sector with automobiles, textiles and chemicals, on the one hand, and powerful trade and quintessentially a complex web of economic relations and 'business' in Bombay installing the entrepreneurial energy operating in the city with increasing factors of capitalist production, on the other (Appadurai 2002b: 62).

Appadurai adds the idea of 'cash', implying the circulation of various kinds of capital, and its new and contradictory manner. On the one hand, it registers the 'post-Fordist Bombay' (2002b: 69), characterizing a broad megacity project of multinational corporations and materiality, consumption and modern domesticity – creating a new 'global' middle class (see Chapter 2). On the other hand, 'cash' also solicits the 'parallel' or 'black' economy (2002b: 60), of which Appadurai further suggests, Bombay's ratio is probably high and also finances the Bollywood film industry. This money is invested in the entire cultural economy giving a dubious character to 'business' by means of smuggling, racket-payments, illegitimate state protection, and so on. The 'business' here revolves around large cash transactions within the economy of black money, implying the deep-rooted circulation of currency that goes hand in hand with materiality, which Appadurai strongly characterizes as 'the commodification of flesh'. Knitting together the complex edifice of cash that circulates in the disorganized sectors, he refers to 'house-related hysteria', its brokers and dealers whose subculture and networking constitutes the fibre of the 'black economy' and the underworld (2002b: 68). These fluid dealings manufacture a notorious space of violence and risk in which the key players are the mafia as solicitors and financers in a discreet pattern of market-making.[7]

Further, the traits of violence characterize the local ethno-politics and Hindu nationalism of the Shiv Sena from the 1960s – Maharashtra's ethno-history and the Maharashtrian self-consciousness, portraying an indigenized strategy to domesticate the local vernacular consciousness in the region (Hansen 2001: 14). The Shiv Sena and its vernacular rendition hold a counter-Bombay imagery, or a niche to its cosmopolitan fervour that translates to a 'Hinduized' city – its ideologies politicized with neo-religious strategies in India and intensely market-driven. The indigenizing strategy further gains impetus with the erasure of the Anglophone name, Bombay, to adopt Mumbai as a 'metonymic' interplay envisioning the regional and vernacular geography of Maharashtra and ethno-nationalism, and conversely multicultural niches to build a specific form of urbanism (Appadurai 2002b: 79).

Cosmopolitanism thus becomes a career for neoliberalism. Corporations envision a united, borderless world ruled by commodity in which geographical differences are conveniently erased by the magic of what David Harvey (2009) calls the 'free market'. This vision is found, for instance, in the steady, unabated march of deregulatory policies and privatization across the planet, welding the world-people as consumers and wreaking devastation on cultures and ecosystems everywhere. As Harvey puts it:

> … neoliberalization has created a flat world for the multinational corporations and for the billionaire entrepreneur and investor class, but a rough jagged, and uneven world for everyone else. (Harvey 2009: 52)

Harvey proposes a reformulated cosmopolitanism – one that takes seriously location, place, space and the biological realm – in short, one that foregrounds the spatial politics of difference and engages conscientiously with 'the banality of geographical evils'. He thus seeks to 'remove the mask that so conveniently and effectively conceals and protects the particularities of the class or ethnic nationalist power hiding behind the noble universal principles' (Harvey 2009: 107).

This book therefore tries to reshape the post-colonial framework that understands the distinct combination of 'high-rises' and 'shanty settlements' that distinguishes this 'frenetic' metropolis. Kidambi, Kamat and Dwyer (2019) account for 'the three-dimensional grid' in capturing the city's 'social landscape', noting the complexity of the relationship between the 'spatial' and 'social stratification' of the city from its making to the present. Bombay, with a certain degree of inter-class mixing quite significantly in its record, offers a vantage point to articulate 'space', 'experiences' and 'capital' that contribute to the rectification of the social class structure. Evoking Robert Rahman Raman's (2019) argument of '*swaraj*-led nationalism' in this city's formation, the political rhetoric is the growing importance of the labour movement and worker's participation. Forced in this collective ritual of the workers' revolution, Bombay encapsulates 'integration' (Masselos 2019). The 'integration' is an overarching entity of the space and the people, reflecting in Jim Masselos' further exploration of the interaction between the 'formal' and the 'informal'. The city's dramatic identity is forged within the episodes of 'interaction' and 'space', drawing attention to ambiguities and stratifications; yet, this 'messiness of everyday life' bolsters the urban prism of 'differences'. A regulated degree of this mixing calls firmly to an intricate connection in shaping the new forms of public action and human relations in contemporary Bombay, as this book tries to capture.

Chapters

Chapter 2 articulates the specific aspect of globalizing modernity and consumer culture that appears to address the understanding of how the marketplace produces desire, and how the 'market' is intrinsically linked to the construction and negotiation of a specific form of identity and subjectivity. This work also draws attention to how sexuality is produced through culturally specific social processes, with an emphasis on the construction of sexuality across time and space, so as to demonstrate the particular framework of a particular subculture – the *hijra*s – and to understand the complex relationship between their sexuality, sexual practices and sexual desires that are embodied and re-represented.

Chapter 3 has made an attempt to construct an anthropological understanding of the spatial and embodied metaphor of violence, in the context of which the *hijra*s try to navigate and manoeuvre their power. It further identifies how power is constructed in that particular space which is symbolic of the political and the embodied ways that the *hijra*s negotiate the particular space. This particular piece of work, in fact, brings evidence of voice and narratives that further add to the theoretical framework of the anthropology of the *hijra*s in conflict, with the 'local' interpretation in the understanding of the community, shifting dynamics of *hijra* identity and the democratic framework of community empowerment. In other words, this chapter in particular is a renewed debate within the anthropology of gender and sexuality in the non-Western context and builds a niche for the new ways of representation of violence in a 'local' transgender community – the *hijra*s.

Chapter 4 recounts anthropological narratives of a carnivalesque culture and a particular sexual subculture in India – the *hijra*s – and their participation adds meaning to the semiotics, symbolic and cultural meanings of the carnival. The festival represents a highly ritualized and ceremonial occasion, adding a nuanced expression of seductive charm, erotic sensuality, libidinal interplay, pleasure and bodily display. The festival brings to light an intelligible account of the community's free expression through the act of excitement, exhilaration and laughter. Sexual symbolism in the festival provides a new interpretation of the extravagant costumes and bodily display – breasts, stylized performances and exhibitionism create the structure of an erotic meaning that further focuses attention on the desires and the desirability of the *hijra*s. Therefore, the celebration as a whole recounts a cultural politics that nonetheless provides a unique interpretation of the erotic and sexual universe of the *hijra*s and their sociability in a carnival culture.

Chapter 5 leads to an argument that could be broadly conceptualized as the understanding of 'cultural citizenship' that effectively creates the possibility of the symbolic presence and the visibility of a particular population in society from a relation of 'marginality' to 'assimilation'. The sense of assimilation of the transsexual subjects is broadly represented in terms of how their citizenship is related to consumerism – emphasizing the consumption of the cosmopolitan lifestyles that could meet their innermost desires. This tacit relationship of the body and the medical marketplace intersects to produce a newly formed subjectivity and agency.

Chapter 6 is based on a framework that contextualizes 'participation' as a tool for the development of community engagement, inviting the possibility of 'self-organization' through mobilization, resistance, participation in governance and decision-making, claiming rights, and so on. Following this perspective, this empirical study has examined the collective efficacies of the *hijra* community that generate a form of 'protest participation', focusing in particular on facilitating 'citizen-to-citizen' deliberations and allowing the group associated with the collective action to form a specific movement or radical political manoeuvring.

Chapter 7 identifies and describes the qualities and characteristics of cosmopolitanism in line with the discursive and material processes of consumption, the city and city-spaces, culture, identity, citizenship and politics. This chapter, in a way, attempts to identify the geographies of the transnational locality with the new configuration of relationships within a specific subculture. The new form of cultural articulation and the public life that Bombay generates demonstrates the strong impetus of 'cosmopolitan urbanism' – reflecting a sense of neoliberal cultural traits and a form of urban life with a specific kind of consumption, lifestyle and cultural sensibility.

Chapter 8 builds on the significance of this theorization to rupture the very idea of the new modalities of these representations and builds multiple sites for the emergence of not only a single sexual category but conceptualizes sexuality beyond sexual subjects and the frames of reference of the globalizing category of the sexual. The representation is increasingly beyond capital's grasp – an attempt to realize the possibility of desire with the newly realized multitudes of consciousness, bodies and gendered geographies. Taking this standpoint forward, this chapter attempts to highlight radical democratic politics as a subject of discussion that provides crucial insights to an anti-essentialist approach to understanding the pluralistic sexual representations in Bombay.

NOTES

1   My aim in this work is to draw evidence via ethnographic research about the sexual subaltern or marginalized population that inhabits the city's spaces. I have related elsewhere (Roy 2017) the impending bourgeois ethos of the city of Bombay and how the cosmopolitan ethos is embodied in everyday life. Also, I have noticed that non-heteronormative lives across social and economic classes are interlinked – be it activism, politics or/and other forms of representation – bringing together these spatial niches to the complex intersection of desire, imagining the city's urbanism that potentially builds a new form of sexual articulation in contemporary Bombay. My scholarly contention is to navigate these spaces and mark as what Binnie et al. (2006: 8) call 'cosmopolitan urbanism', reflecting a sense of neoliberal cultural traits and a form of urban life with specific kinds of consumption, lifestyles and cultural sensibilities. Therefore, my starting point is to understand the anthropology of space and representation – exploring the transgressive politics of gender, body, way of being – the fluidity and plurality of the gendered expressions that transgress sexual differences. The transgression that I aim to portray here is a political stance, quite radically democratic, to understand sex and gender in the contemporary economic and cultural context of Bombay. Accounting for gender transgression corroborates those practices that exceed the boundaries of normativity – to 'transgress' implies the strategies of normalization as response to a form of anomalous embodiment.

2   The Foucauldian understanding of transgression problematizes the anomalous body that poses the imbrication of 'abnormality' and further transgresses and pushes the point of rupture of law and order. In *Discipline and Punish*, *Madness and Civilization* and *The History of Sexuality*, the modern authorities of legality, comprising norms and judicial institutions, incorporate a continuum of apparatuses – medical, administrative, and so on. Yet Foucault sees resistance primarily as a transgressive moment that outlines the response of the 'normative' governmentality. What interests me here is to draw the theoretical impetus of Foucauldian 'abnormality' with sexual 'ambiguity', generating these irregularities of the sexual and bodily representation of the muffled within modern technologies of bodily embodiment. Neither do they call themselves women nor do they identify as 'transgender'. But the Derridean undecidability underlines the inevitable realization of the reflection of the paradox of the peculiar margins of this particular sub-culture. I would also like to draw upon the philosophical lineage of transgression from Thomas Hobbes (*Leviathan*), Immanuel Kant (*Ground of the Metaphysis of Morals*) and Friedrich Nietzsche (*Beyond Good and Evil* and *Towards a Genealogy of Morals*) – situating how ethical representations

are grounded in the universal law, but also how new ethical sensibility overcomes earlier universal ethics. I would further try to draw on other philosophers who have relied on counter universalism, foundationalism and essentialism – namely Martin Heidegger, Max Weber, Theodor W. Adorno and Luce Irigaray – focusing on the field of political theory that attacks Enlightenment universalism situating the notion of the disembodied subject.

3   In the light of ethnography, this piece of work captures the central political argument of 'being feminine', *hijra* femininity and its femaleness. This practice of breaking down the barriers of institutions of dominion and connecting the wider spheres with the art of potentially constitutive bodies and desires ruptures the very idea of the new modalities of these representations and builds multiple sites for the emergence of not a single sexual category, but the conceptualization of sexuality beyond sexual subjects, beyond frames of reference to the globalizing category of the sexual. The representation is increasingly beyond capital's grasp – an attempt to realize the possibility of desire with the new multitudes of consciousness, bodies and gendered geographies.

4   The dominant queer theory colludes with institutional racism, hence reinforcing white privilege. The usual subject-less critique of queer theories rests on the presumption of what Jasbir K. Puar (2007) calls 'freedom from norms' that queer theory tries to impose as a regulatory queer ideal. In addition, Sara Ahmed (2006) revokes queer theory and its movement as a movement based on 'fetish'; perceiving the exclusion of 'other', in terms of an elite cosmopolitan formulation of those who have access to cultural capital and material resources. Again, in the critique of dominant trans-studies, Jack Halberstam's (2018) recent book, *Trans** (with an asterisk), argues that the non-naming of an identity enables the ability to capture unfolding of categories of gender(ed) expressions. Non-naming further implies a transition from a specificity and advances a form of gender variance based on desire and the desirability of one's own representation. Halberstam's political stance of diversity disrupts the classification and norms of identity, breaking away from the binary ideals that the nineteenth- and twentieth-century Western model of sexual taxonomy has established, or the phenomena that involves the reconceptualization of transgenderism and the women's question in the late-twentieth-century feminist debates in the West, explicitly arguing the 'transitional discourse' of the medicalization of the body, its sexed materiality and embodiment, and gender identification.

Decentring the normative gendering, Halberstam proposes the power of new articulation of non-classification – what it means to a gender identity without naming, formulating a gender fluidity without the recognition of any power or regulation. The gendered ambiguity and instability reflect the Deleuzian understanding of the body as a 'liquid set of dynamics' that suggests increased flexibility of the body's representation. The book would thus contribute to the South Asian discourse on the political significance of biological male bodies in transgression, as acquiring gender(ed) and sexual significance of the gender liminal self. However, it does provide a greater emphasis to the *hijra*-identified population in terms of its corporeal transgression; the book would also explore the various spaces across social and economic classes in contemporary Bombay, how and in what ways these transgressive politics are manifested.

My attempt is to subvert the mundane classification of gendering the non-heteronormative sexual self and to constitute the dimensions of performativity, the location of the self and various embodied practices. This further informs the political understandings and associations of the complex conceptualization of commercialism and cosmopolitanism of spatiality – the *hijra*s in contemporary Bombay relate the notion of bodily display, their embodied practices that act as a temporal subversion of the already-given cultural construction (Roy 2016, 2020). Their new performative image further interplays between space and emotions in a very crucial way to discount and subvert historic racialization and the symbolic materialization of the gender(ed) corporeal being (McClintock 1995).

5   Bombay is a milieu of commerce, finance, films, entertainment, and multiple national and international languages and cultures, where there is a competitive marketplace for ideas and experiences (Patel and Thorner 1997: xiii). The city has certain elements of charm and aura that are brought about by its cosmopolitan culture and 'Bollywood' as a worldwide film industry that attracts a large population in India and beyond. Bombay has achieved the status of global commercialization, with a wide range of corporate advertising, business centres and modern industries. Bombay has gained this multicultural and intense corporate environment through the global market of commerce, industry, culture and diverse human relations.

6   Bombay in the twenty-first century has displayed the complex interactions of cultures that inherently represent modernity with specific characteristics of local cultures. The colonial and post-colonial portrayal of Bombay depicts the construction of its urbanity with the hybrid identification of the populace (Patel and Thorner 1997), which seems to reside within and beyond the political boundaries of an Indian nation state. Rachel Dwyer (2000: 62–66) traces the history and the construction of Bombay city, focusing on the migration of the 'business class' from across India, mostly Gujarat, during the nineteenth century. Besides, the Parsis, who are originally migrants from Iran, settled in parts of India and later migrated to Bombay in the eighteenth century and commenced their business. Also, the Muslim population from the Middle Eastern countries came to Bombay at that time for trade and commerce. Dwyer further articulates the fact that these populations became the 'middle men' or the 'working class', working with the East India Company during the British Raj in India. These people became identified as the 'middle class' of Bombay, which gradually became wealthy and prosperous.

7   Bombay is a commercialized city with a high degree of industrialization and urbanity, resulting in the commodifiction of material goods and enterprises (Varma 2004). In fact, Rashmi Varma also notes the fact that modern Bombay is analogous to other big cities in the West, where 'emotions are commodified … capital seems to become human' (Varma 2004). Varma's illustration of the city evokes a representation of the urban context that captures a strong sense of modernity with industrial and mechanized manufacturing, which have ultimately affected human emotions. On the other hand, Appadurai points out

the correlation between industrial development and the effective construction of human identities and relationships.

In the specific context of Bombay, Appadurai observes that the transnational culture, spatial dynamics and material geographies of people, goods and services, production and distribution are commercial, corporate and enterprising (Appadurai 1996, 2001).

BIBLIOGRAPHY

Aboulafia, M. 2010. *Transcendence: On Self-determination and Cosmopolitanism.* Stanford: Stanford University Press.

Ahmed. S. 2006. *Queer Phenomenology: Orientations, Objects, Others.* Durham, NC, and London: Duke University Press.

Alcoff, L. M. 2006. *Visible Identities: Race, Gender and the Self.* Oxford and New York: Oxford University Press.

Appadurai, A. 1996. *Modernity at Large: Cultural Dimensions of Globalization.* Minneapolis: University of Minnesota Press.

———. 2000. 'Grassroots Globalization and Research Imagination'. *Public Culture* 12(1): 1–19.

———. 2002a. 'Deep Democracy: Urban Governmentality and the Horizon of Politics'. *Public Culture* 14(1): 21–47.

——— (ed.). 2002b. *Globalization.* Durham, NC: Duke University Press.

Appadurai, A., and C. Breckenridge. 1995. 'Public Modernity in India'. In *Consuming Modernity: Public Culture in a South Asian World*, edited by C. Breckenridge, 1–22. Minneapolis and London: University of Minnesota Press.

Appadurai, A., and J. Holston (eds.). 1999. *Cities and Citizenship.* Durham, NC, and London: Duke University Press.

Aull-Davies, C. 2008. *Reflexive Ethnography: A Guide to Researching Selves and Others.* Oxon, Canada and New York: Routledge.

Balsamo, A. M. 1996. *Technologies of the Gendered Body: Reading Cyborg Government.* Durham, NC, and London: Duke University Press.

Beck, U. 1992. *Risk Society: Towards a New Modernity.* London: SAGE Publications.

———. 2005. *Power in the Global Age.* Cambridge: Polity Press.

Benhabib, S. 1986. *Critique, Norm, and Utopia: A Study of the Foundations of Critical Theory.* New York: Columbia University Press.

Bhabha, H. 1994. *The Location of Culture.* London and New York: Routledge.

Biehl, J., and P. Locke (eds.). 2017. *Unfinished: The Anthropology of Becoming.* Durham, NC, and London: Duke University Press.

Biehl, J., B. Good and A. Kleinman. 2007. *Subjectivity: Ethnographic Investigations*. Berkeley: University of California Press.

Binnie, J., and B. Skeggs. 2004. 'Cosmopolitan Knowledge and the Production and Consumption of Sexualized Space: Manchester's Gay Village'. *Sociological Review* 52(1): 39–61.

Binnie, J., J. Holloway, S. Millington and C. Young (eds.). 2006. *Cosmopolitan Urbanism*. London: Routledge.

Bourdieu, P. 1986. 'The Forms of Capital'. In *Handbook of Theory and Research for the Sociology of Education*, edited by J. Richardson, 241–258. Westport, CT: Greenwood.

Brunkhorst, H. 2005. *Solidarity: From Civic Friendship to a Global Legal Community*. Translated by Jeffrey Flynn. Cambridge, MA: MIT Press.

Buchbinder, M. 2010. 'Giving an Account of One's Pain in the Anthropological Interview'. *Cultural Medical Psychiatry* 34(1): 108–131.

Calhoun, C. 2002. 'Imagining Solidarity: Cosmopolitanism, Constitutional Patriotism and the Public Sphere'. *Public Culture* 14(1): 147–172.

Campbell, T., and A. Sitze (eds.). 2013. *Biopolitics: A Reader*. Durham, NC: Duke University Press.

Cavarero, A. 2000. *Relating Narratives: Storytelling and Selfhood*. London and New York: Routledge.

Chow, R. 2008. 'Reading Derrida on Being Monolingual'. *New Literary History* 39(2): 217–231.

Deleuze, G., and F. Guattari. 1975 (1986). *Kafka: Towards a Minor Literature*. Translated by Dana Polan. In *Theory and History of Literature*, vol. 30. Minneapolis and London: University of Minnesota Press.

Derrida, J. 1998. *Monolingualism of the Other, or The Prosthesis of Origin*. Stanford: Stanford University Press.

Drabinski, K. 2014. 'Identity Matters: Teaching Transgender in the Women's Studies Classroom'. *Radical Teacher* 100: 139–145.

Dudley, W. 2002. *be Hegel, Nietzsche and Philosophy: Thinking Freedom*. Cambridge and New York: Cambridge University Press.

Dwyer, R. 2000. *All You Want Is Money, All You Need Is Love*. New York: Cassell Publishers.

Elliot, P. 2001. 'A Psychoanalytic Reading of Transsexual Embodiment'. *Studies in Gender and Sexuality* 2(4): 295–325.

Emerson, R. M. (ed.). 2001. *Contemporary Field Research: Perspectives and Formulations*. Long Grove, IL: Waveland Press.

Featherstone, M. 2002. 'Cosmopolis: An Introduction'. *Theory, Culture & Society* 19(1–2): 1–16.

Foucault, M. 1976 (2008). *The History of Sexuality: The Will of Knowledge*, vol. 1. Translated by Robert Hurley. London: Penguin.

Frisby, D. 1997. *Simmel on Culture: Selected Writings*. London: SAGE Publications.

Gemes, K., and C. Janaway. 2009. 'Nietzsche on Free Will: Autonomy and the Sovereign Individual'. https://www.researchgate.net/publication/292547964_Nietzsche_on_Free_Will_Autonomy_and_the_Sovereign_Individual. Accessed in July 2017.

Gillham, B. 2008. *Observation Techniques: Structured to Unstructured*. Bodmin: Continuum Press.

Gilroy, P. 1993. *The Black Atlantic: Modernity and Double Consciousness*. Cambridge, MA: Harvard University Press.

Gupta, A., and J. Ferguson. 1992. 'Beyond "Culture": Space, Identity, and the Politics of Difference'. *Cultural Anthropology* 7(1): 6–23.

Halberstam, J. 2018. *Trans*: A Quick and Quirky Account of Gender Variability*. Oakland: University of California Press.

Hansen, T. B. 2001. *Wages of Violence: Naming and Identity in Postcolonial Bombay*. Princeton: Princeton University Press.

Harvey, D. 2009. *Cosmopolitanism and the Geographies of Freedom*. New York and London: Columbia University Press.

Held, D. 2005. 'At the Global Crossroads: The End of the Washington Consensus and the Rise of Global Social Democracy?' *Globalization* 2(1): 95–113.

Held, D., A. McGrew, D. Goldblatt and J. Perraton. 1999. *Global Transformations*. Stanford: Stanford University Press.

Jenks, C. 2003. *Transgression: Key Ideas*. London and New York: Routledge.

Jones, C., and A. M. Leshkowich. 2003. 'What Happens When Asian Chic Becomes Chic in Asia?' *Fashion Theory* 7(3–4): 281–300.

Kidambi, P., M. Kamat and R. Dwyer (eds.). 2019. *Bombay Before Mumbai: Essays in Honour of Jim Masselos*. Oxford and New York: Oxford University Press.

Knowles, S. 2007. 'Macrocosm-Opolitanism? Gilroy, Appiah, and Bhabha: The Unsettling Generality of Cosmopolitan Ideas'. *Postcolonial Text* 3(4): 1–11.

Lapple, D. 2001. 'City and Region in an Age of Globalization and Digitization'. *German Journal of Urban Studies*. https://citeseerx.ist.psu.edu/viewdoc/download?doi=10.1.1.198.4457&rep=rep1&type=pdf. Accessed in August 2017.

Leahy, M. 2013. 'Ulrich Beck's Cosmopolitanization Thesis: A Philosophical Critique'. *Australian Journal of Political Science* 48(2): 152–163.

Lemke, T. 2010. *Beyond Foucault: From Biopolitics to the Government of Life*. London and New York: Routledge.

Levy, D. 2016. 'Cosmopolitanizing Catastrophism: Remembering the Future'. *Theory, Culture and Society* 30(2): 3–31.

Levy, D., and N. Sznaider. 2005. *The Holocaust and Memory in the Global Age*. Philadelphia: Temple University Press.

Linklater, A., and S. Mennell. 2010. 'Nobert Elias, "The Civilizing Process: Sociogenetic and Psychogenetic Investigations" – An Overview and Assessment'. *History and Theory* 49(3): 384–411.

Lloyd, G. 1996. *Routledge Philosophy Guidebook to Spinoza and the Ethics*. London and New York: Routledge.

Loomba, A. 1998. *Colonialism/Postcolonialism: The New Critical Idiom*. London and New York: Routledge.

Mahmood, K. T. 2008. *Selected Poetry on Women Writers*. New Delhi: Star Publications.

Mahmood, S. 2005. *Politics of Piety: The Islamic Revival and the Feminist Subject*. Princeton: Princeton University Press.

Malinowski, M. *Argonauts of the Western Pacific: An Account of Native Enterprise and Adventure in the Archipelagoes of Melanesian New Guinea*. London: Routledge.

Masselos, J. 2019. 'Remembering Bombay: Present Memories, Past Histories'. In *Bombay Before Mumbai: Essays in Honour of Jim Masselos*, edited by P. Kidambi, M. Kamat and R. Dwyer, 305–314. Oxford and New York: Oxford University Press.

McClintock, A. 1995. *Imperial Leather: Race, Gender and Sexuality in the Colonial Context*. New York and London: Routledge.

Mensch, J. R. 2020. *Decisions and Transformations: The Phenomenology of Embodiment*. New York and London: Columbia University Press.

Merriman, P. 2012. *Mobility, Space and Culture*. London: Routledge.

Nava, M. 2002. 'Cosmopolitan Modernity: Everyday Imaginaries and the Register of Difference'. *Theory, Culture and Society* 19(1–2): 81–99.

Negri, A., and M. Hardt. 2004. *Multitude: War and Democracy in the Age of Empire*. New York: Penguin Press.

Nussbaum, M. 1996. 'Compassion: The Basic Social Emotion'. *Social Philosophy and Policy* 13(1): 27–58.

Ortner, S. 2006. *Anthropology and Social Theory: Culture, Power and the Acting Subject*. Durham, NC, and London: Duke University Press.

Patel, S., and A. Thorner (eds.). 1997. *Bombay: Metaphor for Modern India*. New Delhi: Oxford University Press.

Polletta, F., and J. M. Jasper. 2001. 'Collective Identity and Social Movements'. *Annual Review of Sociology* 27(1): 283–305.

Pollock, S. 2000. 'Cosmopolitan and Vernacular in History'. *Public Culture* 12(3): 591–625.

Prosser, J. 1998. *Second Skin*. Columbia: Columbia University Press.

Puar, J. K. 2007. *Terrorist Assemblages: Homonationalism in Queer Times*. Durham, NC, and London: Duke University Press.

Raman, R. R. 2019. 'Civil Disobedience and the City: Congress and the Working Classes in Bombay, c. 1930–32'. In *Bombay Before Mumbai: Essays in Honour of Jim Masselos*, edited by P. Kidambi, M. Kamat and R. Dwyer, 263–284. Oxford and New York: Oxford University Press.

Rock, P. 2001. 'Symbolic Interactionism and Ethnography'. In *Handbook of Ethnography*, edited by P. Atkinson and A. Coffey, 477–492. London, Newbury Park, CA, and New Delhi: SAGE Publications.

Roen, K. 2001. 'Transgender Theory and Embodiment: The Risk of Racial Marginalization'. *Journal of Gender Studies* 10(3): 253–263.

Roy, A. 2016. 'Sexualizing the Body: Passionate Aesthetics and Embodied Desires'. *Indian Journal of Gender Studies* 24(2): 1–23.

———. 2017. 'Mumbai Fables: Cosmopolitanism and the Sexual Ethos'. *Studies in Humanities and Social Sciences* 2(2): 98–112.

———. 2020. 'Spivak Alert! Conceiving Sexuality from the Subaltern Lens'. *Gender, Place and Culture* 28(2): 1–17.

Said, E. 1994. *Orientalism*. New York: Vintage Books.

Sassatelli, M. 2012. *Festivals, Museums, Exhibitions: Aesthetic Cosmopolitanism in the Cultural Public Sphere*. London and New York: Routledge.

Sassen, S. 2001 (1991). *The Global City: New York, London, Tokyo*. Princeton: Princeton University Press.

———. 2005. 'The Repositioning of Citizenship and Alienage: Emergent Subjects and Spaces for Politics'. *Globalization* 2(1): 79–94.

———. 2008. *Territory, Authority, Rights: From Medieval to Global Assemblages*. Princeton: Princeton University Press.

———. 2012. 'Cities: A Window into Larger and Smaller Worlds'. *European Educational Research Journal* 11(1): 1–10.

Scott, J. C. 1992. *Domination and the Arts of Resistance: Hidden Transcripts*. New Haven and London: Yale University Press.

Shohet, M. 2007. 'Narrating Anorexia: "Full" and "Struggling" Genres of Recovery'. *Ethos* 35(3): 344–382.

Sznaider, N., and U. Beck. 2010. 'Unpacking Cosmopolitanism for the Social Sciences: A Research Agenda'. *British Journal of Sociology* 61(S1): 381–403.

Smith, D. 2007. 'Deleuze and the Question of Desire: Towards an Immanent Theory of Ethics'. *Parrhesia* 2: 66–78.

Tsing, A. 2004. *Friction: An Ethnography of Global Connection*. Princeton: Princeton University Press.

———. 2009. 'Supply Chains and the Human Condition'. *Rethinking Marxism: A Journal of Economics, Culture and Society* 21(2): 148–176.

Urry, J. 1995. *Consuming Places*. London and New York: Routledge.

Varma, R. 2004. 'Provincializing the Global City: From Bombay to Mumbai'. *Social Text* 22(4): 65–89.

Vertovec, S., and R. Cohen (eds.). 2002. *Conceiving Cosmopolitanism: Theory, Context and Practice*. Oxford and New York: Oxford University Press.

Werbner, P. (ed.). 2008. *Anthropology and the New Cosmopolitanism: Rooted, Feminist and Vernacular Perspectives*. London and New York: Routledge.

2

Bioengineering, Beauty and Racial Sensibility

BOMBAY, MALVANI SLUM AND SAKHIYANI

The ladies' compartments on the Bombay suburban railways are usually positioned at both ends of the train. The trains are crowded with passengers all day. The popular 'western line' is frequent and regular, with trains scheduled every three minutes.[1] The platforms swarm with people – passengers, vendors and railway police constables – all jostling past the fast-food stalls, trinket sellers, goods and parcels. To board the train is a challenge – there is every possibility of missing it. It is best to mingle with the crowd and get pushed through towards the train just as it arrives at the platform. Before first light, the train is crowded with fisherwomen and vegetable vendors commuting to the city market from their villages on the urban fringes of Bombay to sell their catch from their village ponds or produce from their fields. At that hour, it seems the trains are no longer passenger trains but chaotic goods trains crammed with fish, vegetables and tradespeople. At seven in the morning, the crowd is replaced by office workers, school children and college students. At midday, the trains are less busy. Then at three in the afternoon the rush begins again, continuing until midnight when the vegetable vendors and fisherfolk return to their villages after their long day in the city.

My usual destination during my fieldwork was Malad, a place in suburban Bombay. After reaching Malad station, it was a twenty-minute autorickshaw ride to Malvani slum. The rickshaw would pass through the busiest areas of Kolad, past shopping malls, office buildings, high-rise apartments and multiplex cinema halls. An activist friend once told me about the history of Malvani. He said that it had always been marked as a notorious place, infamous for murders, underworld gangs, burglaries and various forms of extortion. He added that Hindu–Muslim communal violence was an everyday story. Some ten years ago, he said, the Municipal Corporation of Greater Mumbai (MCGM) 'dumped' the migrant *hijras* in Malvani. They had been scattered 'here and there' in the city. Malvani had such a bad reputation that my friends who are acquainted with the city were filled with anxiety when they heard that I had chosen it as the field-site for my doctoral research. But I knew that this would be the ideal location to study the *hijras*. It provided the perfect blend of slum, urbanity and multi-religiosity (Figure 2.1).

On the first day of my visit to Malvani, all I knew about the slum was its name and the name of a *hijra* community organization, Sakhiyani (Figure 2.2). Geeta, who runs the organization, is a self-identified *hijra* who manages some grants from the Mumbai Districts AIDS Control Society (MDACS) for developing acquired immunodeficiency syndrome (AIDS) awareness among the *hijras* in Malvani.[2] I managed to speak to her twice over the telephone before I met her. She spoke English, revealing her social class – a *hijra* with a sense of modern identity, associated with non-governmental organization (NGO)-activism, sexual health promotion and rights-based issues.[3] The telephone conversation between Geeta and myself was as follows:

Me: Hello Geeta, my name is Ahonaa. I have been asked to contact you by Mr Kishore [a prominent human rights activist]. Is there any possibility that we could meet?

Geeta: Sorry, I am very busy (in an angry voice).

Me: (in a soft tone) Well, it could be some evening after your office hours. Some ten minutes would do. Please?

Geeta: Call me next week!

Me: Geeta, I forgot to give you some brief introduction of myself. I want to research on 'the community' in Malvani. And please do not misunderstand me. There would be no misrepresentation – written or spoken – about your community by me. Promise.

Geeta: *Baas!* (That's enough!) (in a rebuking tone) *Saab aise hi bolte hain!* (Everyone says that!) I have seen many researchers like you who exploit us, we poor *hijras*.

Me: Hmmm.

Geeta: OK. Visit me next Tuesday after 4 p.m. in my office. (tone settling and becoming softer) But remember, I will give you only half an hour.

Me: Thanks so much. How should I reach your office?

Geeta: Where would you be coming from?

Me: Vashi, Navi Mumbai [New Bombay].

Geeta: Bitch! You live so, so far. It takes nearly two hours to reach my office.

Me: Yes, I am aware of that.

Geeta: Reach Malad station. Come to the 'West'. Hire an autorickshaw and ask for Malvani *5 numbar gali, police chowki ki samne* (Malvani, lane number 5, in front of the police station). *Phir pahunch keye phone karnaa, mein kisi ko bhejungi tumhe leye aney keye liye.* (And when you reach, call me; I will ask somebody to go and pick you up.)[4]

Me: *Dhanyavaad.* (Thank you.)

Geeta: *Aur suno, yeh autorickshaw wale bahut harami hote hain; 30 rupiyee lagte hain humare idhar pahunchne mein. Jada paisa mat dena* (And listen, these autorickshaw drivers are bastards. The usual fare is 30 rupees to reach my office. Do not pay more than that.)

Me: *Dhanyavaad.* (Thank you.)

I reached Malvani the following Tuesday. I stood in front of the *police chowki* (police station) and called Geeta. Over the telephone, I mentioned to her the colour and type of my dress as a mark of identification – blue *salwar kameez* (a south Asian women's dress comprising a long tunic and loose pants, and a scarf or stole called *dupatta*), with a brown bag and a file in my hands. In ten minutes, a thin man, wearing grey trousers and a white shirt, with leather slippers on his feet, came up to me and asked, 'Aap Ahonaa ji[5] ho? Mera naam Prateek hain, Geeta neye bheja hain aapko office mein leye jaane keye liye' (Are you Ahonaa? My name is Prateek; Geeta asked me to pick you up and bring you to her office).

Prateek walked me through a tangle of lanes, on a muddy and uneven road flanked by shoddily constructed shops. We passed fast-food shops selling *pakoras*[6] and stale-looking *samosas*.[7] Women were walking by in their *burkhas*,[8] shopping at roadside vegetable stalls. I felt bewildered. The local butchers stood at their open butcheries, and the smell was putrid and somewhat repulsive; I wondered whether Malvani's residents were used to this. There were low-budget garment shops, and amidst all this, 'video centres' that cater to the local 'male' population with films with names like 'Meri Biwi ki Jawani' (My Wife's Lust). I later asked Prateek about this, and he replied, 'Idhar adult film chalta hain' (They show adult films here).

MALVANI SLUM AND ITS NOTORIOUS HISTORY

Malvani is infamous for fights and theft, and is an area in the western suburbs of Bombay recording one of the highest crime rates in the city. This dense slum was a rehabilitation site with *kachhi jhopris* (temporary shanties) at the time of the communal riots in Bombay in the early 1990s. Drugs and narcotic consumption and trade are a major problem in the area and part of the wider nexus of drug peddling in the city. The local slum dwellers mentioned links to the Middle East and also Pakistan and Afghanistan. Their narratives are substantiated by the fact that there are some fishermen from India as well as Pakistan who meet in the Arabian Sea and engage in criminal activities. The slum also sees tragic deaths in the dingy alleyway next to the *kabristan* (graveyard). The slum dwellers also mentioned the murders of people every other day. There are instances of local goons in league with the underworld gangs of Bombay. They extort substantial *hafta* (protection money) from local shop owners. If there is resistance, the shopkeeper is called to a nearby alleyway at night and shot. The local police are aware of these incidents but the wider nexus of the perpetrator with bigger gangsters leads to suppression, and the deaths remain unnoticed.

The slum dwellers avoid walking in the alleyways near the *kabristan*. These alleyways are menacing even during the day. The local goons play cards, smoke, consume drugs and create a noxious atmosphere. At night they drink alcohol openly and engage in various wrongdoings. The area in and around Malvani slum records the highest number of murders almost every year.

Rival gangs of two notorious underworld gangsters, Dawood Ibrahim and Chota Rajan, had years ago fought violent, bloody battles for control of the area. Today, while the gangs and their leaders are no longer active, slumlords who pledge loyalty to these gangsters still call the shots. Almost all officials in the northern part of the city said the gang culture among the slum population contributed to the crime pattern in the city. Theft was the most commonly reported crime in the nearby police station. The slum dwellers warn each other to keep their doors locked from inside even during the day. The Malvani slum area is illegal in the sense that the slum is built on unauthorized land. The slumlords sell small shanties to vulnerable immigrants who have no other shelter in the city. The slum dwellers live in dire poverty, compounded by illiteracy, poor sanitation and open drains with sewage flowing into the lanes. Huge mounds of garbage are seen in every corner of the dingy by-lanes, with rodents scurrying through and street dogs and pigs scavenging for food. Children play cricket in the narrow lanes during the day, with cricket balls often falling into the drains. The children climb down into the drain to fetch their ball, now covered with dirt, wash it and resume their game.

Geeta's community-based organization (CBO) – Sakhiyani – is located in one of these lanes in the slum. Besides families that live in the slum, there are single women who live in a community. These are sex workers who travel across the city for work. *Hijra*-identified persons also live as a community. This mixed population is scattered across the slum. Geeta rented the ground floor of a two-storied house. One could always hear loud music being played inside the office from outside. Visitors went in and out, with a row of their slippers on the tiny veranda in front of the house. There are loud noises – sounds of laughter, cacophony or sometimes arguments – that one cannot miss if one passes by in the lane.

Figure 2.1 *Kothi*s and *hijra*s with their *panthi*s (boyfriends) from Malvani slum, Bombay, socializing at Aksa Beach near the slum
Source: Photograph by the author.

BEAUTY, SPACE AND CONSUMER CULTURE

Henri Lefebvre's (1991) classic account of the city invigorates the idea of urban space and urban structures. It establishes the perspective of how a city's space manoeuvres the people and the social context – in the way in which the 'city' is represented. However, the city as a context of everyday practices provides a valuable account of the ways in which human experiences are conducted. The feminist interpretation of the city's space and spatiality marks the importance of the positionality of the gendered(ed) being in mediating that space and the ways in which those spaces are navigated and re-imagined (Rose 1993). It further brings in the conceptualization of the city and its urban spaces which are enmeshed with multiple contingencies of gender forms and categories that are performative enactments, adding meaning to a concrete spatial context. Elizabeth Grosz (1995) draws attention to the tacit interconnectedness between the body and the city – as Grosz observes, both are 'mutually defining', with a fundamental involvement of ideas, knowledge, practices, systems and processes, so as to assign a particular meaning to the 'boundary of that space'.

Globalizing modernity has marked a discrete understanding of the city's space (McGrew and Held 2002; Soros 2002), with a significant emphasis on the effect of globalization in the construction and rearticulation of gender and sexuality (Altman 2004). The new processes of modernity project a contemporary conception of a particular characteristic, a new form of production and consumption that further leads to the formation of a new form of self and identity (Appadurai 1996; Ngai 2005). This form of social and cultural structure manifests in a pattern of interaction of market-driven mechanisms, with an expression of a discrete progressive modernization. These traits are further manoeuvred within the life of people – a political engineering and the management of the politics of the body and disciplinary techniques by which market knowledge is imbibed and embodied (Ong 2006: 12–14).

My point of departure in this piece of work is to articulate the specific aspect of globalizing modernity and consumer culture that appears to address the understanding of how the marketplace produces desires, and how the 'market' is intrinsically linked to the construction and negotiation of a specific form of identity and subjectivity. This work also draws attention to how sexuality is produced through culturally specific social processes, with an emphasis on the idea of how sexuality is constructed across time and space, so as to demonstrate a particular framework of a particular subculture – the *hijra*s – and to understand the complex relationship between their sexuality, sexual practices and sexual desires that are embodied and re-represented.

Theorizing on the link between capitalist society and consumer culture, anthropological literature looks into the empirical evidence on how newly formed identities are created, based on consumption, desires and sexual practices (Parker 1991; D'Emilio 1998; Turner 1996; Vickers 2006; Gamson and Moon, 2004). A political economy of desire begins to substantiate the linkages between 'market' and 'consumption', so as to understand capitalism and the free flow of commodities; 'desire' builds into the interpretation of the self-engineering and self-enterprise of a market-driven mode of governing, a constantly shifting discourse on the economic landscape and the political restructuring of materiality and its emergent processes (Curtis 2004; Parker and Gagnon 1995; Jackson 2003). This adds to the argument of Haug (1986), who analyses the 'aesthetics of commodities' in the period of late capitalism, and the 'erotic' interpretation of commodities. Commodities build into a libidinal metaphor and consumption practices evoke the desires that are produced – a complex interplay of what Haug terms the 'sexualization of commodities' and the human appetite to perceive and consume.

This leads to the argument that desire is a social phenomenon produced by the market economy (Turner 1996; Boellstorff 2007). Modernity and the interpretation of desire are linked to the foci of how 'practice' builds into the evidence of 'recognition' and the 'reflection' of self-formation (Hall et al. 2000: 16–20). This self-efficacy of consumption and the construction of one's individual body and the self further attempts to deploy commodity and the idea of fetishism (Bristow 1997; Adkins 2002; see also Beck 2006). From an anthropological point of view, fetishism draws attention to erotic signification and the politics of pleasure suggesting an illusionary experience of either consumption or experience or both. This brings in the idea of the 'commodification of identity' in the context of which Debra Curtis (2004) refers to the market economy and the continuous processes of human desires via the urge to self-seeking consumption that ultimately becomes a socially and discursively produced cultural artefact.

TRANSGRESSION AND THE VANITY OF DESIRE

Transgenderism in non-Western societies is particularly explained based on the multiplicities of gender configuration (Kulick 1998), postulating on the particular cultural spaces which they inhabit. Anthropological inquiry on contemporary transgender communities (Prieur 1998; Kulick 1998; Boellstorf 2005; Sinnott 2011; Johnson 1997) reinforces the idea of the erotic practices and urban lifestyle within these communities and their spaces, and establishes how discrete identity categories are formed based on their self-defined gender and performativity. The subjects exhibit certain forms of beauty and consumption practices that reveal elements of capitalist and cosmopolitan traits and yet strongly cling to their local culture. To name a few, the *fakaleiti* in Tongo in Western Polynesia, the *travesti*s of Brazil, the *jota*s of Mexico and the *kathoey*s in Thailand demonstrate a unique interpretation of transgender culture and identity that posits the meaning of how these populations embody the symbolic and material association of cosmopolitan traits with a competing correlation of the global and the local. For example, Niko Besnier (2002) demonstrates that the *fakaleiti*, transgender people in Tongo, in their fashion, dress and bodies, exhibit a considerable feminine comportment; with reification of symbolic feminine performativity and the consumption of female hormones, they achieve more feminine appearances. Their cosmopolitan traits further manifest in the *fakaleiti*s' participation in beauty pageants; the extravagant glamour with which they fashion their overall performances demonstrates skilful understanding of their aesthetic and interactional display. This highlights how transgender sexuality in the non-Western context constitutes a new expansive notion of beauty, identity and body that proposes a logic of aesthetics, closely bound with the notion of heterogeneity of consumption practices, yet creating a re-representation in how they retain their localized cultural traits to showcase a new way of identity politics.

In a similar fashion, radical transgender politics in the Latin American context provides an important idea of the transgression of conventional gender and body norms, to a large extent, by body image acquired through feminine physical attributes (Prieur 1998; Kulick 1998). For example, in Brazil, the *travesti*es, the local transgender community, do not identify as women; they are homosexual males who desire men, but who irretrievably alter their body by injecting female hormones so as to generate female bodily features like breasts, rounded body parts, and so on.

What is interesting to note here is, the social organization of desire through capitalist lifestyle choices – the multiple transgender communities in the non-West like the *jota*s, *travesti*s, *fakaleiti*, *kathoey*s and *banut* have developed a specialized erotic world for themselves, constituting a specific erotic schema that consciously regulates their particular context.

Among the more intriguing cultural–political developments in modern South Asia (Bose and Jalal 2017), sexuality and conditions of gender pluralism generally have a long history (Roy 2020). The 1990s witnessed projects of modernity during economic transformation, presupposing a social engineering that developed a modernist discourse, emphasizing urbanization, technology, economic progress and industrialization and, most notably, institutional and cultural rationalization with the rise of market economies (Roy 2017).

This chapter undertakes a comprehensive analysis of gender(ed) pluralism, developing an interpretative framework of broad indexicality of subjects with feminine traits. Through a lower social and economic stratified subcultural study, I plan to understand and theorize on the experiences of beautification and transformation. I focus on historical transformations of identities and representations to build a framework conducive to culturally interlocking domains that critically envisage the conditions of pluralism.

Gender and sexuality in modern South Asia are 'wrapped in micro-corporeality' (Chatterjee 1999). Discourses of embodiment domesticated by various intermediaries of historical contingency and post-colonial revolutionary politics lie heavily contested within the intersections of national belonging – politics, sociality, identity and class – engaging further with questions of democratic rights and dissent (Shah 2019; Mazarella 2017; Menon 2007; Mukhopadhyay 2017).

However, Anjali Arondekar (2015) traces the historical archives pointing in particular to South Asian colonialism entangled with race. Arondekar (2006) further premises 'race' as situated within a rhetoric of interchangeability in complex global systems. And to these differential racial logics, sexuality is an invocation of a new form of racism – transnationally and trans-historically. That is to say, tracing its genealogy, the imperial archive forces us to rethink colonial exclusion of gender transgressors within the lexicon of erasure, silence and liminality (Arondekar 2005, 2009). The historiography of colonial sexuality sets the grid on white enslavement and colonial fear – a matter of considerable political gravity that eschews imperial race (Sinha 1995; Lamb 2000; Puri 1999; Gupta 2001). Such experiences of subversion render a system of control laid down by colonial lawmakers enforcing policies in their own interest. This deeply concerns questions of violence and power, further corroborated by systems of evidence, granting subjectification under the law. Legal jurisprudence in the colony ruptures the distinction between 'sovereign and disciplinary power' – a mechanism in which 'sovereignty' becomes 'the discourse of discipline' that is the basis for the code of law (Stoler 1995). However, the eulogy of race is never justified. Race gradually became confiscated by society at large with the nobility occupying a significant class position (McWhorter 2004). Race regimes produce subjugated bodies outlining the distinct realm of experience that occurs in isolating a tactical component within the population. Paul Gilroy's (2000) anti-essentialist theories of black identity build the argument on race as an objective condition to polarize identity. This problem diminishes the culture of the complex and the effective within political and moral languages, let alone the corrosive power that assigns an inferior position in the enduring hierarchies that raciology creates (McClintock 1995).

The implication of Black critique in the colonial–racial line responds to the political core of the imperial figure, pointing to the oppressive system of the rising Euro-American capitalist hegemony (Grzinic and Tatlic 2014: 94). This began with 'Negro labour', especially slave trade which formed the basis for a large market for British manufacture, and laid the foundation for the integration of the world and a new commercialization, opening new vistas for empire (du Bois 1899). In mapping the progress of industrial modernity, the matrix of racialization sustained a homogenous system of control over heterogenous ideological approaches (Grosfoguel 2000; Perez 1999: 128). Thus, race developed as a taxonomic enterprise tantamount to differences. The problematics of these differences shifted from 'race' to 'population' in the wake of World War II which witnessed biological selection of the 'population' entangled with a politically powerful classificatory regime (Haraway 1989, 1997). Race as a concept in the mid-twentieth century was framed around biological determinism grounded in the commitment of post-genomic scientific enterprise, potentially entangled with scientific and social practices of racial politics within social projects (see Byrd and Hughey 2015).

THE DRESS THAT MATTERS

Prateek is in his late twenties, is of short height and has a wheatish complexion. He has a sharp pointed nose and protruding upper teeth. Prateek identifies as a *kothi*. He works as an accountant in the Sakhiyani office. He has decided to resign from his job there as he is to marry a girl from his native village. The marriage is against his wishes, but he is being compelled to do so by his parents. Prateek said that his family expected the birth of a male child after his marriage to continue their family lineage. His parents were aware of his *kothi* identity.[9] They knew that Prateek had some kind of physical or emotional relationship with a young man of his age in their neighbourhood. Prateek's father believed that everything would become 'normal' after the marriage: 'Sab theek ho jayega shadi keye baad' (Everything will be all right after the marriage). His mother, on the other hand, had pleaded with him to get married and father a child and told him that after that Prateek could lead his life as he wished to.

During the day, the Sakhiyani office is busy with visitors. The *hijra*s come to share the joys and sorrows of their everyday lives, exchange amusing jokes, socialize, drink tea and play indoor games; sometimes they dance to the rhythm of Bollywood songs, having adorned themselves with make-up and jewellery (Figure 2.3). While dancing, some call to their *hijra* friends and colleagues and ask cheerfully, 'Am I not just like so-and-so, the beautiful Bollywood heroine?'

Figure 2.2 *Hijra*s socializing in the Sakhiyani office of Malvani slum, Bombay. Madhu (extreme left) and Sruti (second right).

Source: Photograph by the author.

Sakhiyani outreach workers Shamma, Chappi and Rajni encouraged the *hijra*s to use condoms when engaged in *pan* (sex work). In the *hijra* language they say, 'Waater dhurane keye time chocolate istemaal karna' (When engaging in anal sex, use condoms). Here *waater* means buttocks while *dhurana* means having intercourse. *Chocolate*, in the *hijra* language, stands for condoms. They prefer to use the *hijra* language among themselves. Shamma *mammi*, an elderly *hijra* who lives in the slum, explains that *hijra rewal*, or *hijra* language, is useful when the *hijra*s are being chased by the police when out for *pan*. The language, which is alien to outsiders, safeguards their communication with one another.[10]

Sakhiyani is a Hindi word, which means female friendship. The office maintains strict records of the *hijra* AIDS patients in the slum and prompts them to visit local government hospitals for regular check-ups. The staff distributes condoms for safer sex and organizes government-supported sex education workshops. Geeta is the founder member of the organization. She is herself a *hijra* but does not socialize with the other *hijra*s in the slum. She is a high-school graduate who speaks fluent English and prefers to involve herself in *hijra* activism and work to promote sexual health. Geeta says she started Sakhiyani as a community set-up with the idea of subverting the popular programmatic work related to AIDS. Her aim is to construct an informal space for *hijras* based on dialogue and communication. She believes that the exchange of casual and informal conversation on the topics of health, sexual activities, love, emotions, ornaments, *panthis* (male lovers or clients) and AIDS will engender a strong sense of community and friendship among the *hijras*.

In the evenings, the office premises become home to some of the *hijra* employees of Sakhiyani. Chappi, Shamma and Rajni sleep there after they return from their *pan*. They dress in the office and leave for their *pan* on the nearby expressways that connect Bombay to other cities of India. Otherwise, they prefer to perform *mangti* (begging) on long-distance trains. Shamma explains that they prefer the 'Punjab Mail' because the train has *chissa-panthis* (handsome men). According to them, North Indian men are *ariyaal chissa* (very handsome) and they respect, love and become physically attracted to *hijras*.

Figure 2.3   *Hijras* applying make-up and getting dressed before leaving for sex work one evening

Source: Photograph by the author.

Prateek calls herself 'Priya' while out for *pan*. She dresses in a colourful *sari*, make-up and ornaments, and joins her *hijra* colleagues, either in suburban railway stations or at appointed places. From there, they form groups and leave for their respective destinations. Their allotted places or zones for sex work are determined by *nayak*s, who are the heads of the *hijra* community. The *nayak* acts as the lawmaker of the community and decides which place would be allotted to a particular *hijra*. These zones are not fixed but are rotated among the community.[11]

Chappi, who has also worked as an accountant in the Sakhiyani office, seemed to me to be scared to join the *hijra*s for sex work. She worried that if she is caught by the *gori* (police) while out for sex work, she would be unable to get away. She is neither confident in using the *hijra rewal* nor does she know how to trick police officers by seducing them with oral sex on which the officers leave the *hijra*s alone; she has heard about these tricks from other *hijra*s in the community. Furthermore, she is also scared that if her biological father (with whom she stays in Bombay and to whom she presents herself as male) discovers her affiliations with the *hijra*s and hears that she is involved in these activities, he would kill her. One evening, under pressure from her *hijra* colleagues, she decided to join them. Their team for work was divided into two. One of the groups, comprising Chappi and Prateek, planned to perform *mangti* (begging) on trains. According to them, the act of *mangti* is less vulnerable to police investigation because the work is not directly related to performing sexual activities in public. Moreover, it is not considered a criminal offence like *pan*, whereas for the latter, *hijra*s are harassed and beaten brutally.

Rajni and Shamma planned to visit Naygaon Chowk beside the expressway that connects the city of Bombay to the city of Surat in the neighbouring state of Gujarat. They sought *panthi*s among the long-distance truck drivers who stop for food and rest at nearby inns. The locality has many dance bars which are visited by local gangsters and men for recreation. Young men from Surat and Bombay also visit resorts that are situated by the seashore. These young men often look for sex at night when resort owners are unable to provide contact with female sex workers. The *hijra*s have gradually become known to these men in the Naygaon area for *pan*.

That evening, they dressed differently, according to the purpose for which they were going out. Shamma and Rajni dressed in jeans and sleeveless tops and put on loud and appealing make-up: foundation to hide their stubble, thickly applied eyeliner, pink eyeshadow and red lipstick. Prateek changed her name to 'Priya', associated with her female identity, for *pan*. Chappi, on the other hand, prefers to wear Indian clothes like *salwar kameez* and *sari*s. Dress, they say, is an important mechanism for attracting clients. Their dress symbolizes their profession according to tradition or modernity. Shamma explains that clients for sex work prefer to have someone dressed in Western or modern attire. Conversely, begging, or *mangti*, is symbolic of a traditional occupation for the *hijra*s: it is associated with respect for the community and public fear of visibility of the hijra identity. For each of these purposes, dress is important.

Both groups dressed to highlight their breasts. Some *hijra*s in Malvani slum have developed breasts by consuming hormonal supplements, and others have undergone breast implant surgery.[12] Besides this, many *hijra*s put pads inside their bras to enhance the shape of their breasts and add to their femininity. It signifies the erotic capital of their bodies. Rajni said that many of her male clients or *panthi*s understand how breasts are enhanced with padded bras. When some of the *panthi*s realize that the breasts are not real, they refuse to pay the *hijra*s for their services. If the *hijra*s protest against non-payment, the *panthi*s threaten to report their activities (prostitution) to the police.

Besides their breasts, *hijra*s enhance their lips and eyes with intense make-up. They feel that their lips and eyes are sought by the *panthi*s while making eye contact that leads to the deal. They linger at Naygaon Chowk and look for men in the busy areas of the street, where the inns and bars are situated. When a man repeatedly tries to stare, the *hijra* knows the art of enticing him by returning his glance. They keep looking at him. Such interaction proceeds secretively, and both parties are conscious of hiding it from public attention. Only the *hijra* and the man know their mutual purpose and the means to achieve it. From her corner, the *hijra* delivers a sign of sex through her glossy lips, which she has painted with red lipstick and lip gloss and outlined with a contrasting colour like black or deep blue. Her eyes are highlighted with thick, black eyeliner and mascara to make her eyelashes prominent. Sometimes she sprinkles her eyelashes with glitter to make the eyes even more prominent and appealing. She may make a subtle pout with her lips, simulating a kiss, or push her tongue between her lips to indicate her willingness to offer oral sex. Shamma confidently adds that seeing such gestures would arouse any man.

While putting on their make-up that evening, Shamma narrated an incident:

Ahonaa ji, kaal Naygaon mein jab pan karne gaye, tab jharion mein gori aaya tha bila karne. Mein neye usko khomat kaar di. Gori khush, mein bhi khush. Par mujhe sirf bees rupiyee diye. Par aur eek panthi mila jo meri kaam aur adao seye khush hokey panch sau rupiyee diya. Panthi mere adaon peye fida ho gaya. Mujhe bola Bombayee mein mujhse milne keye liye. Panthi bahut ameer thaa lagta thaa. Mota soney kaa chain galey mein, aur ariyaal thappar. Unoneye mujhe 500 rupiyee diye, sirf khomat keye. Par sale gori neye sirf bees rupeyee diye kal pan peye.

Ahonaa, when we went for sex work in Naygaon, a policeman came into the bushes to harass me. So, I pleased him with oral sex. He was happy and I was also happy. But he offered me only 20 rupees. Later, I met another client who was so pleased with my services and feminine charms that he asked me to meet him in Bombay later. The client was very rich as *ariyaal thappar* [in hijra language]. He was wearing a thick gold chain. I just served him with oral sex, and he offered me 500 rupees. But the bastard policeman only paid 20 rupees.

Chappi and Priya were also excited to narrate some incidents that took place in the train during their *mangti* on the day before. Chappi said:

Priya aur mein jor seye tali bajate hain. Sab ki samaj mein aa jata hain, hijra ayaa hai train mein. Saab toh thoda thoda dar jate hain, par panthi logo mein bahut shararat jagta hain. Mein to gana gaate gaate godi mein jaa keye baithti huin. Koye koye panthi meri dhamni dabaa deta hain. Bhaut sare panthi aachey paisee dete bhi hain. Jaubaan paisa hota hain mangti mein.

Priya and I clap our hands intensely. This lets the passengers know that *hijra*s have boarded the train. Some of them are scared of *hijra*s, but the *panthi*s [men who are sexually interested in *hijra*s] are excited and act mischievously with us. I always sing songs and sit on the men's laps. Some of them squeeze my breasts. Many pay good money. Good money is generated in begging.

After they have finished dressing and applying make-up, the *hijra*s hurriedly make their way to start their evening of *pan* and *mangti*. They buy chewing gum from the tea stall adjacent to the Sakhiyani office. Walking down the lanes of the slum in their glamorous, high-heeled shoes to reach the main road, they entice the local young men with erotic looks. According to them, their high-heeled shoes add more glamour to their appearance. The shoes are hard to walk in, but these *hijra*s wear them every day and have learnt to manage. Their vanity bags swing at their sides, they toss their long hair which they keep loose, and sway their hips as they call out to each other: 'Dhandhey peye chaley?' (Shall we go for work?)

THE BIOPOLITICS OF BEAUTY

The central argument of this chapter relates to the inherent characteristics of appearance that signal a new political rationality of beauty within these sexual subcultures in Bombay. 'Race' is concerned in this beauty project with the largely imagined potential for beauty enhancement within the spectrum of commercialism and the ideals of cultural aesthetics. And this cannot avoid the recognition of corporeal identification as an effective domain of 'disciplinary' power – beauty emerges as a complex explosive symbol of 'aestheticized' and 'eroticized' consumption practices that positions these gender liminal identities within the regimes of capitalism (Edmonds 2010: 31). The rise of the culture of beauty leads to a new argument to rethink the social hierarchy of these subjects – 'race' arguments pause to indicate the key element of historic–colonial exclusion in the management of the population (Hinchy 2019: 204). Situating the subcultural identity within racial politics is a power exercise – describing a population ('criminal tribe') within the nation state, which enacts governmentality and a political economy of domination (see Foucault 2004). It could also be argued that Michel Foucault's analysis of 'power over life' establishes the link between 'state racism' and biopolitical rationality that focuses on control over relations of power. Foucault dwells on this in the *Order of Things* (1970 [2001]); the analysis of taxonomies would legitimate a discourse that is based on power and 'relations of force' (Fujita 2013). This opens up a historico-political field, in which telling 'the history' deciphers the constitution and management of populations within the elements of bio-politics, whereby, race-laden norms emerge as a trope, arguably conceptualizing a society or nation as a 'social body' (Muller 2011). These complex processes of surveillance in the regulation of bodies relate to Foucault's 'governmentality'.

The point of reflection of 'race' and bio-politics, which is also noteworthy in this chapter, prefiguring Martin Heidegger's reflection on 'machenschaft', or machination, develops a critique of Foucault's account of bio-politics and also a critique of Giorgio Agamben's presentation of bio-politics as the metaphysical foundation of Western political rationality (Crowell and Malpas 2007). Heidegger's mediation on the essence of modern technology presents an intriguing remark on the convergence of 'technological ordering', 'biological existence' and 'enhancement of power' that are constitutive of the concept of bio-power and bio-politics (Blitz 2014). Articulation of this modernity suggests the modern conception of natural self-production and the technical construction of 'beings' (Feenberg 2010). Thus, for Heidegger, modernity is 'blind to machenschaft' – the 'objectification and subjectification' of being that defines technological nihilism (Geertz 2018). Heidegger's 'being' can reckon with the productive depiction of the collective ordering that is representable within the purview of sociopolitical dimensions of modernity. Therefore, Heidegger's 'machination' is an ontological account of the way beings are disclosed and rationally ordered in modernity. While Heidegger hints at the significance of life, understood as will to power, as an element of power and technological control, the connection becomes explicitly articulated only with Foucault's conception of bio-power.

Foucault consistently uses bio-power and bio-politics as synonyms for 'the regulation of the life of populations' (Lacombe 1996). Foucault's analysis of the 'Right of Death and Power over Life' indicates the transition from a pre-modern to modern regime of power over life. Again, modern power develops into an 'anatomo-politics' of the human body, organized through disciplinary techniques, aiming at the optimization of the body's capabilities, forces and docility that eventually develops into a 'bio-politics of the population' – a regulatory power centred on the species; the body imbued with the mechanics of life, serving on the basis of biological processes (Collier 2009; see also Arnason 2012). Foucault's 'technologies' of power focus on the 'ontic' level of 'organized' techniques of power that concerns the technological ordering of life to a historically specific analysis of 'the biosocial management of populations' that powerfully functions in modern society (Cisney and Morar 2015).

Foucauldian 'bio-politics' however reflects an abandonment of the critical–theoretical perspective, favouring an exploration of the aesthetic–ethical practices of self-fashioning. This possibility might involve Foucault's remark on 'bodies and pleasures', gesturing towards sexual subcultures and the resistant form of bio-power that I will explain in Chapter 5. This further departs from the understanding that subjects are able to resist and subvert. Agency is made possible by a kind of potential self-reflexivity, implying a particular kind of relation to oneself which is based upon the practices of subjectivation. Foucault uses 'freedom' as a situated practice of choice-making within structured conditions. According to him, 'Power is exercised only in free subjects, and only in so far as they are free…. Power and freedom's refusal to submit cannot therefore be separated' (Foucault 1982). This situated practice of freedom or self-reflexiveness further aims to analyse anti-authoritarian struggles as a form of resistance to power (Allen 2011: 29–30). This form of modern self-governmentality suggests Foucault's 'ethical turn' in his interpretation of 'Care of the Self' as a practice of freedom (Milchman and Rosenberg 2011). This 'ethical turn', as Robert Sinnerbrink (2006) affirms, concerns 'pragmatic practices of ethical self-formation'.

It is also tempting to suggest Agamben's thesis on the bio-political essence of modernity that mediates the 'quasi-Hegelian Aufheben (Shilliam 2009). Yet Agamben tempers the overt formalized character of Heidegger's theory of machination, appropriating further the historically particularistic approach of Foucault's genealogies of bio-power. Agamben profoundly questions the bio-political foundations of modernity without succumbing to a utopian messianism. That said, Agamben interchanges the political dimensions of bio-power – resistance and various forms of bio-political control into a 'messianic politics' (Cimino 2016).[13] Again, Agamben's messianic politics is a kind of 'synthesis' of the Heideggerian 'metanarrative of Being' into a 'metanarrative of biopolitics'. That latter takes 'the exposure of bare life to sovereign violence', exemplified by the camp, as manifesting the fundamental ontological structure of Western political modernity; a parlous condition that can only be overcome through a messianic overturning of existing law and politics in favour of a utopian community to come (Sinnerbrink 2006).

AESTHETIC CONCEPTUALIZATION

Hijra beautification techniques raise certain issues on the focus on the body and the connection to their embodiment that describes the body's subjectivity in importantly different ways. These beautification practices can create and evoke certain narratives of experiences which in a way raise the issue of the phenomenological analysis of a particular process of beautification (Cahill 2003). The beautification of the *hijra* body can be understood in terms of Elizabeth Grosz's (1995: 104) contention of how the body is 'a unity and cohesiveness through physical and social inscription of the body's surface' – allowing the inscription of 'sexed/gendered bodies' through the embodiment of bodily practices. The embodied practices develop a form of cultural image that serves a type of 'representational' constellation to a form of space that adds meaning to the subject (Joyce 2005; Hogle 2005; Adkins 2002: 62; Orlie 2002).

Mary Douglas in her path-breaking work, *Natural Symbols* (2003 [1970]), considers the symbolic significance of the body. Douglas argues that human agency has a strong sense to 'replicate' the social context in a symbolic order that draws certain bodily metaphors. Given this articulation and view of the body that symbolically manifests the social – Douglas presents reflexive accounts of the body as a 'social text' that draws a complex representational perspective of society. The body, as she argues, generates the meaning inscribed by cultural forces to deliver culturally specific meanings. Many other social theorists of the body observe that 'feminine beauty and embodiment' is a cultural artefact that builds an ideal aesthetic and beauty regime, and further serves as a mechanism of 'social power' to discipline and demonstrate the desired body image (Bordo 1993).

Elizabeth Grosz (1995: 104) recounts the archaeological composition of the body with specific focus on dress, ornamentation and body modification, demonstrating the construction of gendered bodies with an embodied sense of bodily practices (see also Joyce 2005; Hogle 2005; Clark 2003). These social entities of embodied practices mark the assumption of the significance of the embodying elements, indicating how dress and ornamentation contribute to 'public legibility', so as to 'textualize' and give meaning to the body's surface with an articulation of the social presentation of the body (Barney 1992; Gremillion 2005). The techniques of inscription demarcate a 'gender-specific costuming' – highlighting a symbolic allegory that displays certain specific ideas and discrete subjective meanings of the physicality and the performative model that the subject inhabits.

In a similar fashion, Enid Schildkrout (2004) discerns several theoretical positions in her discussions on the 'archaeology of the body'. On the one hand, she identifies the body as a 'scene of display' – reckoning 'posture', 'gesture', 'costume', 'sexuality' and 'representation'. On the other hand, Schildkrout borrows her idea from Anthony Giddens to relate the body as an 'artefact', referring to the representational metaphor of the body in relation to larger social contexts. The narratives of *hijra* beautification for sex work reinforce the view of their body and their appearances, so as to evoke a corporeal dimension that seeks to build a cultural legitimation, as to how their bodily inscription of dress, ornamentation and make-up marks and appropriates the cultural regimes of society in terms of feminine beautification. Western and traditional clothing as a point of departure for their sex work conform to certain representational and material dynamics of the body and its embodied practices. These perceive the construction and production of the body and its discursive materialization based on 'market' regimes of social organization of their sexual and everyday life. This is to say, the hijra body and beautification bring into evidence a 'market-like' character that installs certain attributes of eroticism emphasizing the socially constituted artefacts that transpose the institutional dynamics of the feminine body, mannerisms, beautification and other corporeal sites that are observable, and induce masculine pleasure (Greenberg 1988; Negrin 2002; Cahill 2003; Reischer and Koo 2004).

Their sense of dress and appearance also seeks to recall and represent a powerful embodied effect that conceals as well as reveals their body, with a gendered corporeal identification. Their feminine embodiment is to generate attractiveness through the means of make-up and beautification, and to hide any surface reality of male and masculine bodily attributes – evoking a sense of identification that is integral to their desires and fantasies. The *hijra* sense of being celebrates their feminine attributes with the articulation, construction and representation of the material embodiment of beautification. Further, their dress becomes the cultural expression of their embodied being by which the significance of their male bodily attributes is reduced. The multiple material forces of how they dress in varied spatial contexts further promote the idea of corporeal expressions demanded by spatiality.

Maurice Merleau-Ponty in his idea of body-image and space (1962, 1963, 1964) writes of the implication of the body in a particular spatial context; how the body inhabits that space; and how its movements and its limits create a 'corporeal schema' or 'body image' which is located in that space. The space is a conscious invasion of the subject that permeates the reflection of the subjects' action. In other words, the space and the subject are built through a series of relations in which the body situates itself in that space.

My contention on space, body and sexuality attempts to locate the nuances of the interaction between the *hijra*s and their clients during solicitation. The erotic display, visual interplay and facial expressions as a sign of solicitation bring in the erotic and eroticizing perception between the *hijra*s and their clients – rendering an intimate exploration of the sexualization of the *hijra* body with a standardized erotic prize. The erotic capital that the *hijra*s possess pertains to an attribute that is reflexive to the erotic response that they receive from their clients in the spaces they visit for sex work. Moreover, the sexual attraction that is formed involves the eroticization of their body and performances in a particular erotic style that configures erotic passion. In the words of Merleau-Ponty, eroticized perception is the desirability of one body to another, in the context of which the 'physiognomy' is perceived through a set of signs, and the cultivation of a libidinal metaphor based on 'sensibility', 'affectivity' and 'perception'. In relation to this argument, sexuality according to Merleau-Ponty is not reflexive but 'intentional' – a conscious effort, and the interplay of instinct, impulse and perception (Merleau-Ponty 1962, 1964, 64).

In terms of the erotic schema and the analysis of a sexual subculture, Pierre Bourdieu's theorization of 'habitus' and 'field' (1977, 1980), and Erving Goffman's (1959) social psychological emphasis of the presentation of self builds a framework on 'self-presentation' and 'sexual practice', so as to construct a relationship between the structural constellations of the erotic actors in a particular social structure, and the spatial nodes and positions in which they present themselves. Bourdieu's 'habitus' as related with the 'erotic habitus' is the configuration of a historically and symbolically devised social structure which is embedded with fantasy and desire. The structure of desire is formulated in a designated space or site – the 'field' that manifests an organized set of signs and significations to pattern a definite set of interactions. In relation to this, Goffman's social–psychological focus on 'self-presentation' lays emphasis on image or impression – the manner in which the bodily features convey a critical understanding of the 'micro-level interactions' within this particular social context.

Bringing Bourdieu's and Goffman's analyses together, Adam Isaiah Green (2008) develops a 'sexual field framework' that outlines a context in which the actors negotiate in that field by developing a 'reflexive' understanding of their practices, the ways they present themselves, articulating a structure that is organized within a systematic interplay of the representational matrix.

The understanding of this theoretical apparatus relates to the logic of the contextual relations of the *hijra*s and their negotiations for sex work. Their beautification to develop erotic capital evokes a salient characteristic of the corporeal politics of these individuals. It further adds to the notion of the spatial schemata where their erotic disposition inhabits a particular space to cater to a particular taste – leading to the sexualization of a particular interactional pattern.

The extravagant beautification of the *hijra*s, such as highlighting their lips, wearing glossy lipsticks and glittering eyeshadows, their overtly sexual gestures, eye contact and pouting lips are evidence of the structural context premised on the spatial metaphor as organized in the arenas of their erotic world; constituting a pattern of their gender, identity and class, with their desired representation that adds to their erotic price, and physical traits to allure a specialized audience. The symbolic and the sexual metaphor illuminates the management of their sexual practices and their micro-level interactions – the *hijra*s and their clientele render an enduring representational metaphor of an erotic and sexual organization that further crystallizes into the analysis of the symbolic and sexual life of the *hijra* subculture.

RECOGNITION OF BEAUTY

The key to this comparative theoretical taxonomy on bio-politics suggests a prevailing logic of the reality experienced by these gender transgressors in Bombay – a semantic conceptualization of the representative figure of a 'state of exception', where laws, naming and prescriptive value blur the big principles and identity-calling. This radical challenge restores the sovereign mandate of the constitutive condition of their political existence. The politics posits an indispensable destabilizing of the body image; transformation acknowledges both situated knowledges and shared public knowledges on beauty. In other words, the stories in Malvani slum recorded here testify to the bio-political utility of beauty that charts several facts. First, the new regimes of beauty consumption assert an economic management of the subculture – that is to say, how attractiveness is correlated to their production and financial profit. Their new modes of beautification make their sex work economically more productive. And again, 'to look good' captures the material capacities of the body that ultimately integrate 'the body' into a system of economic productivity. Their stories of beautification also render a function of the body's performances (Roodenburg 2004) – corporeal beauty to look good and the quest for an image of feminine modernity. These make them striking to their male clientele (*panthi*): a sexual provocation that welcomes entertainment and sexual acts. Beautification and sex work go hand in hand, reflecting an aesthetic ideal of a new claim of 'affective turn' (Jarrin 2017: 13). This point relates to my second argument of Foucault's 'ethical turn' that I have explained before. In this context, the changing constellation of the body and how embodied practices to beautify have built in materiality and affectively attuned re-appropriation of their subjective construction are relevant. Also, this section draws on the possibilities to rethink beauty with another aspect of global homogenization – how beauty has emerged as a monolithic category. Beauty's promise as a certain form of regularity to new domains of experience marks the process in which appearance becomes the principal form of capital. Again, appearance bears the 'value' that might position class culture within the hierarchies of market-embedded networks of power and privilege – so much so that the 'value of appearance' constitutes the power of erotic legitimacy within the newly formed moral–national lexicon of Indian society.

The spectacle of dress and ornamentation as described amongst the gender transgressors signals a new symbolic cultural value that remains particularly charged with new representations of femaleness and traits of femininity. The body and its representation are attached to a historical and racialized gender(ed) image – *hijras* in contemporary Bombay transgress the stability of their racialized gender to embody dress-styles with multicultural dimensions. Adopting Western dress has two-directional influences: first, it influences the creation of new types of universalized identity; second, it creates an aesthetic appearance leading to a visual consumption of the body and ultimately 'a utility' – further enhancing their body's significance in terms of labour and economic value for sex work. The embodiment of Western dress thus becomes a cultural transgression within the subculture, with implications for the identity–culture nexus. Crossing this border of strict racialized gender practices and the body's stylization, Western attire symbolically transfers them (temporarily) from a homogeneous rigid space of their own nativity to a new order of spatialized gender that disrupts the status quo. Although such embodiment does not directly lead to a change, but the momentary transgression leads to an alteration that reflects a democratic sex appeal. This new pattern of conduct and form of expression builds their desirability, in terms of a modern or Western or liberated domain of femininity, aspiring to which they free themselves within the city's cosmopolitan space wherein their dress and femininity could align with cosmopolitan identity.

STORIES OF BREASTS

Dhamni, or breasts, are a popular topic of conversation among the *hijras* in Bombay. In social gatherings like the Urs (an Islamic religious festival) or *jarat*,[14] *hijras* sit after the festival and discuss their *dhamni*. They talk about hormones, and if one of the *hijras* has more developed breasts, then the rest of the group is eager to know about the particular hormones they have taken. Silicone implants, and where to get them, are popular topics as well. They talk about *hijra*s who have undergone breast implants and hence earn more through prostitution, and clients who are attracted by big breasts and therefore pay more. They also discuss how women have well-developed breasts that give their bodies a feminine shape, and, in their view, how women in the slum are envious of *hijra*s with big breasts. The *hijra*s also say that women in the slum feel a sense of insecurity and ask their husbands not to be friendly with the *hijra*s (especially those with big breasts) and not to look at them as they walk down the streets. *Hijra*s believe that it is because of their breasts that the *marad*s, or husbands, do not leave their wives and buy them gifts like *sari*s and gold jewellery.

*Hijra*s in Malvani spend hours discussing *harmones ki goli* (hormone tablets). Some of them had heard about hormones from their *hijra* friends in Kamatipura. Their friends told them that 'Harmones ki goli seye dhamni badi hoti hain' (Hormone tablets enhance breasts). The idea of being able to consume something that would feminize their bodies thrilled them, and they were curious to know more. They believed that these hormones had magical properties and would dramatically enhance their breasts, making them look beautiful. They also thought that *harmones* (hormones) would feminize their skin texture, and they would become fairer-skinned, gaining a much-desired feminine beauty. According to their beliefs, fairer and lighter-skinned feminine beauty is much desired by *panthi*s.

Young *hijra*s in Malvani are particularly preoccupied with hormones and breast development. They have learned the names of the relevant hormones that some of them buy over the counter in drug stores. Also, they have learnt from their *hijra* friends elsewhere in Bombay that hormones can be more effective if injected. This leads them to visit a local doctor in the slum, who can assist them with the therapy. In the process of their hormonal therapy, the *hijra*s are delighted to meet each other and compare their breast sizes and engage in various mischiefs. This excitement is related to how the *hijra*s link breast development to the elements of embodiment of femininity. The *hijra*s consider breast development as something extraordinary and magical.

The padded brassieres that *hijra*s wear when out for sex work give them the illusion of a feminine body shape – a form they would like to acquire through the use of hormones. Breasts become their symbolic capital when they are looking to attract clients. Furthermore, breasts become the essential body part that appeals to men. Sometimes men promise love and affection based on the sexual gratification from *hijra*s' breasts.

When seeking clients, Nitu, one of the *hijra*s in Malvani, said that they usually make eye contact with the *panthi*s (potential clients). Thereafter, they wait for the man to reciprocate and communicate his intentions similarly.

The *hijra* and the man thus reach an agreement on sharing physical intimacy. Then, also by means of eye contact, she asks the man to follow her to a more private place. The initial meeting usually takes place in the high street or on the highways. When they have moved to a less populated place, the *hijra* and the man negotiate payment, depending on the degree of intimacy the man desires.

Nitu says that after her breast implant surgery, *panthi*s usually pay her 100 rupees for one hour, but before her breast surgery men paid her only 20 rupees. She used to use pads and sometimes got beaten by her *panthi*s, who became especially aggressive when they found out that her breasts were not real. In many cases, *panthi*s ask the *hijra*s for oral sex. The rate for this varies from 20 to 50 rupees, depending on the pleasure the man receives. Nitu also remarked that certain sex acts cannot always be performed as they require the availability of discreet places and the elements of safety associated with them. These acts are usually performed in places like bushes, under a tree, public toilets and beaches – places that are usually dark and not frequented by the public.

As concerns the consumption of hormones, two hormone tablets every day is the most common dosage taken by the *hijra*s. This amount is not prescribed by any doctor or clinician; the *hijra*s learn this from other *hijra*s who consume similar hormones. These tablets are usually anti-androgen tablets in strong doses.[15] If the *hijra*s do not have much money, they usually buy contraceptive pills. The pharmacists at local drug stores are sometimes apprehensive about selling the pills to them as they are concerned that such strong dosage may affect the health of the *hijra*s. In this situation, the *hijra*s try to acquire the drugs by means of coercion. They either try to persuade shop owners with sexual overtures or resort to threats and abuse to realize their wishes.

Before her breast surgery, Nitu used to visit the local drug store in the slum to buy hormones to enhance her breasts. The attendants in the drug store were concerned about selling the tablets to her; they said that these strong drugs had a high chance of making her ill. However, she refused to listen to them and insisted they give her the medicine. When Nitu realized that there was no other way to persuade them, she began to entice an attendant with sexual conversations and body contact. Nitu asked the youngest attendant in the shop, who was in his late twenties, to visit her house late one night. When the attendant arrived, Nitu invited him to indulge in sexual acts, performing oral sex on him. The man was pleased and often visited Nitu's house in Malvani for the same purpose. In return, he provided Nitu with the hormone tablets whenever she needed them.

Nitu told her close *hijra* friends about her physical intimacy with the shop attendant. This news spread among the other *hijra*s in Malvani slum. They went to the shop and asked for hormone tablets over the counter; the shop attendants refused. They complained to the shop owner mentioning how Nitu obtained the pills from their shop attendant secretively and demanded the pills. The shop owner rebuked his employee and threatened to dismiss him from his job. Despite their efforts to convince the shop owner to give them the pills, he refused. In response, they called all their *hijra* friends from Malvani slum – about thirty of them. Together they stood in front of the drug store and started abusing the shop attendants and the owner. Their behaviour became aggressive, and as a sign of discontentment, they clapped their hands loudly and pulled up their *saris* (common gestures used by *hijras* to threaten or extort money in public places, often from shopkeepers). The situation became so chaotic that the local police were called in. The *hijras* were so obstinate that they refused to leave the shop until they received the pills. The policemen requested the shop owner to provide the *hijras* with the medicines, as they wanted to avoid any sort of chaos and confrontation, and settle the matter. In such situations it becomes hard for common people and the police to confront the *hijras*. *Hijras* often take advantage of these situations as they are aware of this fact; they often say, 'Hijra kanun keye bahar hain' (*Hijras* lie outside the domain of law).

Hum Neye Jumbo, Jumbo Dhamni Banaye (I Have Developed Huge, Huge Breasts)

Hijras know that hormones are not the only way of obtaining the feminine body shape they desire. They are aware of silicone breast implants. Leela, the *hijra*-guru, had her surgery in Bombay. She developed a good rapport with a doctor, and many other *hijras* from Bombay undergo the same procedure with this doctor. The *hijras* say that other doctors are reluctant to admit *hijra* patients in their hospital as they believe that it would bring shame to the hospital. Young hijras from Delhi visit Bombay for silicone breast implant surgery. Leela assists these *hijras* by introducing them to the doctor. She also negotiates the surgery rates on behalf of her *hijra* friends, and if the doctor disagrees with her, she threatens him with her power from her affiliation with local gangsters. The *hijras* ask the doctor for large breasts, according to Sruti. From their point of view, the bigger the breasts the better, as these enhance their erotic appeal; they talk of *jumbo jumbo dhamni* ('huge, huge breasts').

In Malvani slum, there are some *hijras* who have undergone breast implant surgery. They are mostly young *hijras*, and some identify themselves as 'upper-class' because they engage in highly paid sex work. They are beautiful, speak English and earn fairly good money. These *hijras* have a regular clientele during the week and work for rich patrons. These rich *hijras* undergo breast implant surgery in private hospitals in Bombay. They sometimes seek help, asking Leela to introduce them to a plastic surgeon. Most of the other *hijras* in Malvani slum earn less and cannot afford to undergo breast implant surgery in private hospitals. However, their strong desire for bigger breasts is fulfilled by the lower cost of the surgery in government hospitals. According to them, the surgery is essential for their sex work, because it brings in higher rates from their clientele.

Many *hijra*s say that they are treated differently by their clients during physical intimacy after breast implant surgery. The men bring gifts for the *hijra*s and buy them gold for special occasions and festivals like birthdays, Eid and other religious festivals, as their emotional attraction for the *hijra*s increases. The *hijra*s feel that these men receive extra pleasure and satisfaction when they see breasts during sex; this is expressed as a feeling of happiness and results in love and care for the *hijra*. For example, the *hijra*s describe how their clients show greater intimacy and also concern, inquiring about any material needs the *hijra*s may have. The acquisition of breasts by the *hijra*s adds a different dimension to their sexual life. Some *hijra*s also report that in certain contexts, if a *hijra* sex worker stands with a female sex worker in the high street, men may choose the *hijra* rather than the female sex work because of the former's breasts.

Sometimes in the Sakhiyani office, the *hijra*s have cheerful chats in the afternoons and exhibit their enhanced breasts. When Chumki reported to her *panthi* (her lover with whom she lived in Malvani slum) about a milk-like substance discharging from her nipple, he was excited and showed more affection towards her. This process of breast development is based on those facets of femininity that are linked to the *panthi*s experiencing an illusion of the *hijra*s as 'female-like'; stories of 'milk' discharging from breasts are a common narrative.

In certain respects, the physicality of breasts creates such a strong impression of femininity for the *panthi*s that they may 'ignore' the fact that the *hijra*s are not conventionally women. Komal, a *chela* (disciple) of Leela, has acquired breasts through silicone implants. She also consumes female hormones (Figure 2.4). She believes that *nirvan*, or castration, is an act against nature and says, 'Kudrat neye jo diyaa ussseye khush raho' (Whatever nature has given, be happy with it). When she dresses in a *sari* and uses make-up, she does not resemble a *hijra* because she does not clap her hands; nor does she walk down the streets swinging her hips to attract attention – in the particular style adopted by many *hijra*s. Komal performs sex work for financial reasons. Leela believes that Komal is a rich *hijra* because of her high income from sex work. She has said that one of her *panthi*s, who lives in *bahar gaon* (different country) in *Amrica* (referring to America, or the United States), has given her a huge sum of money to buy a house. When asked about her male genitals, she says that her *panthi*s are more concerned with how she performs during sex, and her breasts excite them. Moreover, the feminine features of her body, like her round buttocks and feminine facial features (such as smooth skin which is significantly enhanced by hormone consumption) make her *panthi*s identify her as a woman.

Figure 2.4 Komal wearing make-up and dressed in Western clothes before leaving for sex work one evening

Source: Photograph by the author.

The elements of feminine embodiment by *hijras* include their practices of breast development, hair removal, hormone consumption, and so on. These practices are based on the 'presentation' of a visual character that is not female but 'female-like'. According to the *hijras*, there is no standard way to acquire female-like attributes although most *hijras* in Bombay believe that the development of breasts enhances the feminine beauty of their body. Different *hijras* have alternative ways of portraying their *hijra* identity, based on their personal logic. Thus, *hijra* beautification is not a fixed set of categories.

THE BODY AND THE EROTIC

Breast development by *hijras* via certain enhancement technologies invokes cultural assumptions of femininity based on their desires and social conditions. The newly formed physical appearance of the *hijras* establishes a cultural importance in terms of their re-identification and their construction of beauty – particularly the argument which is situated in the discourses and practices of the symbolic transgression of their *hijra*-hood and being. Rosemary A. Joyce

(2005) contends that the contemporary scholarship on the body metaphor largely draws attention to 'lived experiences' and corporeal inscription, and this interpretation occupies a very important position in social theory. The 'lived experiences' of the body, according to Thomas J. Csordas (1994), recall the phenomenological perspective of embodiment –describing the perspectives of identity to highlight the attributes of being and the ways of its embodied practices, which are either psychic or material. In this way, breasts signify a beauty myth amongst the *hijra*s that leads them to adopt modern medicines and surgery. Embodiment of breasts further installs a new expansive notion of *hijra* identification, a new way of representation that would further allow them to renegotiate broader changes and transformations in their social and sexual relationships. These sorts of embodied practices provide a new perception of *hijra*s in contemporary Bombay, with a certain type of medical management of their sexuality that is directly connected to a pattern of consumer lifestyle. Alexander Edmonds (2007, 2010), in his brilliant scholarship on plastic surgery and beautification amongst the non-elite in Brazil, recounts how beautification and body enhancement are a form of capital that allow elevation of 'social position', arguing that the these capital formations free the body by means of market mechanisms. Desires that are formed with the reframing of the body in the milieu of cosmopolitan culture expose a new horizon with a liberatory potential and a sense of consumption techniques – which in a way contest the traditional and the stereotype. Edmonds further borrows from Bourdieu in articulating the fact that the construction of beauty threatens and creates tensions in conventional social hierarchies; attractiveness allows the distribution and the evenness of capital. The point which is recognized by Bourdieu is the interpretation of 'body' and 'class' – the construction of beauty which he calls 'fatally attractive' ensconces bodily attributes with an aesthetic and erotic ideal, a 'tactic' to 'seduce' every social class, possessing a 'democratic appeal' (Edmonds 2007).

These arguments recall the stories of the breasts of the *hijra*s, providing evidence of how their breasts serve as a benign symbol of beauty, aesthetics and eroticism, adding value to their femininity, which is in a way culturally constituted, and provide the opportunity to look beautiful and feminine and attract their male clientele. Breasts further augment their 'market' value for sex work, in a context in which they are paid in proportion to the pleasure they offer their clients. Further, embodiment of breasts serves as a sexualized trait for the masculine entertainment culture, focusing on 'labour' in relation to the body (Yang 2011). The concept of labour, in this framework, draws attention to another aspect of the 'market' – enhancement procedures that are commodified in pursuit of 'profit' – the *hijra*s and their breast development become the material signifier in the context of beauty as well as economy, rendering the proposition Green (2008) terms as a 'structural feature of sexual sociality', suggesting the logic of 'exchange' or the marketable value of the object that here constitutes erotic value and a definite cultural pattern, establishing institutionalized utility for sex work. Therefore, breasts as an eroticized representation of beauty and feminine embodiment mark a specialized sexual niche of *hijra* embodiment that draws a unique significance of power, bodily signification, gendered position, economy, class and subjectivity.

BREASTS, EROTIC FETISHISM, NATIONAL IDENTITY

Breast enhancement further marks aesthetic ideals, addressing the gendered trope and characterizing aesthetic hierarchy within the disenfranchised *hijra*s. Refashioning the subculture that was historically 'despised', breast embodiment transforms the image of their inequality to a complex interlocking logic of their social class. The news of breast enhancement spreads across the *hijra*s in Malvani slum and even across the community in Bombay. Other *hijra*s visit those who have undergone surgery. They are awestruck with the body's transformation and its exotic image. However, the embodiment of the implants is arguably seen as a kind of notorious erotic reshaping; a new domain of experience that is subjected to a sexual market. The image of this beauty has a bio-political dimension; the niche standardization of categorical alignment of the body's aesthetics. Thus, breast enhancement builds a sociocultural stereotype of 'beauty' (Epstein 2007: 135).

The transformation of bodies under the authority of modern bio-politics is structured around embodied experiences (Lee 2016). That is to say, beauty embodiments rely on the neoliberal logics of 'self-possession', a sense of ownership constituting powerful economic and social relations. This implies further an alluring aspect of their beauty, what Alvaro Jarrin (2017: 195) calls 'secular magic'. The qualities of these embodiments traverse from a local to global phenomenon that functions as a transnational bio-political discourse (Edmonds 2010). Breasts are often considered 'assets' – an exoticism improving the body's image, a material or erotic appeal – in modernity's consumer encounter with the possibilities of market-driven logic. For the *hijra*s, these consumptions build an erotic-led enjoyment, as they happily express the fact that they receive lavish 'compliments' from their *panthi*s. Also, those *hijra*s who have developed bigger breasts are a threat to those who do not. Those who have received more attention are more in demand in the 'market'.

There has been a surge of characters in Bollywood films who highlight breasts. From yesteryears films of the 1970s right up to modern times, female actors wear Indian clothes that distinctly highlight their breasts. More so,

Bollywood film dances often involve moving the upper part of the body. The consumption of films and potential relation to soap operas and films are a part of Indian familial sentiment. Spectators often watch these characters and aspire to and emulate their aesthetics. The popular understanding of beauty works in tandem with the fetish attached to the actors' body type, lifestyle, beauty and various beauty-related consumptions. Therefore, beautiful breasts become a feminized attribute of the body, constitutive of a sexualized and racialized symbol of the body's image. Breast reconstruction automatically uplifts the body's appearance, so much so that it meets the popular aesthetic evaluation of the nation. Big breasts are largely accepted – a perceptible ideal of beauty, and a purchase of acceptance and assimilation to Indian beauty imagery. This archetypical embodiment becomes a particular ideal of the female or feminine, which could also avoid various kinds of social exclusion. Therefore, enhanced breasts are seen as an exceptional quality every *hijra* wants to acquire – to stand differentiated, noticeable and alluring to their *panthi*s.

CONCLUSION

This chapter builds an argument on India's modernity, with special reference to the city of Bombay, and as to how, in this space, there is a quest for a modern identity with new forms of appearances, addressing bio-political engineering, of which varied beauty consumptions are emblematic. Understanding sexuality that is entangled with the logic of the market, the chapter has highlighted the central argument of body and beautification – that is, a new sexual culture formed by eroticized, visualized and commodified traits. Merleau-Ponty's radical reflection and his ontological dimensions of embodiment start with the premise of understanding 'flesh' (1968: 35). 'Flesh' according to him is the most elementary characteristic of the being that constitutes an effect of 'reversibility' – describing the fundamental reflexivity that illustrates the 'subjective' and the 'objective' dimensions of the being. With more specific understanding of the body, Merleau-Ponty talks of 'flesh' as a 'mirror phenomenon' (1968: 240), describing the perceptible dynamics of the 'seer in the visible' and proposing frames of reference for the subjective and the objective dimensions in techniques of visibility. In other words, as he proposes, to see entails being seen by other subjects – theorizing the very essential component in techniques of embodiment. This act of reflexivity adds value to the most radical formulations in the phenomenology of perception, bringing stronger evidence of the material existence of the 'image' or bodily metaphor. The subject–object dimension of the flesh pertains to the idea of interrelated systems, constituting interdependence as well as differences.

This further moves to the assertion of the phenomenology of the body and space, in which context Merleau-Ponty (1962: 102) reckons that the body always tries to inhabit a space in which the subjective space is fundamentally linked to the objective corporeal being, giving an 'active' meaning to that space.

This chapter has made an attempt to understand body and embodiment from epistemological and ontological perspectives – drawing heavily from the narratives of the *hijras* and their everyday lives in contemporary Bombay. Theorizing the link between consumer culture and sexuality, the chapter notes how consumption is central to the new ways of identity and subjective representations based on desires and fantasies. This provides further evidence of the fact that desires are socially produced and independent of any specific social framework. In this context, desires are redressed by the market which in turn establishes an individual's subjective experience of the desire. In other words, it delves into the consumption of commodities as an artefact of desire and provides an overview of how these desires shape sexuality – producing an erotic and corporeal signification of the *hijra* subculture.

This anthropological study especially draws attention to the unfettered corporeal embodiment and sexual relations with certain traits of globalizing modernity of the popular transgender culture in India –the *hijras*. The focus is on the construction of micro-level interactions, and the meanings deciphered by means of construction of such narratives, which are related to the phenomenology of the body and embodiment, further revealing broader accounts and experiences of gender and sexuality of the *hijra* subculture.

NOTES

1   The longitudinal character of Bombay city has given rise to three parallel railway lines that stretch east to west across the city. The rich and poor essences of Bombay can be traced through the settlements that run along the 'western line' of the Bombay railway track.

2   MDACS, or the Mumbai Districts AIDS Control Society, is a governmental body that was established in 1998 by the Municipal Corporation of Greater Mumbai (MCGM) for the control and prevention of HIV/AIDS. It undertakes multisectoral and bilateral collaborations with government agencies, non-governmental organizations (NGOs) and CBOs, international non-governmental organizations (INGOs) and private sector organizations working in healthcare. This body is aimed at offering comprehensive healthcare facilities with regard to AIDS and related sexual-health measures. The MDACS works on 'targeted interventions' for sexual health promotion among 'high risk' groups – female sex workers, *hijra* sex workers and truck drivers – who could be affected by HIV/AIDS and other sexually transmitted diseases.

3   During my fieldwork it was noticed that the speaking of English by any *hijra* is an embodiment of social class and higher status and a way to an influential

position. They can seek NGO and activist work and negotiate and communicate with government officials in various meetings in local, regional and even national contexts. Geeta exemplifies one such *hijra* associated with this kind of work, which shapes her identity as well.

4   Autorickshaw is a form of public transport usually seen in South and Southeast Asia. The vehicle has the capacity to accommodate four–eight passengers, depending upon its size. It is a box-shaped vehicle that tapers down in the front, slightly resembling a frog's mouth. Unlike in many other parts of India, where these vehicles run as a 'shared' service whereby different commuters along a definite route can share it, in Bombay (and most large cities), the services of the autorickshaw are similar to those of taxis in the sense that a single passenger has to hire the entire vehicle to reach their destination.

5   Adding *ji* after the name typifies a sense of respect among Hindi-speaking Indians.

6   Deep-fried vegetables coated in chickpea-flour batter.

7   Deep-fried snacks consisting of triangular pastries filled with spicy mashed potatoes and other vegetables.

8   A garment worn by Muslim women covering the entire body, with a veil over the face and a net eyepiece to see through.

9   *Kothi*s usually refer to effeminate homosexuals in India; they adopt female mannerisms, make-up and sometimes female clothes, and prefer to be the passive recipient in their sexual practices (Khan 2004; Reddy 2005a; Rowkavi 2007). Khan (2004) notes that the shift in identity of *kothi* subjects, pointing to the change in behaviour and mannerisms from effeminacy to more masculine conduct, depends on the social situation and surroundings. Their masculine disposition is more prominent in public spaces (the workplace and home), while there is a shift in identity and behaviour in the sexualized spaces of parks and CBOs. Sexualized spaces create a social environment where *kothi* subjects socialize and exhibit their female mannerisms. These spaces are also utilized by them in carrying out their sexual practices, sometimes in search of male partners for emotional gratification and also for socializing with other homosexual-identified men (see Khan 2001, 2004; Boyce 2007). With special attention to *kothi* subjects in Bombay, Rowkavi charts how these subjects are classified in respect to their behaviour and identity (2007: 392). He classifies these effeminate homosexuals as *kothi*, *dhoru-kothi* and *pav-bata-wali-kothi*. The latter two classifications are usually applied with respect to their sexual behaviour and the dual relationships they maintain. In that respect, Rowkavi states that *dhoru kothi*s sometime take the role of the penetrating partner in sexual practices, while the *pav-bata-wali-kothi*s usually maintain dual relationships – marrying and having children at home on the one hand, and having *kothi* partners in sexualized spaces on the other. This dual identity and sexual behaviour of *kothi* subjects is termed 'double-decker' in northern India (Khanna 2007: 179). But *kothi*s usually desire to have *panthi*s as their sexual partners as they regard the latter as 'real men' who take the penetrating role in sexual practices (Khan 2001, 2004; Reddy 2005b; Cohen 2005). The *kothi–panthi* model is what Serena Nanda (2000) calls

'gendered homosexuality' in male same-sex relations, where the gender binary of male–female is reinforced in male–male relationships, behaviours and sexual practices.

The *kothi* subjects are representatives of Indian homosexual identity (Khan 2004; Rowkavi 2007). They are usually from lower-middle-class Indian families, and previous evidence shows that *kothi*s are most vulnerable to HIV/AIDS and other sexually transmitted diseases (Khan 2001, 2004). Boyce (2007) notes how a certain 'language' creates certain meanings of homosexual socialization, friendship and sexual practices. In that respect, *line e nemechhi* or *line ee esechi* (meaning, joined the club or profession) signifies the affiliation of *kothi* subjects to the *kothi* community and sexualized spaces. Again, the language of sexual practices creates a discrete meaning whilst the *kothi* subjects try to authenticate their body and identity as women. The sexual tensions and practices between these subjects and their 'masculine' male partners are described by terms imbued with derogative meanings, such as *gaard-marwana*, *pode-bamboo* or *ghusana* (Hazra quoted in Cornwall and Jolly 2006: 99). *Gaar* is a Hindi word which means the bottom, and *marwana* means getting penetrated. These words and phrases usually imply the anal-sex culture in male same-sex relations in India. The words and phrases not only signify and underline sexual practices and gendered homosexuality in Indian society, but also how men and the masculine disposition are portrayed and performed in sexual acts. Again, the act of penetration signifies gender superiority as only a man's ability. Besides, certain languages and terms are used both among effeminate homosexuals and *hijra* subjects (Reddy 2005a).

In this chapter I revisit *kothi* subjects. I support Khanna's argument that there is no fixed homosexual identity and subjectivity, and identity is the voice or desire of the soul (see Khanna 2007: 167). Therefore, negotiating effeminate homosexual identity, my ethnography concentrates on the voices and desires of their soul. Moreover, my ethnography strictly explores the nuances of the expression of their behaviour and their identity – not as two separate categories but as ones that are interlinked. Understanding the strict heteronormative social environment in Indian society, I explore the politics of shift in their identity. With close rapport with them and by gaining their confidence, my ethnography extends from the sexualized spaces to the public spaces where they interact. My gay (activist) friends in Bombay, whom I knew earlier through the Humsafar Trust (a Bombay gay support group), introduced me to the social spaces where *kothi* subjects meet. This also allowed me to explore the macho men, or *panthi*s, whilst understanding how and to what extent emotions and commitment play a role in male same-sex partnerships in India. In addition, CBOs provided an important place to explore *kothi–panthi* identities and behaviours. In fact, these organizations gave me an idea of the engagement of the *kothi* subjects in development- and policy-based works. Understanding *kothi*s to be from the lower economic sections of society (see Boyce 2007), the ethnography of CBOs reveals how and in what position *kothi* subjects are recruited in sexual-health work. This question opens up the degree and extent of their sexual relations and practices, with special emphasis on HIV/AIDS intervention.

Unlike *kothi*s, which is a recent construction of a category of homosexual subjects in Indian society, *hijra*s are as old as the Indian epics (see Pattanaik 2002). The term *hijra* usually referred to male hermaphrodites who took care of and protected the queens in the medieval and Mughal reigns (Pattanaik 2002). They held a high status and were quite respected – until the colonial period in India when they were termed and ostracized as a 'criminal tribe' (PUCL-K 2003). Today, *hijra*s are the most stigmatized and socially and politically neglected class of Indian society (see Reddy 2005a). In the contemporary *hijra* culture and way of living, these subjects usually live in communes, after leaving their biological families, and earn their livelihoods from street performances such as dancing, clapping and begging (Nanda 1990; Reddy 2005b). They also collect money by dancing and singing at childbirths and marriages, which is commonly seen as highly auspicious and is part of rituals in both the Hindu and Muslim traditions in India (Ibid). With special reference to *hijra* subjects in Bombay, Rowkavi (2007) points to two categories – *nirvana hijra*s and *jogta*s. The former are castrated *hijra*s, and in the context of activism and HIV/AIDS intervention work they are one of the most vulnerable sections of society (Rowkavi 2007: 397).

10   It is important to understand the politics of *hijra rewal* (*hijra* language). Their clapping, signs and utterances give meaning to an identity or a social situation. Clapping among the hijras is a sign of difference and distinction; not only do they clap their hands, they pull up their saris to show their genital mutilation and use specific hijra language to authenticate their identity.

Kira Hall, an American linguist who has worked extensively on the *hijra* language, states that *hijra*s speak in a hybrid language by integrating 'he' and 'she', the two categories of gender identification. Although they prefer to be referred to as 'she', Hall asserts that *hijra*s 'imitate and parody binary construction of gender in an effort to gender themselves' (Hall and Donovan 1996). The politics of language among the *hijra*s is based on a different dialect and parlance used by the community to create a mark of differentiation. The *hijra* language and conversations create a sense of confidentiality, solidarity and authenticity among them, which become especially useful at times when they want to escape the police while out for sex work, for example. The origin of this language is indeterminate. During fieldwork, the *hijra*s stated that their *rewal* (dialect) is so deeply rooted in the past that no modern *hijra* could be certain of its primary source. Hall notes that:

> Their use of language in particular reflects a life constantly self-defining: they study, imaginate and parody dichotomous constructions of gender in an effort to gender themselves. Not only do they switch between feminine and masculine morphological forms in their everyday discourses, they also employ a mixture of conversational styles variously associated with either femininity or masculinity. (Hall quoted in Cohen 2005: 276)

Hall's observations on *hijra* identities reflect a challenge to and subversion of the norms of the dominant, patriarchal structure of Indian society. Through their gestures, styles and behaviour, *hijra*s construct their own identity, social space and gender. Clapping their hands and pulling up their *sari*s, as proof of their castration, become natural and ritualized acts (Reddy 2005b) and a politics of subversion to male hegemony and patriarchal structure. The use of a discrete language by the *hijra*s has a strong sense of political significance: the negation of dominant patriarchy and heteronormativity in Indian society. This *hijra* language has also been extended to the *kothi* community (Cohen 2005).

Hall further states that by using both genders in self-reference, they un-identify themselves: they are neither male nor female. Moreover, the *hijra* identity is further established by the way they represent their bodies and how they use other means of communication. Their bearded faces, deep male voices and typical masculine ways of smoking *bidi*s (indigenous cigarettes) substantiate their masculine identity, whereas wearing *sari*s and feminine adornments, applying make-up and engaging in prostitution substantiate their femininity. Finally, Hall's identification of derogative words, a practice adopted by *hijra*s when they use masculine expletives suggests a sense of maleness and hyper-(*hijra*)masculinity, whilst preferring to be referred to as 'she' further affirms the *hijra* dual identity (Hall and Donovan 1996).

11   Throughout Indian cities and centres, each *hijra* community is divided into seven houses. The head of all the houses in a city is called the *nayak*. In Bombay, the houses are 'Laskarwallah', 'Chaklawallah', Lalanwallah', 'Bendi Bazaar', 'Poonawallah', 'Ballakwallah' and 'Adipur' (Nanda 1990: 39), and each house has its inherent rules and separate code of conduct.

The *guru* is the head of the house (usually the owner), and she has her *chela*s (disciples) who live in the same house with her. After the *rit* ceremony, a *hijra* formally joins the community; she becomes a member of a particular house and her avenues for livelihood like *badhai* (childbirth and marriage-blessing ceremonies), *mangti* (begging) and *pan* (prostitution) are restricted to a specific area. These activities are organized in order to provide equal opportunities to all *hijra*s from each of the seven houses. Every city or centre has a *nayak* (chief hijra), and the *nayak* holds *jamat* (meeting) with other senior members of the *hijra* community to discuss issues of community welfare and the overall governance of the *hijra*s.

The *guru–chela* relationship is based on mutual benefits and reciprocity, like a mother–daughter scenario. The *chela*s refer to themselves as *guru-bhai* (sisters), and the *guru*'s *guru* is referred to as *nan-guru* or *nani* (grandmother). The *guru* ensures that her *chela*s have security and protection during *nirvan*. She lends her *chela*s money for the operation and performs all household chores including bathing, cooking, feeding and other activities to support her *chela*s during the recovery period. At the end of this period, the *guru* organizes a *daawat* (feast) and invites other *hijra*s in the area to celebrate. As a disciplinary mechanism, a *guru* keeps close surveillance over their *chela*s and rebukes and chastises them when they make mistakes. In return, the *chela*s support their *guru*s by handing over substantial amounts of their income.

Based on this evidence, Gayetri Reddy (2005a) says that the *hijra* community has a strong sense of familial association and cohesion. They are bonded by love and affection and term their relationship *pyar ka rishta* (relationship based on fondness and devotion). The hijras support each other in times of need and defend against any threats to their unity from outsiders (Reddy 2005a: 161–164).

The other side of the *guru–chela* relationship is based on a sense of power and hierarchy. The *gurus* employ coercive power over the younger *hijras* in order to establish a form of authority. With regard to their authoritative control as a form of power, the senior *hijras*, who are higher in status in their kinship and lineage structures, often confiscate a large part of the possessions and wealth of the younger *hijras* on the grounds that this provides revenue for the *hijra* community and political structure. Their sense of power is also based on their seniority and creates authority over the *chelas* because of the support and shelter given to them in their *gurus'* houses.

12   The development of breasts as part of *hijra* self-modification is elaborated in a subsequent section in this chapter. It will talk about their consumption of female hormones and the various means and ways by which they undergo treatment. The section also talks about silicone breast implant surgeries, especially in government hospitals in Bombay.

13   Agamben's 'messianic politics' invokes not only a non-Marxist Benjaminian 'messianism', but also a post-political Heideggerian Gelassenheit.

14   *Jarat* is the third day after the day of burial of the *hijras*, observed according to Islamic rules, when other *hijras* from the city or town or from nearby places gather to commemorate the death. But *jarat* among the *hijras* is also observed with certain elements of celebration; they mark the day with good food (for example, eating meat and rice) and rejoice the fact that the *hijra* who has died has renounced this hard and difficult life, and has been emancipated from the pains of *hijra* life and existence.

15   Transgender women's experience of consumption of anti-androgen medications is largely perceived as 'hormonal therapy' in the gender transition process according to clinical dictionaries. This process of medication is often called HRT, or hormone replacement therapy, and is associated with conditions of gender transition from male to female. Hormone replacement therapy does not necessarily lead to a surgical process of transition but, in the case of anti-androgen therapy, does lead to physical changes or the outward feminization of bodies – like breast development, rounded body parts, feminization of skin texture, and so on.

BIBLIOGRAPHY

Adkins, L. 2002. *Revisions: Gender and Sexuality in Late Modernity*. Maidenhead: Open University Press.

Allen, A. 2011. 'Foucault and the Politics of Our Selves'. *History of the Human Sciences* 24(4): 43–59.

Altman, D. 2001. *Global Sex*. Chicago: University of Chicago Press.

———. 2004. 'Sexuality and Globalization'. *Sexuality Research and Social Policy* 1(1): 63–68.

Appadurai, A. 1996. *Modernity at Large: Cultural Dimensions of Globalization*. Minneapolis: University of Minnesota Press.

Arnason, G. 2012. 'Biopower (Foucault)'. In *Encyclopaedia of Applied Ethics*, edited by R. Chadwick, 2nd edition, 295–299. Cambridge, MA: Elsevier.

Arondekar, A. 2005. 'Border/Line Sex: Queer Postcolonialities or How Race Matters Outside the US'. *Interventions: International Journal of Postcolonial Studies* 7(2): 235–249.

———. 2006. 'Entangled Histories'. *Economic and Political Weekly* 41(3): 3409–3411.

———. 2009. *For the Record: On Sexuality and the Colonial Archive in India*. Durham, NC, and London: Duke University Press.

———. 2015. 'Queering Archives: A Roundtable'. *Radical History Review* 122: 211–231.

Barney, R. 1992. 'Appearances and Impressions'. *Phronesis* 37(3): 283–313.

Beck, U. 2006. *The Cosmopolitan Vision*. Cambridge and Malden: Polity Press.

Besnier, N. 2002. 'Transgendersim, Locality, and the Miss Galaxy Beauty Pageant in Tonga'. *American Ethnologist* 29(3): 534–566.

Blitz, M. 2014. 'Understanding Heidegger on Technology'. *New Atlantis* 14: 63–80. https://www.thenewatlantis.com/publications/understanding-heidegger-on-technology.

Boellstorff, T. 2005. *The Gay Archipelago: Sexuality and Nation in Indonesia*. Princeton: Princeton University Press.

———. 2007. 'Queer Studies in the House of Anthropology'. *Annual Review of Anthropology* 36: 17–35.

Bordo, S. 1993. *Unbearable Weight: Feminism, Western Culture and the Body*. Berkeley, Los Angeles and London: University of California Press.

Bose, S., and A. Jalal. 2017. *Modern South Asia: History, Culture, Political Economy*. London and New York: Routledge.

Bourdieu, P. 1977. *Outline of a Theory of Practice*. Translated by Richard Nick. Cambridge: Cambridge University Press.

———. 1980. *The Production of Belief: Contribution to an Economy of Symbolic Goods. Media, Culture, Society* 2: 261–293.

———. 1991. *The Political Ontology of Martin Heidegger*. Cambridge: Polity Press.

Boyce, P. 2007. '(Dis)locating Male-to-Male Sexualities in Calcutta: Subject, Space and Perception'. In *The Phobic and the Erotic: The Politics of Sexualities in Contemporary India*, edited by B. Bose and S. Bhattacharya, 399–416. New Delhi: Seagull Publications.

Bristow, J. 1997. *Sexuality*. London and New York: Routledge.

Byrd, W. C., and M. W. Hughey. 2015. 'Biological Determinism and Racial Essentialism. The Ideological Double Helix of Racial Inequality'. *British Journal of Sociology* 661(1): 8–22.

Cahill, A. J. 2003. 'Feminist Pleasure and Feminine Beautification'. *Hypatia* 18(4): 42–64.

Chatterjee, I. 1999. *Gender, Slavery and Law in Colonial India*. Oxford and New York: Oxford University Press.

Cimino, A. 2016. 'Agamben's Political Messianism in "The Time That Remains"'. *International Journal of Philosophy and Theology* 77(3): 102–118.

Cisney, V. W., and N. Morar. 2015. *Biopower, Foucault and Beyond*. Chicago: University of Chicago Press.

Clark, S. R. 2003. 'Representing the Indus Body: Sex, Gender, Sexuality, and the Anthropomorphic Terracota Figurines from Harappa'. *Asian Perspective* 42: 304–328.

Cohen, L. 2005. *The Kothi Wars: AIDS Cosmopolitanism and the Morality of Classification*. In Sex in Development: Science, Sexuality and Morality in Global Perspective, edited by V. Adams and S. L. Pigg, 1–38. Durham, NC: Duke University Press.

Collier, S. J. 2009. 'Topologies of Power: Foucault's Analysis of Political Government Beyond Governmentality'. *Theory, Culture and Society* 26(6): 78–108.

Cornwall, A., and S. Jolly. 2006. 'Introduction: Sexuality Matters'. *IDS Bulletin* 37(5): 1–11.

Crowell, S., and J. Malpas (eds.). 2007. *Transcendental Heidegger*. Stanford, CA: University of California Press.

Csordas, T. J. 1990. 'Embodiment as a Paradigm of Anthropology'. *Ethos* 18(1): 5–47.

——— (ed.). 1994. *Embodiment and Experience: The Existential Ground of Culture and Self*. Cambridge: Cambridge University Press.

Curtis, D. 2004. 'Commodities and Sexual Subjectivities: A Look at Capitalism and its Desires'. *Cultural Anthropology* 19(1): 95–121.

D'Emilio, J. 1998. *Sexual Politics, Sexual Communities*. Chicago: University of Chicago Press.

Douglas, M. 2003 (1970). *Natural Symbols: Explorations in Cosmology*. New York: Routledge.

du Bois, W. E. B. 1899. 'The Negro in the Black Belt: Some Social Sketches'. In *Bulletin of the Department of Labour*, no. 22, edited by C. D. Wright and O. Weaver. Washington, DC: Washington Government Printing Office. https://fraser.stlouisfed.org/files/docs/publications/bls/bls_v04_0022_1899.pdf. Accessed in June 2018.

Edmonds, A. 2007. '"The Poor Have the Right to be Beautiful": Cosmetic Surgery in Neoliberal Brazil'. *Journal of the Royal Anthropological Institute* 13(2): 363–381.

———. 2010. *Pretty Modern: Beauty, Sex and Plastic Surgery in Brazil*. Durham, NC, and New York: Duke University Press.

Epstein, S. 2007. *Inclusion: The Politics of Difference in Medical Research*. Chicago: University of Chicago Press.

Feenberg, A. 2010. 'Meaning, Being and Technology in Heidegger and Marcuse'. https://www.sfu.ca/~andrewf/books/MeaningBeingTechn_HC_NYC.pdf. Accessed in June 2018.

Foucault, M. 1982. 'The Subject and Power'. *Critical Inquiry* 8(4): 777–795.

———. 2004. *Security, Territory, Population: Lectures at the College de France, 1977–1978*, edited by Michel Senellart. Translated by Graham Burchell. London: Palgrave Macmillan. https://link.springer.com/content/pdf/bfm%3A978-0-230-24507-5%2F1.pdf. Accessed in June 2018.

Fujita, K. 2013. 'Force and Knowledge: Foucault's Reading of Nietzsche'. *Foucault Studies* 16: 116–133.

Gamson, J., and D. Moon. 2004. 'The Sociology of Sexualities: Queer and Beyond'. *Annual Review of Sociology* 30: 47–64.

Geertz, N. 2018. *Nihilism and Technology*. London and New York: Rowman & Littlefield.

Gilroy, P. 2000. *Against Race: Imagining Political Culture Beyond the Colour Line*. Cambridge, MA: Harvard University Press.

Goffman, E. 1959. *The Presentation of Self in Everyday Life*. New York: Anchor Books.

Green, A. I. 2008. 'The Social Organization of Desire: The Sexual Fields of Approach'. *Sociological Theory* 26(1): 25–50.

Greenberg, D. F. 1988. *The Construction of Homosexuality*. Chicago: University of Chicago Press.

Gremillion, H. (2005). 'The Cultural Politics of Body Size'. *Annual Review of Anthropology* 34: 13–32.

Grosfoguel, R. 2000. 'Developmentalism, Modernity and Dependency Theory in Latin America'. *Nepantla: Views from the South* 1(1): 347–374.

Grosz, E. 1994. *Volatile Bodies: Towards a Corporeal Feminism*. Bloomington: Indiana University Press.

———. 1995. *Space, Time and Perversion: Essays on the Politics of Bodies*. London and New York: Routledge.

Grzinic, M., and S. Tatlic. 2014. *Necropolitics, Racialization and Global Capitalism*. Lanham, MD: Lexington Press.

Gupta, C. 2001. *Sexuality, Obscenity and Community: Women, Muslims, and the Hindu Public in Colonial India*. New Delhi: Permanent Black.

Hall, K., and V. Donovan. 1996. 'Shifting Gender Positions among Hindi-speaking Hijras'. In *Rethinking Language and Gender Research: Theory and Practice*, edited by V. Bergvall, J. Bing, and A. Freed, 22–266. London: Longman Press.

Hall. S., D. Held, D. Hubert and K. Thompson. 2000. *Modernity: An Introduction to Modern Societies*. Oxford: Blackwell Publishers.

Haraway, D. 1989. *Primitive Vision: Gender, Race and Nature in the World of Modern Science*. New York and London: Routledge.

———. 1997. *Feminism and Technoscience*. New York: Routledge.

Haug, W. F. 1986. *Critique of Commodity Aesthetics*. Minneapolis: University of Minnesota Press.

Hinchy, J. 2019. *Governing Gender and Sexuality in Colonial India: The Hijra, c. 1850–1900*. Cambridge: Cambridge University Press.

Hogle, L. F. 2005. 'Enhancement Technologies and the Body'. *Annual Review of Anthropology* 34: 695–716.

Jackson, P. A. 2003. 'Space, Theory and Hegemony: The Dual Crises of Asian Area Studies and Cultural Studies'. *Journal of Social Issues in Southeast Asia* 18(1): 1–41.

Jarrin, A. 2017. *Biopolitics of Beauty: Cosmetic Citizenship and Affective Capital in Brazil*. Berkeley: University of California Press.

Johnson, M. 1997. *Beauty and Power: Transgendering and Cultural Transformation in the Southern Philippines*. Oxford: Berg Publishers.

Joyce, R. A. 2005. 'Archaeology of the Body'. *Annual Review of Anthropology* 34: 139–158.

Khanna, A. 2007. *A Critical Engagement with the Postcoloniality of Sexuality*. In *The Phobic and the Erotic: The Politics of Sexualities in Contemporary India*, edited by B. Bose and S. Bhattacharya, 159–200. New Delhi: Seagull Publications.

Khan, S. 2001. 'Culture, Sexualities and Identities: Men Who Have Sex with Men in India'. In *Gay and Lesbian Asia: Culture, Identity, Community*, edited by G. Sullivan P. A. and Jackson, 99–116. New York: Harrington Park Press.

———. 2004. *MSM and HIV/AIDS in India*. New Delhi: Naz Foundation International.

Kulick, D. 1998. *Travesti: Sex, Gender and Culture Among Brazilian Transgendered Prostitutes*. Chicago: University of Chicago Press.

Lacombe, D. 1996. 'Reforming Foucault: A Critique of the Social Control Thesis'. *British Journal of Sociology* 47(2): 332–352.

Lamb, S. 2000. *White Saris and Sweet Mangoes: Aging, Gender and Body in North India*. Berkeley: University of California Press.

Lee, S. H. 2016. 'Beauty Between Empires: Plastic Surgery, Global Feminism and the Trouble with Self-esteem'. *Frontiers: A Journal of Women's Studies* 37(1): 1–31.

Lefebvre, H. 1991. *The Production of Space*. Translated by D. Nicholson-Smith. Oxford: Blackwell.

Mazarella, W. 2017. *The Mana of Mass Society*. Chicago: University of Chicago Press.

McClintock, A. 1995. *Imperial Leather: Race, Gender and Sexuality in the Colonial Context*. New York and London: Routledge.

McGrew, A., and D. Held (eds.). 2002. *Governing Globalization: Power, Authority and Global Governance*. London: Polity Press.

McWhorter, L. 2004. 'Sex, Race and Biopower: A Foucauldian Genealogy'. *Hypatia* 19(3): 38–62.

Menon, N. 2007. 'Living with Secularism'. In *The Crisis of Secularism in India*, edited by A. Dingwaney and R. Sunder Rajan, 267–293. Durham, NC, and London: Duke University Press.

Merleau-Ponty, M. 1962. *The Phenomenology of Perception*. Translated by Colin Smith. London: Routledge.

———. 1963. *The Primacy of Perception*. Evaston: Northwestern University Press.

———. 1964. *Signs*. Evaston: Northwestern University Press.

———. 1968. *The Visible and the Invisible*. Translated by Alphonso Lingis. Evaston: Northwestern University Press.

Milchman A., and A. Rosenberg. 2011. 'Michel Foucault: An Ethical Politics of Care of Self and Others'. In *Political Philosophy in the Twentieth Century*, edited by Catherine P. Zuckert, 228–237. Cambridge: Cambridge University Press.

Mukhopadhay, M. (ed.). 2017. *Feminist Subversion and Complicity: Governmentalities and Gender Knowledge in South Asia*. Chicago: University of Chicago Press.

Muller, B. J. 2011. 'Governmentality and Biopolitics'. *Oxford Research Encyclopedia of International Studies*. https://oxfordre.com/internationalstudies/view/10.1093/acrefore/9780190846626.001.0001/acrefore-9780190846626-e-50. Accessed in May 2018.

Nanda, S. 1990. *Neither Man nor Woman: The Hijras of India*. Belmont, CA: Wadsworth Publishing Company.

Negrin, L. 2002. 'Cosmetic Surgery and the Eclipse of Identity'. *Body & Society* 8: 21–41.

Ngai, P. 2005. *Made in China: Woman Factory Workers in A Global Workplace*. Durham, NC, and London: Duke University Press.

Ong, A. 2006. *Neo-liberalism as Exception: Mutations in Citizenship and Sovereignty*. Durham, NC, and London: Duke University Press.

Orlie. M. A. 2002. 'The Desire for Freedom and the Consumption of Politics'. *Philosophy of Social Criticism* 28(4) : 395–417.

Parker, R. 1991. *Bodies, Pleasure and Passions: Sexual Culture in Contemporary Brazil*. Boston, MA: Beacon Press.

Parker, R. G., and J. H. Gagnon. 1995. *Conceiving Sexuality: Approaches to Sex Research in a Postmodern World*. New York: Routledge.

Pattanaik, D. 2002. *The Man Who Was a Woman*. New York: Harrington Park Press.

Perez, E. 1999. *The Decolonial Imaginary: Writing Chicanas into History*. Bloomington and Indianapolis: Indiana University Press.

Prieur, A. 1998. *Mema's House, Mexico City: On Transvestites, Queens and Machos*. Chicago: University of Chicago Press.

PUCL-K. 2003. *Human Rights Violation Against the Transgender Community: A Study of Kothi and Hijra Sex Workers in Bangalore*. http://pucl.org/sites/default/files/reports/Human_Rights_Violations_against_the_Transgender_Community.pdf. Accessed in March 2018.

Puri, J. 1999. *Women, Body, Desire in Post-colonial India: Narratives of Gender and Sexuality*. New York: Routledge.

Reddy, G. 2005a. *With Respect to Sex: Negotiating Hizra Identity in South India*. New Delhi: SAGE Publications.

———. 2005b. 'Geographies of Contagion: Hijras, Kothis and the Politics of Sexual Marginality in Hyderabad'. *Anthropology and Medicine* 12(3): 255–270.

Reischer, E., and K. S. Koo. 2004. 'The Body Beautiful: Symbolism and Agency in the Social World'. *Annual Review of Anthropology* 33: 297–317.

Roodenburg, H. 2004. 'Pierre Bourdieu: Issues of Embodiment and Authenticity'. *Etnofoor* 17(1–2): 215–226.

Rosalyn, D. 1997. *Evictions: Art and Spatial Politics*. Boston: MIT Press.

Rose, G. 1993. *Feminism and Geography: The Limits of Geographical Knowledge*. Minneapolis: University of Minnesota Press.

Rowkavi, A. 2007. 'Kothis Verus Other MSM: Identities Versus Behaviour in the Chicken and Egg Paradox'. In *The Phobic and the Erotic: The Politics of*

Sexuality in India, edited by B. Bose and S. Bhattacharya, 391–398. New Delhi: Seagull Publications.

Roy, A. (ed.). 2020. *Gender, Sexuality, Decolonization: South Asia in the World Perspective*. London and New York: Routledge.

Roy, T. 2017. *The Economy of South Asia: From 1950 to the Present*. London: Palgrave.

Schildkrout, E. 2004. 'Inscribing the Body'. *Annual Review of Anthropology* 33: 319–344.

Shah, S. 2019. 'Sedition, Sexuality, Gender and Gender Identity in South Asia'. *Samaj: South Asia Multidisciplinary Academic Journal* 20. https://journals. openedition.org/samaj/5163. Accessed in June 2020.

Shilliam, R. 2009. 'Hegel's Revolution of Philosophy'. In *German Thoughts and International Relations: The Rise and Fall of a Liberal Project*, 88–118. London: Palgrave Macmillan.

Sinha, M. 1995. *Colonial Masculinity: The 'Manly Englishman' and the 'Effeminate Bengali' in the Late Nineteenth Century*. Manchester: Manchester University Press.

Sinnerbrink, R. 2006. 'From Machenshaft to Biopolitics: A Genealogical Critique of Biopower'. *Critical Horizons* 6(1): 239–265.

Sinnott, M. 2011. 'The Language of Rights, Deviance and Pleasure: Organizational Responses to Discourses of Same-Sex Sexuality and Transgendersim in Thailand'. In *Queer Bangkok*, edited by Peter Jackson, 205–228. Hong Kong: Hong Kong University Press.

Soros, G. 2002. *Globalization*. New York: Perseus Book Group.

Stoler, A. L. 1995. *Race and the Education of Desire: Foucault's History of Sexuality and the Colonial Order of Things*. Durham, NC, and London: Duke University Press.

Turner, B. 1996. *The Body & Society: Explorations in Social Theory*. London: SAGE Publications.

Vickers, E. 2006. 'Queer Sex in the Metropolis? Place, Subjectivity and the Second World War'. *Feminist Review* 96: 58–73.

Yang, J. 2011. 'Nennu and Shunu: Gender, Body Politics and the Beauty Economy in China'. *Signs* 36(2): 333–357.

3

Contesting Violence, Constructing Power

This chapter draws the trajectory of the contemporary conflict in the lives of the *hijra*s in Bombay, exploring the ways in which hegemony, resistance and terror play out in the reality of organized social relations. With ethnographic storytelling, the stories of the characters – Leela, Geeta and Saleem Khan, and Nitu – reveal the social fabric of their everydayness, delineating a unique perspective of violence. A deep ethnography offers here a different and much-needed view of the power politics within the subculture that further responds to a form of political propaganda as an enactment of resistance in their experiences. Situating this context within the modern struggles of power, these powerful subjects impinge on the analytical framework of power and domination to impose discipline. And again, their disciplinary techniques are confined to the level of cultural manifestation of contemporary consumption, erotica and certain political expressions of resistance.

Anthropological scholarship on violence is largely linked to the study of the cultural implications of conflict (Whitehead 2004), and little attention has been given to the study of violence from the point of view of the nuances of the act of violence. The task of the anthropologist is to explore the interpersonal relationship of the performers, adding to the meaning of the interplay of power relations that builds on new experiences and also new anthropological denotations. David Riches in his book, *The Anthropology of Violence* (1986), attempts to underline the fact that the very act of violence bears a core political motive of establishing the hegemony of power. Riches' purpose is to understand violence on a 'tacit pre-empting', to secure the assumption of micro-politics and the broader notion of the infliction or coercion of the perpetrator and the ways to defend against them (Riches 1986: 5). This raises the crucial issue of attempting to understand that power is intrinsic to social relationships and also unavoidable. Further, the act of power has no midway, but the weakening of the less powerful by those that hold more power. Riches provides a deeper understanding of violence, referring to it as an imagery construct or a scenic metaphor that he calls the 'dynamic triangle of violence'. This triangular potency calls for the legitimacy of the interplay of the perpetrator, victim and witnesses, wherein the crucial point draws upon the contesting politics of 'legitimacy' to manoeuvre power, so as to mark the visibilities and the effectiveness of violence that build into the form of a particular discourse (Riches 1986: 11–13).

Veena Das (2007), takes forward Riches' theorization of violence, and points to the metaphor of the 'symbolic' as the loci of the cause and effect that ultimately pertains to 'goal appropriateness' in the instrumentation of the action. Das, who is much more impressed with the 'symbolic', makes her logical argument delineating the symbolic from the 'instrumental'. The former implicates varied agencies and social conditions – space, language and actors – as vexing the rigour of the violence based on performance and engagements. Das adds to the understanding of the latter, primarily referring to the position of the 'territoriality of the body' as significant in the understanding of violence – in the moment of which the analytics of the corporeal significance to its spatial context, arrangements and meanings are derived.

The notion of violence is, however, quite contested, with multiplicities in form, for identifying social, cultural, psychic and bodily experiences (Jenkins 1998). The discourses on violence thus rest on the deployment of multiple forms of coercion and power that are either 'psychological' or 'structural–symbolic' (Nagengast 1994), or certain 'cultural' and 'political' practices (Warren 2004), or a sort of terror (Scarry 1985), or the identification of certain experience, representation and interpretation of a wider context of violence in which one form intersects with the other (Haraway 1991; Sluka 1992; Scheper-Hughes 1992; Moser 1998).

The phenomenological understanding of violence seeks to address intersubjective perception, so as to constitute the 'lived-experiences' of the body that provide a deeper grasp of embodiment and infliction in the context of violence. Merleau-Ponty's (1968) 'intentional analysis' is further related to his idea of the 'third dimension' – looking into the nuances and intricacies of the subjective and objective analysis of human experiences. This intersubjective element digs deeper to open the possibilities of the symbolic, code structure – making sense of the world that is beyond and before the embodied metaphor – a 'pre-reflexive' knowledge of the subject that explicitly forms an account of the imperative understanding of the social, symbolic and psychological constitution of the embodied subject (Stoltzfus 2003).

With similar thoughts, this chapter brings forth an intelligible understanding of power and violence through narrative-building that further makes sense of an intersubjective perception of violence, with a primary focus on experience, cultural and symbolic understanding, and the process of embodiment of the subject; this provides an integrative account with a rich description and the complexities of how *hijra*s negotiate power in their everyday practices. The ethnography builds a collection of evidence that constitutes the reality of their social and cultural conditions, providing an epistemological and ontological tool to interrogate the complex relationships of their lives, the practical and the political imageries of their experiences, and the nuances of how they manoeuvre power to build a niche of their identity and self.

*HIJRA*S AND MAFIA NETWORKS

One afternoon, when I visited Leela's house in Bombay, I saw her dressed in a white *salwar kameez*,[1] dangling earrings and a thick silver necklace. She also wore flamboyant make-up, including glossy red lipstick. Moreover, her *salwar* (trousers) was not loose, as is common in this part of South Asia, but tight fitting. It was three-quarter length, reaching halfway down the calf muscle. The *kameez* (tunic) was loose, but with a modern, umbrella cut that accentuated her body shape, and intricately embroidered in silver.

That afternoon, we went on a journey in her car. Leela sat beside her driver in the front passenger seat. Behind them, in the middle row, sat three men I had never seen visiting Leela before. I sat on the third row of seats beside Leela's male assistant, Atharva, who often accompanies her on official visits or to formal meetings. On these occasions, Leela normally introduces Atharva as *mera beta* (my son).[2] As I supposed, Leela consciously chose Atharva to accompany her. In this way, she was representing a modern *hijra* identity – one that could be publicly associated with a man, albeit in a maternal role, without any sexual overtones. In other words, Atharva's association is a non-intimate one; Leela needs to be accompanied by a man to showcase to the outside world a form of familial togetherness that she situates within her subculture: as a *beta* (son). In addition, Leela consciously seeks to cultivate a modern identity and free herself from the restrictions of the traditional subcultural occupations of begging and sex work. Her identity is manifested in her behaviour and an ability to speak a 'foreign' language – English – a strong communication skill that would work to her advantage in achieving her goals.

Leela and Geeta have bonded over activism and community feeling. Yet they have a professional conflict, especially in terms of who can seek more attention among the political leadership and the movement. Leela lives in Thane, a district adjacent to Bombay. She has been gradually becoming famous through her appearances in the Indian media and multiple television shows and films. She is often seen filming and photographed with Bollywood actors, and her social positionality has metamorphosed from the traditional *hijra* identity. Leela lives with her natal family and travels widely, attending meetings for international and national governance-based programmes. Her ability to speak English allows her to establish her leadership, and further to represent, share ideas and develop community-based programmes for sexual minorities across India and South Asia and also globally.

On the day of my visit, Leela asked me to accompany her on a journey she was in a hurry to start. While I sat with Atharva, I was quite anxious and uncomfortable about the other men in the car. They were well-built and relatively tall, with thick beards on their faces. The windows were closed in the middle row of the car. And strangely, the men wore sunglasses even after sunset. They also kept their heads down facing the floor of the car, as though trying to hide their faces; moreover, their heads and the sides of their faces were covered with a scarf.

Atharva mentioned to me that we were on our way to meet someone called Baba, in the South Bombay area. After a while, he whispered in my ears: The Baba he was referring to is a gangster closely connected with one of India's most wanted fugitives, D. Ibrahim. Ibrahim's syndicate is often referred to as 'D Company' for his vast properties, extensive ventures and wide-ranging criminal activities like drug dealing, extortion, illegal currency, sex trade, and so on. D. Ibrahim does not live in India, but he is believed to be hiding either in Dubai in the United Arab Emirates or in Karachi in Pakistan after fleeing the country in 1993 following the infamous terrorist attacks in the city of Bombay that killed nearly 300 people. The popular belief of the government and the people of India is that 'D Company' was involved in the attack.

Atharva told me that the three men seated in the car were also linked to the mafia and had at some point escaped prison. They were privy to important internal information about 'D Company' and would be valuable to the government, if caught. My understanding was that Leela was in some way safeguarding these men from the police and was helping them by taking them to Baba. Leela was therefore serving a useful and important role within the Bombay underworld. As the protector of these three men, she was undertaking a task which Baba and his fellow gangsters would have had great difficulty in doing by themselves, especially discreetly. It seems that Leela's identity as a *hijra* enhances her position to undertake this task because she is unlikely to be challenged or questioned by popular society. She often remarked, 'Hijra kanun keye bahar hain' (*Hijra*s are outside the law). Her awareness of her positionality allowed her to capitalize on her social position and defend the mafia from the threat presented by the police.

It is unheard of for *hijra*s to be imprisoned in India. More commonly, they might be kept in legal or police custody for several days during which time they may well be physically tortured and sexually harassed before being allowed to return to their community. Leela undertook this work because of her vested interests as she shares a reciprocal and mutual relationship with Baba. In undertaking this task, Leela earns favour that she can exploit in times of need. In this way, Baba is not only a symbol of defence for her, but also a real physical safeguard who can protect Leela from any local challenges she might could face in Bombay. She needs to establish this kind of defence for herself because, in some ways, she poses a threat to other *hijra* leaders in her region and in other parts of India. In some cases, Baba's 'men' (read: gang) return her favour by checking threat, fear and abuse from other local gangsters who may try to antagonize Leela. On these occasions, Leela uses Baba symbolically as her defence.

At the beginning of this particular journey Leela told me that we were proceeding to the Mulund Police Station. This happened to be where a number of her *hijra-chela*s were being held in custody. Leela's task was to sign bail (custodial release) for her *chela*s, so that they could be freed. The car pulled up near the police station. Before getting out of the car, Leela warned the driver to keep all the car windows closed. She went alone into the police station. It is often seen that there is a very strong community feeling within the *hijra*s. They support and stand by each other during times of distress. Although that there are several groups and discrete *hijra*-lineages in the community, and individual community-led ideologies, they stand by each other in solidarity.

In fact, several *hijra*s had rushed to the police station to support and plead the release of their *hijra* friends who were locked up. They were angry, standing in unison and protesting. They came running as soon as they saw Atharva and made sexually offensive remarks. Others broke into laughter. Their laughter was soon checked as a policeman come out and began to hit the *hijra*s with his cane. The officer admonished Atharva and then lifted his stick to strike Atharva too. All the *hijra*s were frightened, so they dispersed and hid.

VIOLENCE IN THE UNDERWORLD

From the Mulund police station we continued our journey to visit Baba. Baba lives in Masjid Bandar, a place in South Bombay. The area has a sub-locality called Dongri. Hussain Zaidi, in his book *Dongri to Dubai: Six Decades of the Mumbai Mafia* (2012), talks about the incubation of mafia gangs in the city of Bombay, from local thugs to organized crime. Dongri as a place holds the history of the underworld, the home for the evolution of Bombay's mafia. Shootouts in broad daylight, contract killings, sex trade, drug dealing and human- and child-trafficking are prevalent, though run covertly in the area. Zaidi further touches on the importance of geopolitics, tracing its notorious by-lanes which are sites for nefarious crimes. It is an area populated by Muslims and often referred to as South Bombay's 'ghetto'; kebab shops at every corner, several mosques and prayer zones, men in traditional Islamic attire and women in *burkha*s, signboards mostly written in Urdu – a place exemplifying mystery, danger and edginess. Further, the place has a history of smuggling since the 1950s, and notorious Muslim mafia gangs and leaders emerged from the area. It is South Bombay's 'other' – a ghetto in the imagination of upper-middle-class Bombay residents and termed 'mini Pakistan' by staunch Hindus. The area was allegedly the site for various activities of the mafia. D. Ibrahim's story from a small boy from the lanes of Dongri to his massive 'D Company' is significant in this area.

As we entered Dongri, there was a growing sense of fear. Everybody in Bombay knows about the place. It is not common practice for ordinary people to walk in the area, even in broad daylight. The atmosphere was strange – remarkably different from elsewhere. I saw through the dark glazed car window an elderly *thelawala* (rickshaw puller) being thrown onto the side of the road by a gang of ruffians. Some men on the street were standing and smoking something, attempting to conceal what they were doing from public attention. 'This is nothing but cocaine,' Leela remarked. It became clear that we had entered Baba's *dera* (secret hub or neighbourhood).[3] The men were all smoking. Dense fumes of cocaine filled the air with a noxious smell. I found it difficult to breathe. Leela's driver, Mishra, was not familiar with the street. She spoke to someone over the phone, explaining, 'Meri gaadi maroon colour ki Bolero jeep hain' (My car is a maroon-coloured Bolero jeep). Soon, Leela pointed to men on motorbikes, who had seemingly appeared out of nowhere, following her car. Leela asked her driver to follow the motorbikes.

Baba's *dera* was located in one of the narrow lanes of Dongri which is inaccessible to cars and other four-wheeled vehicles. So we had to leave the car outside and walk down the lane. The lane was so dark and dingy that the men who were guiding us on their motorbikes had to shine a torch to help us see the way. Although we were walking carefully, the way was muddy and waterlogged, with many potholes, and mud splattered onto our clothes. Listening to the men talking, I became aware that Baba did not seem to be his name, but a way of addressing him with respect, honour as well as fear.

Baba's *dera* was a space in the corner of the ground floor of a dilapidated building. The front porch was covered with asbestos. There were chairs placed on the covered porch, which was lit by a neon light. In the corner, Baba had a small room in which men's clothes were displayed for sale. This is what he called his 'shop'. He said that the garments were imported from Dubai. Soon after, I reflected on the possible rationale for establishing a shop in a place so inaccessible to the public; it acted as a shield to protect Baba and his gang in the event of a sudden police raid. Baba, on such occasions, could tell the police that there were people gathered there because of the garment shop. In addition, the shop acts as a further defence for Baba – in providing a legitimate face for the proscribed fiscal transactions between him and 'D Company'.

Baba greeted us with a smile and in the traditional Islamic way, saying, 'As-salamu aleykum'.[4] Baba and Leela hugged each other and said it had been a long time since they had met. Their hug also seemed to have romantic implications. Baba had different *chela*s inside the *dera*. Some were young, wearing jeans, t-shirts and informal shoes. They were well-built and urbane. Others were middle-aged men wearing traditional clothes, like Afghani *kurta-*pajama.[5] In addition, they all had long beards in the typical Muslim way.

There followed a conversation between Leela and Baba:

Leela: *Janemaan kaise ho?* (Darling, how are you?)

Baba: *Baas aap ka hi intezaar tha.* (I have been looking forward to your arrival.)

(They hugged and kissed each other quite intimately in front of everyone.)

Leela: *Yeh saab chore keya karte hain idhar? Saab to ek seye badh kar ek maal hain.* (What do these young men do here? All of them are equally handsome.)

Baba: *Araam seyee baith!* (Sit comfortably!)

Leela: *Haiii. Tab seye to log mere upar diwane hain. Itni bari bari dhamni kidhar milenge. Aaoo mere janeman. Kab seye mere gale nahi mile ho. Mein pyasi huin, diwani huin, tumhara rog hain mujhme.* (People are mad for me since then [since she got breast implants]. Where else will they see such big breasts? Sweetheart, beloved, come to me. How long it has been since you were in my arms. Come on, come on. I am infected with love for you, in my body, in my heart, I long for you.)

Leela was sitting quite intimately with Baba. It was more than flirtatious. Baba looked shy and awkward because of the way Leela was getting intimate with him.

Baba: *Sun, kuch problem solve karni hain. Yeh Aftaab mere saath bahut din seye kaam karta hain. Woh Canada mein tha, job kaar raha tha choto motaa, aur ek Canadian ladki keye saath shadi kiya. Abi bechara mushkil mein paar gaya.* (Listen, you have to help me regarding something. This boy, Aftaab, has been working with me for a long time. Poor man. He was in Canada, working there, and he married a Canadian woman. Now he is in trouble.)

Leela: *Haan. Usko meri office bhej do. Mein dekhti hun keya kiya jayee. Bahut time lagega iss problem ko solve karne mein. Do raat rukhna padega shayad Aftaab ko.* (Hmmm. Send him to my office. Let me see what can be done. But solving this problem will take time. Aftaab might have to stay for two nights at my place [to get it solved].)

(Leela blushed.)

Baba: *Iskaa Canadian biwi keye taraf seyee ek beta hain, jo ki biwi neye apne hifazat mein rakh liya. Abhi bachha dena to dur ki baat, bachha dekhne bhi nahi deti Aftaab ko. Aftaab to bachhe ki baap hain; uska haak hain India bachha ko leye aane ka.* (Aftaab has a son from his Canadian wife, who she has in her care. Now, this is the conundrum: Aftaab's wife will not allow him to see his son, let alone give him to Aftaab. But she is forgetting that Aftaab is the father of the child. Therefore, he has every right to bring his son back to India.)

Leela: *Tum chinta mat karo. Sab theek ho jaiga. Dilli mein mere political contacts hain. Ek baar phone karne seye, Aftaab ko bachha mil jayga.* (Do not worry about this issue at all. I have good political contacts in Delhi. One phone call, and Aftaab will have his child.)

Baba: *Chalo tumne meri chinta dur kari. Atharva aur Ahonaa ko, Aftaab, raste mein ghumane leye jao. Kuch thanda pilao. Ghumo tum log.* (Now you have relieved some of my worries. Aftaab, take Atharva and Ahonaa to roam outside. Offer them some cold drinks.)

The association between Baba and Leela highlights how violence is constructed through the mechanism of the hegemony and political power of mafia leaders. The role of Leela in this context is to enhance the power of the underworld through an indirect relationship and as a passive agent. Her confidence with the mafia leaders is based on a mutual relationship and an interdependence of power by which Leela expects to receive help from Baba during her time of need. This in turn demonstrates the reciprocal means by which they exchange power based on their positionality in society. Baba's hegemonic power is related to his status as a mafia leader. On the other hand, Leela's power is related to the fact that she is a *hijra* leader who has not only acquired a dominant position in the *hijra* community but has also developed prominence and fame in popular society. Leela and her public image as a *hijra* leader have been showcased on television and in the newspapers, making her identity increasingly prominent (Donaldson 1993; Hogle 2005).

Her breasts as a signifier of her femininity entrench further an erotic symbolism that Leela trades to reconfirm her hegemony within the mafia (Brickell 2006). In other words, her power could be related to the Gramscian notion of hegemony in the context of which Petersen (1997) charts hegemony as a 'political technique'. The power is hence 'political', in the sense that she is quite hopeful of meeting her goals. Further, her symbolic construction of the feminine builds a comprehensive meaning of her identity that Julie Hanson (2007) calls 'framing the body' within a particular cultural configuration. The non-traditional dress builds a discrete feminine identity to re-symbolize her with reference to modern cosmopolitan traits of consumption. Her breasts also play the role of unremittingly fascinating Baba and his gang. They further project an unusual erotica wherein a woman(-like) person embraces political authority on the one hand, and sexual suggestiveness on the other, actually building an extraordinary sense of power. But an anthropological lens allows us to perceive an exchange in power relations: body and the erotic on the one hand, and an act of defence on the other. This semiotics of exchange centres around the conditions of recognition of the social conceptualization of political authority (Hearn 2007; Hakim 2010, 2011).

Building an argument from Marcel Mauss' (1969) logic of exchange in social life beyond the economic vision enables this study to enunciate the ritual symbolism involved in interpersonal relationships. Symbolic functions provide a political context to a systematic orientation of the symbolic action – a sense of 'reciprocity', implicating exchanges based on dyadic back-and-forth transactions; an exchange of equally valuable goods (Appadurai 1988). To emphasize further, the transaction in a specific way has value as 'incarnated signs' to the 'necessities' of politically charged complexities (Appadurai 1988: 38). This further builds on the complex consumption processes that fundamentally excite meaningful dimensions of exchange, articulating the aesthetics in perceptibility and labour. The quest for this act is the potent suggestion in convincing a rampant fetishism that is intertwined with the cultural grid – 'labour' becomes polemic to the political location of the sensitivities of the embeddedness of the exchange in culture. This analysis of the 'value' of the power of breasts generates a charismatic authority with a highly political circulation, by giving a Maussian analysis of 'charisma' that objectifies social power to an entity.

Thus, these economies of exchange between Baba and Leela are recognized within a typical closeness of kin, apparently ensconced with affectivity, but this kinship translates into an economically structured organization of rank and hierarchy that balances the market demands of the reciprocal debt and obligation defining their exchange (see Levi-Strauss 1978). Thus, the circulation of exchange presupposes an expansion of trust and affective value that prescribe a constant mutual commitment to each other, also realizing the history of their respective lineages. Keeping this in mind, their putative relationship, though apparently social, is significantly dominated by materiality and self-interest – a possibility established to trade the commerce of emotions and the erotic in multi-layered interfaces.

Again, eroticism is described by Deborah Elliston (1995) as a 'cultural practice' which might not only lead to an 'erection', but any physical sense of genital transformation for the act of being sexual. For her, eroticism as a 'ritualized practice', such as performing sex, could also be analysed as an emotional and expressive means by which to construct an affinity and attraction. Hence, in the words of Richard Parker, eroticism is a 'social and cultural system' that is not just libidinal (Parker 1989). Parker's analysis lies within a symbolic allegory of bodily traits and performances overtly constructing the political interplay of the act. Eroticism thus constructs the social element of thrill and excitement that ultimately becomes pleasant and pleasurable.

Furthermore, the agreeable relationship constructed between Aftaab and Leela, in which she decided to help him with her political contacts to regain his paternal rights, signifies the symbolic meaning of power of an agency and their control over the state. In this case, Leela's assertion of having networks in Dilli (Delhi) made emphatic in her statement 'Dilli mein mere political contacts hain' (I have political contacts in Delhi), which signifies her political authority confirming her power to be able to appreciate and manipulate rules and regulations. This symbolizes a fictitious sense of power demonstrating certain elements of hegemony and control over the law that she can manoeuvre in her self-interest. Again, those elements of hegemonic power that she has gained over the state are the fruits of her activism and the public symbol of modern *hijra* identity which she shares with her mafia associates. Further, in acting as an imperceptible liaison between the legitimate political rule of the state and the contrasting unlawful mafia practices, Leela situates her self-interest through her use and abuse of power. Her frequent remark, 'Hijra kanun ke bahar hain' (*Hijra*s are outside the law), indicates illegitimate political claiming of rights and situated representation; her sexual distinctiveness outlines the power to overthrow popular judicial perceptibility.

Baba's *dera* evokes a sense of space – dark and hidden – that generates mafia violence by maintaining privacy, silence and secrecy. It is a space in which antisocial behaviours are discussed, mapped and verbally executed, setting out plans for violence and aggression. In this way, it represents a space based on hierarchy, authority and political control, where mafia power is imagined and contemplated to construct further, anarchy and disorder in popular society. In other words, it symbolizes an enclosed area, away from public sight and knowledge, which develops the mafia's political technique of shaping power. In analysing such an architectural space, which is characterized by a gendered meaning and constructs a sense of hegemonic masculinity, Jane Rendell (1999) discusses the instance of club culture in London. Clubs generate the meaning of a private space, which starts to construct a 'civil society' distinct from the 'public' domains of the streets and workplace and the 'private' domains of family life. In doing so, club culture has been able to build a sense of individuality and personal choice. Drawing from this analysis, the *dera* represents an architectural space that can be 'masculinized', constructing a social intimacy of these actors that further reinforces their masculinity. The *dera* constructs a form of spatial location based on secrecy where mafia power is imagined and contemplated to construct new forms of hegemony and masculinity based on their performative acts, and a symbolic allegory through which violence and threat become part of social anarchism. Thus, private space ultimately becomes the logic of public disorder, as the mafia's 'political technique' increases their dominance and supremacy.

It was getting dark. Baba's *dera* was becoming busier as time passed, and he was becoming aggressive and hostile with his supporters. We had a few snacks to eat, which Baba offered us. As we were about to leave his *dera*, he invited Leela to meet his family living nearby in Dongri. So Baba came with us in her car and we stopped at his home, which was in an old apartment building. Baba lived on the fourth floor. In keeping with traditional architecture, the apartments had long common balconies that ran along either side, both front and back. On the front balcony were doors leading to each individual apartment or set of rooms, one of which belonged to Baba and his family. Baba had a wife and five children. Four of his children were daughters while the youngest was a son.

Baba's wife was a well-mannered, gentle and pleasant woman. She was born in a Catholic family in Bombay, but after their marriage she converted to Islam. Inside the family home, she preferred to wear a *dupatta* (long scarf), which covered her head as a symbol of femininity and female honour in Islam. She offered us dates to eat and mentioned they were from Dubai. Her lingua franca was English, and as Baba's wife she took care of his children, seeing to their education and schooling, besides other household chores. It was, however, getting late in the night, and it was time for us to depart. The same motorbikes escorted Leela's car on the way back to the main street, safeguarding us from Dongri's notorious lanes.

MASCULINITY, POWER AND GENDER RELATIONS

Baba and Leela's romantic friendship outlines the multiple configurations of gender relations (Schippers 2007). While there are attempts to theorize female masculinities (Halberstam 1998; Messerschmidt 2003) and hegemonic and subordinate femininities (Pyke and Johnson 2003), the chapter reformulates the conceptual hierarchies of femininity. R. W. Connell's (1995) seminal work, *Masculinities*, builds the idea of 'gender' and 'gender relations' with the practices of corporeal experience that cut across multiple masculinities and femininities, featuring a social arena of desire and sexuality (see Connell 2000). I want to suggest here a re-conceptualization of Connell's (1995) model of masculinity and gender hegemony.[6] In relation to Baba and Leela's power interplay, masculinity and gender hegemony are not a reductionist approach to understand gender relations. Instead, their relationship implicates gender(ed) hegemony, leaving aside the male–female binary. Establishing the relationship of gender hegemony begins to feature multiple configurations of masculinity and gender hegemony. For example, Leela establishes her hegemony by means of organized femininity that emerges through multiple symbolic constructions: vis-à-vis her corporeal construction, political authority and dominance and popular cultural representation through the media. Precisely, her identity challenges the classical relationship between masculinity and femininity. The gender meanings thus formed do not perpetuate male dominance as hegemonic. Moving away from the defining variation in gendered practice, power and masculinity between *hijra*s and the mafia suggest the key discourse of transgressive power relations, leading to an understanding of 'resistance'.

Working within the Foucauldian framework that corresponds with several resistance techniques, the peculiarities of power decide how resistance can be conducted (Heller, 1996). Again, Foucault's classical model of power as 'juridico-discursive' calls for a closer inspection of the moving and ever-changing sets of unequal, anarchic force relations. In this view, power is defined as a process of continual struggle within a variety of social relations. These relations function as the undergirding support, articulating the force relations that crystallize rigid, intransigent hierarchical relations.

A closer look at Foucault's power relations conceives a state of disequilibrium – 'a position of exteriority in relation to power' (Thompson 2003). Thus, Foucault's resistance is purely an instrumental relationship with multiple sorts of struggles that constitute force relations. Critical discourse conceives this shift in the configuration of power and enters into a tactical conflict (Thompson 2003). It is in these terms that Foucault considers critical resistance as carrying out 'tactical reversals' (Thompson 2003). Defining this, Foucault seems to overturn the repressive obstacles to sexual liberation in his move into 'bodies and pleasure'. It is on this prong of 'tactical reversal' that the model of resistance is historically situated and politically effective – a challenge to carry out a vigilant countering of a specific force.

Leela and Baba's power relations are likewise constituted on a force relation of resistance that instigates an engagement of contestations and entanglement of alliance and sexuality. The purpose is to resolve problems through political connections – an agenda that seeks to shape individual acts and circumstances in accordance with regimes of governmental practices. Thus, the 'act' attempts to comply with principles that favour both, to sustain their existence, and thereby accords a fundamental role to resistance with autonomy and self-formation (see Hartman 2003; Thompson 2003; Hoy 1999).

In relation to this argument, the fundamental semiotics that mediates this relationship also builds the core of 'the pragmatic' and the 'semantic meaning' (Mertz 1994). The structure of discourse here is an 'extra-linguistic context', meaning the actualities of the 'signs' referred, and carries a broader understanding within the social praxis. The contextual relationship between the sign and the object is a culturally imputed connection through actual spatiotemporal contiguity with the object. Drawing on this structure of discourse, *hijra*–mafia social relations point to multiple 'object-based' indexes that circumscribe the semiotic mediation of its referentiality. That said, 'breasts', Dilli (Delhi) and *dera* (secluded space) characterize a sign vehicle and an interpretation of the representational vehicle of the object and the sign-value. Thus, the symbolic character of these builds a particular meaning in connection to the negotiation of spaces.

VIOLENCE, THREAT AND *HIJRA* MENACE

One morning, during a visit to Geeta's office in Sakhiyani, I noticed that her *chela*s and employees were hostile to each other. Unlike most other days – when they were busy playing indoor games, or listening to music and dancing along, or doing the week's accounts, or allocating condoms to the *hijra* employees to distribute in the slum later – on this particular morning something seemed different. The curtains were pulled, and the room was dark. Chappi, Shamma and Rajni, all employees, were lying on cushions on the floor. Shamma and Rajni were asleep. Chappi was playing with her mobile phone.

Geeta was not there. The front door was partly open, and the heavy curtains were drawn neatly closed, which was fairly unusual for the Sakhiyani office and their members. The environment was low-spirited, so much so that it resembled a space stricken with grief. Chappi whispered in a terror-struck voice that Geeta and her *hijra-guru*, Saleem Khan, had had a vehement argument. The fight was intense to the extent of verbal abuse and even physical violence. It is never heard of that two *hijras* of the same kinship, and especially in a *guru–chela* relationship, confront each other. *Hijra* kinships are reverence-based, with filial ties.

Geeta suddenly appeared in the Sakhiyani office from her short visit to the slum. She overheard Chappi narrating the incident to me. She seemed to be quite troubled and emotionally unstable at that point:

> *Tu kyun Ahonaa ko bata rahi hain mere aur Saleem keye beech mein jo hua? Mein hi bata deti Ahonaa ko.* (Why are you telling Ahonaa everything that has happened between me and Saleem? I would have told her myself.)

> *Saleem Khan ko log pahchante hain bahut khatarnaak hijdo keye naam seye. Mumbai keye gunde bhi darte hain usseye. Bhaut hijdo ko jaan seyee mara usneey. Bahut chedta hain hijdo ko. Jor-julum kar keye paisa leta hain, peetta hain. Saleem ka badhe badhe mafia keye saath contact hain Mumbai mein. Badhe badhe hijde bhi uski baat sunten hain. Paar kaal meine uska ghamand utaarr diya. Saali, hijdo seye paisa mangti hain zabardasti. Mere chelo seye mahiney mein paach hazaar rupiyee mange. Kaal mein uskee ghaar gayee Ghatkopar mein. Mujse mahniyee mein daas hazar rupiyee mange, aur bahut buri tara seye baat ki. Mein kyun sunu uski baat? Aaj mera NGO* [non-governmental organization] *hai. Saab saath mein hain. Mumbai mein bahut badhe bare sarkari officers keye saath meri jaan pehchaan hain. Woh kabhi sooch bhi nahi sakti mera kuch bigadneye ka. Aur mera bhai gora*[7] *hain. Uskii himmat bhi nahi hogi mera kuch bigadneye ka.*

Geeta explained that Saleem Khan is known to be a very notorious *hijra* in Bombay. 'Saleem' is a male name which she had before becoming a *hijra*. But she retained the name even after, so as to arouse terror and panic and create an image by which other *hijras* and even the mafia would be disconcerted. Also, it is often said that even Bombay gangsters are scared of her. She has killed many *hijras*. She intimidates and coerces other *hijras* and extracts money from them. She tries to make others' lives miserable. She also has contacts with nearly all the mafia in the city. Every *hijra* in Bombay is terrified of her. Saleem Khan had demanded 10,000 rupees every month from Geeta. The *guru–chela* relationship and the kinship structure within this subculture also extends to a transactional relationship. The *chelas* give *hafta* (protection money) to their *guru*. The *hafta* annoyed Geeta, and she refused to pay. Geeta believes that *hafta* is a form of brutal extortion, where the *guru* does not undertake any labour to earn income. Further, she feels that she has partially renounced the *hijra* community. She has become a national activist on *hijra* rights and often appears on television, in newspapers and even Bollywood-film-based events. Geeta, like Leela, has a close association with Dilli (Delhi). She attends various government meetings as part of national and regional sexual-health programmes. Her decisions are taken into account, and the authorities acknowledge her opinions. Unlike other *hijra*s in Bombay who are petrified of Saleem Khan, Geeta has gradually overcome her fear. Geeta contests the former's threat to cause her harm through her underworld mafia associates, with her newly formed power and larger political connections. Geeta is aware of instances where Saleem Khan has persecuted, even attempted to kill, many *hijra*s who did not comply with her wishes. There are also other instances where she has chopped a finger and pushed one of her *hijra-chela*s from a speeding suburban train. Geeta's resistance to Saleem Khan's claim is quite uncommon within the community. She has also threatened to report the former's illegal activities to the government.

The argument between Geeta and Saleem Khan depicts contestations based on power relations in the *hijra* community. Saleem Khan, an infamous *hijra-guru* and a senior *hijra* in rank, maintains her hegemony with her close liaison with the underworld. Her hegemony is represented by acts of terror based on violence and murder. Her power relates to Jeff Hearn's (2004) 'radical power' that establishes an intense mechanism of coercion and force, ultimately aiming to sustain self-interest. This coercive power is precisely to contest and supersede the dominant social and political rule, hegemonizing ideological consciousness to overthrow the popular power nexus. Again, contextualizing Gramsci's hegemony in relation to *hijra* masculinity negates the economic determinism of Marx, but conceptualizes 'economic culturalism' (Hearn 2004; Andersson 2008). In Gramsci's analysis, 'hegemony' involves the role of certain social actors both individually and collectively, aiming to dominate the political and cultural structures of society with certain ideological objectives (Hearn 2004; Burr and Hearn 2008). This sense of power is embodied in the case of Saleem Khan who provokes violence. Also, the embodied practices are based on the attributes of the specific gendered structure in relation to how a *hijra*'s body constructs a symbolic metaphor of the material as well as the performative by means of which they act (see Connell 2002). Further, Saleem Khan's power in the form of violence adds to Amir Kordvani's (2002) understanding of dominance, linking it to the infiltrator's power-laden supremacy over a hegemonic and authoritative regime, where the rules are dictatorial and dangerous.

On the other hand, Geeta's power, derived from her political authority, anticipates a sense of counter-hegemonic practice that defies the power and hegemony of her *hijra-guru*, Saleem Khan. Geeta's power is related to what Scheper-Hughes and Bourgois (2004) refer to as the construction of 'structural violence' – a context in which power is related to a form of coercion and threat, but not to any sort of force or assault. Further, Geeta's sense of power is 'structured' within legitimate socially valued and morally endorsed practices (Scheper-Hughes and Bourgois 2004: 1–4). In other words, her power is based on the institutional regimes of political and social support of the government that she uses as a symbol of 'threat' to contest Saleem Khan's power. Geeta's power is 'strategic' so as to mean a sense of obscurity in the power she embodies with regard to the dominant political authority of the state.

Again, Geeta's revolutionary practices are also related to 'protest masculinity', contextualizing power and masculinity as evoked through a sense of 'protest' based on acute indignation and resentment due to constant discrimination and prejudice (Walker 2006). Protest masculinity in this instance applies to a definite set of dogmatic rules of the state's political authority. It is based on this set of rules that Geeta formulates her power to challenge Saleem Khan's *hijra* hegemony. In this way, Geeta's remonstrations create a rupture in the *hijra* hegemony which is exploitative and transform the classical *hijra* hierarchy and dominance. Her protest thus gives an idea of how the hierarchies in the subculture could be subverted and strategically contested.

Geeta once introduced me to Saleem Khan at one of their festivals. It was during the time of *jarat* when the *hijra*s grieve in the form of a celebration on the third day after the death of someone in the community. The festivity includes a feast with mutton (goat) curry and rice, and song and dance performances. This is typically a *hijra* practice in which they follow Islamic beliefs. Saleem Khan's *guru*, Sita, had died due to old age, and many other *hijra*s from Bombay attended the commemoration. Saleem Khan is nearly six-feet tall, of slim-build and with a dark complexion. Her body was so thin and skinny that her silicone breasts seemed to protrude unbecomingly. Her hands were bony resembled those of a skeleton, and two of her front upper teeth jutted out. But when she spoke loudly, the room full of *hijra*s fell silent with fear; her deep male voice could eclipse that of any other man.

Saleem Khan had invited some male guests to the gathering. These men were from mixed social backgrounds; some were well-dressed in trousers or jeans with their shirt tucked in and expensive shoes. Others were wearing similar clothes but had more colloquial and local accents, speaking the regional language: Marathi. The commonality was only in the use of verbal abuse and foul language. Some had red vermillion marks in the middle of their forehead, indicating criminal elements and mafia from the Hindu community. Some were chewing betel leaves and nuts, and some, other substances.

Chappi who was also present at the gathering murmured in a soft voice: 'Yeh saab bhai log hain Saleem Khan ke' (They are all *bhai*s of Saleem Khan). *Bhai* translates to 'brother' in literal Hindi and additionally connotes a human agency that safeguards and shields in times of distress. However, *bhai* also means *gunda* (goon), who establishes masculinist appeal by means of power, control and unlawful practices. In Bombay, *bhai* is the common term used to refer to or address a gangster. *Bhai* characters are quite prevalent in Bollywood films as 'villains' fighting the 'hero'. Conclusively, the struggle between the two brings forth aspects of justice by defeating the disruptive and antisocial and ultimately establishing 'good citizens'.

 Bhai for the *hijra*s is an instrument of terror. Moreover, *bhai*, in the *hijra* context, refers to a metaphor constructing their own cultural truth, a tool to safeguard their personal security. In this way, *bhai* portrays a shield or defence on which they build their hegemonic power, further creating a sense of terror to achieve their self-interest. Not only that, the simple mention of *bhai* creates a symbolic terror – *bhai* here evoking imagery, an imaginary masculine symbol and a cultural analogy of domination within the gendered notion of masculine identity. Thus, *bhai* arouses a sense of supremacy of the (male) gendered imagery that is associated with male, masculine supremacy as a cultural analogy of patriarchal domination. Such referential illustrations of *bhai* have no factual significance but celebrate the symbolic defender. This image is discursively gendered, assigning to it certain elements of power and authority that would try to form a vanguard for support and defence in the imaginary. This relates to Bourdieu's concept of 'habitus' that rests on the metaphor of the cultural importance of 'man' to maintain their hegemony by repetitively acting as a masculine project in determining other subordinate gender(ed) groups (Bourdieu 1991).

LUST, SEX, VIOLENCE: NARRATIVES OF DANCE BARS IN BOMBAY

Nitu often visits Geeta's office, Sakhiyani. She is a 'bar dancer' in a night club in the central suburban area of Bombay. Nitu graduated from a *hijra*-identified person to a bar dancer. She fled her parental home and came to Bombay at the very young age of 14. Nitu visits Geeta for several reasons. First, Geeta helped her when she initially came to Bombay. She allowed Nitu to stay in her house for a year when she was struggling to make money. Second, Nitu is a *hijra-chela* to Geeta and often buys expensive presents for her.

 Nitu lives in a posh neighbourhood in the city in a shared rental apartment. She rents with other female bar dancers. She works for four nights in the bar and earns good money on which she lives extravagantly. She also sends a share of her income to her natal family in her village. Nitu has attractive features and stands five-feet tall, with a fair complexion, chiselled nose, attractive eyes and a well-defined jawline. The most eye-catching thing about her is her smooth and bright skin; she also has a beautiful feminine voice. She has undergone silicone implants to enhance the femininity of her body. It would be nearly impossible to ascertain that she was part of the *hijra* community once and, as I reckoned, she had been castrated like other *hijra*s.

Nitu evokes a new form of gender transgression. Her present sense of self is neither a *hijra* nor a woman. She is a bar dancer, and her profession and performativity establish her sense of self. She does not associate with other *hijra*s; nor does she live with the *hijra* community. She socializes with other female bar dancers. Her clients are affluent. The days when she does not perform, she goes out for sex work and is usually picked up in a car by her clients and taken to hotel rooms or their houses, or, in some cases with romantic ties, her clients take her on holidays. Her identity as a bar dancer evokes a sense of how she prefers to create her own space and detachment from the *hijra* community. According to her, she has made a conscious choice to disassociate herself from her past ties, cultivating a new identity which is a far more respectful than the former. However, she has continued sex work because the profession is lucrative. Again, she feels that a bar dancer who is into sex work is more *izzatdaar* (respectful) than a *hijra* sex worker. Nitu's clients also take her to luxurious hotels and pay her generously.

Nitu took me to her dance bar on various occasions. Weekends were busier. She emphasized the fact that dance bars are not strictly zones of prostitution, but male customers take pleasure in watching the girls dance. The dance poses are sensuous with staged dances on the podium, usually to the tunes of Bollywood songs. The facial expressions of these women convey erotic displays: biting their lips, looking with sensuous gazes and pouting lips, also moving their tongue in and out to please the male customers. Although there are stern boundaries permitting no physical touch, an unsanctioned practice follows the dance performances, and as the guests are about to leave, some are permitted to 'pick' and take home someone. A pimp makes the deal backstage. The chosen dancer earns an extra amount while sharing a portion with the proprietor of the bar and the pimp.

The inside of the dance bar glittered with multi-coloured lights. Several round tables with chairs were positioned around the space facing the podium. Alcohol, snacks and food were served as desired by the customers. The visitors range from young men in their early twenties to much older ones. Women's entry is strictly forbidden, and it was only after Nitu sought permission from the owner that I could enter for my research. She introduced me to her colleagues: Madhuri, Sridevi, Hema, Pamela and Angelina. These names as Nitu surmised are stage names taken from those of female Bollywood and

Hollywood actors. Nitu further added, in the *dhanda* or *bizness* (referring to business or sex work), often the names of female actors is seen to add an exotic appeal. The *custamars* (customers or clients) develop the illusion that they are becoming intimate with a film star. She expressed this in a colloquial way, saying, 'Humare yeh naam seye chutiye custamaar ko lagta hain woh koyee film star ke saath sex kar raha hain' (By these names, the bastard clients feel that they are having sex with a film star). She then laughed.

By 9.30 p.m., clients started to appear in the dance bar. The men who visit the bar cut across social classes, from the rich to the not-so-rich. They enjoy dancing to the tunes, and frequent visitors seem to have developed a rapport with the manager. A few clients resembled provincial thugs with typical bearded faces and red vermillion marks on their forehead. During the dance performances, the floor was sparkling with crystal lights which reflected on the girls' dazzling dresses and the jewellery they were wearing. They danced collectively on the common podium. The fundamental motive was erotic – girls being showcased to be picked and taken home by men after the show. The seats were arranged so as to maintain a physical distance between the clients and the dancers. During the dances, clients happy with the dancers' performances, showered currency notes, aiming at particular dancers. The room smelt heavily of alcohol. The men also whistled and shouted at every song. While the girls were dancing, eye contact between the dancers and the men was evident. That started the initial deal.

Nitu said that when she was new to this profession, she had to face many hardships. For one, she was a castrated *hijra* who was making an attempt to be a full-fledged bar dancer. When her clients prepared to have sexual intercourse with her believing her to be a woman, they were often surprised to discover her real identity. In such circumstances, she was sometimes threatened to be killed or often harshly beaten by her client. Also, her client often refused to pay her money but forced her to perform oral sex and anal intercourse. She had scarce choice and agreed to her clients' wishes, bearing with the terror to save her life.

Nitu's employer was aware of her identity, but in such bars in Bombay, managers have to cater to their clients' varied erotic needs. The manager once said, 'Koi koi aadmi ko hijra pataney mein bhi pasand hain, eesi liye dance bar mein hijre bhi kaam karte hain' (There are many men who are inclined to befriend *hijras*, and for that reason *hijras* also work in dance bars). Subsequently, Nitu's 'market value' at work started to surge, especially when she was open about her identity to her newly acquired clients. She was appealing and extraordinary to certain clients whom her female peers failed to fascinate. Nitu eventually earned great repute in the bar dancing industry in the Bombay region and obtained affluent clients in her sex work.

Nitu recalls that she was eighteen years of age when she began bar dancing. She was encouraged by a man named Amir, who was her *panthi*. Amir had a friend who had a dance bar at Mira Road, a neighbourhood on the urban fringes of Bombay. During those days, she was bullied and disrespected by her colleagues. They often intimidated her because of her identity, claiming she will never receive any male attention on the 'floor'. But when men started to like her, her female colleagues became envious.

Instances are common of abrupt police vigilance occurring during performances. It is often the case that the police are part of the clientele and visitors, but this is of no concern in their work. As part of their vocation, such raids are expected at the dance venue. At such times, the officers harass the girls. They may also set fire to the bars and put the managers and girls in confinement. While operating a dance bar is illegal in Bombay, such places continue to run by bribing local political leaders. At the time of elections, however, vigilance becomes severe with the idea of creating an impression of law and order. The law enforcement tries to build a 'good image' in the public eye, showcasing strong moral values (see Agnes 2005; Anandhi 2010).

The construction of violence in relation to the dance bar is based on the idea of the aggression and fierceness associated with the profession. This is concerned with the understanding of what Anandhi (2010) refers to as interrogating 'the social position' of bar dancers and relates to their everyday lives which are based on subordination. Adding to this, Prabha Kotiswaran (2010) has tried to visualize bar dancing and commercial sex work as 'female tasks', reinterpreting female-hood and feminine labour, which were historically and culturally viewed from a masculinist lens based on masculine pleasure and erotic needs. Also, it is important to note here that Bombay after the 1990s saw the rise of liberalization and rapid economic growth, with powerful capitalist consumption influencing the performing and entertainment industry (Morcom 2013). In other words, consumer capitalism in middle-class India influenced the legitimacy of 'new money' and expenditure – bar dance and its eroticized performances ride the same wave of neoliberal logic, expanding the logic of entertainment in English-speaking as well as vernacular middle-class Bombay (Morcom 2013).

Nitu's story is important to note here. Her social mobility from 'a *hijra*' to 'a bar dancer' is built on applying the economic logic of the intensive transformation of capital to herself: a character she has acquired in contrast to the despised and tabooed *hijra* and that is embedded in her newly formed social class; the ecologies of reshaping herself; her affluent clientele; and her ability to rent an apartment in an up-market neighbourhood in Bombay. In the most direct sense, this echoes David Harvey (2005): '… neoliberalisation has led to burgeoning realms beyond the control of classes'. In other words, the logic of money, analysing the trajectories of class consolidation, has brought about a discrete middle class with an open-mindedness associated with social and sexual liberation (see also Harvey 1985).

CONCLUSION

Each of these ethnographic vignettes reveals a different aspect of the lives of the *hijra*s in contemporary Bombay. Each story represents a context within which they negotiate different spaces, and the ways in which they navigate relationships with men and their masculine domination in these spaces. The *hijra*s featured in this chapter demonstrate the different aspects of violence which they are part of and the ways in which power manifests or becomes the agency in these circumstances by contesting hegemonies of male power. For example, Leela was able to claim a kind of power over Baba by dallying with him, and also because she offers some of his men a kind of protection – a protection she is able to offer because of the social space and latitude she claims through her role as a reputed *hijra* (Figure 3.1).

Figure 3.1   Leela with Baba and his family in Mumbai
Source: Photograph by the author.

Similarly, Saleem Khan's terror and dominance conceptualizes a framework of repression in which her oppressive laws are upheld within the subculture. And her aggression that targets the victim's body demonstrates a sense of how violence could be an embodied practice and part of a particular gendered gesture that could potentially produce a hegemonic symbolism linked to dictatorial governance. And finally, Nitu's story of bar dancing patterns an emerging change in the subcultural politics, led by economic transformation in the wake of neoliberal India. Bombay's commercialization symbolizes a pervasive capitalism – a private act of erotica sequestered within the four walls of the bar, steeped with the culture of performative libidinal enterprise between the 'commodities' and their consumer. Taken together these stories offer some important insights into the everyday lives of *hijra*s in contemporary Bombay, especially the ways in which they negotiate power and violence. Further, *hijra*s represent their identities in new and contemporary ways, each of which disrupts established cultural archetypes. These stories travel beyond previous anthropological studies of the subculture.

NOTES

1   *Salwar kameez* is a South Asian dress. It is the most common ethnic wear in India, besides the *sari*. It comprises a long tunic, with usually half or full sleeves, and trousers that are loose (*salwar*) or fitting (*churidar*).

2   In *hijra* culture it is often the custom to 'adopt' someone. This does not involve a legal or formal adoption but a custom among this community; a person whom they verbally refer to (and sometimes consider) as 'my son' or 'my daughter'.

3   *Dera* is a colloquial Hindi word referring to a private or hidden space where antisocial activities and conversations take place.

4   'As-salamu alaykum' literally means 'peace and blessings upon you'. The pronunciation often varies subtly across regions.

5   Afghani *kurta*-pajama refers to men's traditional attire in Afghanistan, which is also worn commonly amongst the Muslim population in South Asia. This comprises baggy trousers that taper down at the ankle with a tunic which falls below the knee.

6   In Raewyn Connell's *Masculinities* (1995), masculinity comes to be connected to the dominant sexuality of the male body, especially the penis. Therefore, male impotency, whether biological or otherwise, especially male impotency when questioned in the public arena, is a threat to masculinity. In contrast, the perception of women's bodies is as passive-submissive, to be dominated through sustained violence. The study also critiques the feminist oversimplification of men's experience and manifestation of masculinity in a similar manner, irrespective of cultural differences. Here she introduces the concept of hegemonic masculinity: a pattern of 'doing things' – coercion, culture, violence and its institutionalization – that allows men to sustain dominance over women, subordinating women

and demeaning any other alternative form of sexuality. In other words, there is not just one form of masculinity but competing masculinities, with hegemonic masculinity being the idealized form. Men who are lacking hegemonic masculine traits are marginalized.

7   *Gora* in *hijra* or *kothi* language refers to a police officer or an individual attached to state surveillance.

BIBLIOGRAPHY

Agnes, F. 2005. 'Hypocritical Morality: Mumbai's Ban on Bar Dancers'. *Manushi.* http://www.manushi-india.org/pdfs_issues/PDF%20Files%20149/Flavia%20Agnes.pdf. Accessed in July 2018.

Alexander, J. C. 2011. *Performance and Power.* Cambridge: Polity Press.

Anandhi, S. 2010. 'Feminist Contributions from the Margins: Shifting Conceptions of Work and Performance of the Bar Dancers of Mumbai'. *Economic and Political Weekly* 45(44): 48–54.

Andersson, K. 2008. 'Constructing Young Masculinity: A Case Study of Heroic Discourse on Violence'. *Discourse Society* 19(2): 139–161.

Appadurai, A. 1988. *The Social Life of Things: Commodities in Cultural Perspective.* Cambridge: Cambridge University Press.

Banerjee-Guha, S. 2009. 'Neoliberalizing the "Urban": New Geographies of Power and Injustice in Indian Cities'. *Economic and Political Weekly* 44(22): 95–107.

Bhowmik, S. K. 2006. 'Making of a City'. *Economic and Political Weekly* 41(32): 3506–3507.

Blackwood, E. 2005. 'Transnational Sexualities in One Place: Indonesian Readings'. *Gender and Society* 19(2): 221–242.

Bourdieu, P. 1977. *Outline of a Theory of Practice.* Cambridge: Cambridge University Press.

———. 1990. *The Logic of Practice.* Cambridge: Polity Press.

———. 1991. *Language and Symbolic Power.* Translated by G. Raymond and M. Adamson. Oxford: Polity Press.

Brickell, C. 2006. 'Sexology, the Homo/Hetero Binary, and The Complexities of Male Sexual History'. *Sexualities* 9(4): 423–447.

Brighenti, A. 2007. 'Visibility: A Category for the Social Sciences'. *Current Sociology* 55(3): 323–342.

Brooks, A., and L. Wee. 2008. 'Reflexivity and the Transformation of Gender Identity: Reviewing the Potential for Change in a Cosmopolitan City'. *Sociology* 42(3): 503–521.

Burr, V., and J. Hearn. 2008. *Sex, Violence and the Body: The Erotics of Wounding.* Houndmills and New York: Palgrave Macmillan.

Carroll, W. K. 2010. 'Crisis, Movements, Counter-hegemony: In Search of the New'. *Interface* 2(2): 168–198.

Chan, J. 2000. 'The Status of Women in a Patriarchal State: The Case of Singapore'. In *Women in Asia: Tradition, Modernity and Globalization*, edited by L. Edwards and M. Roces, 39–58. Crows Nest, AU: Allen & Unwin.

Chatterji, R., and D. Mehta. 2007. *Living with Violence: An Anthropology of Events and Everyday Life.* New Delhi: Routledge.

Coles, T. 2009. 'Negotiating the Field of Masculinity: The Production and Reproduction of Multiple Dominant Masculinities'. *Men and Masculinities* 12(1): 30–44.

Connell, R. W. 1987. *Gender and Power.* Cambridge, MA: Polity Press.

———. 1995. *Masculinities.* Cambridge: Polity Press.

———. 1998. 'Masculinities and Globalization'. *Men and Masculinities* 1(1): 3–23.

———. 2000. *The Men and the Boys.* Oakland, CA: University of California Press.

———. 2002. 'On Hegemonic Masculinity and Violence: Response to Jefferson and Hall'. *Theoretical Criminology* 6(1): 89–99.

Das, V. 1987. 'The Anthropology of Violence and the Speech of Victims'. *Anthropology Today* 3(4): 11–13.

———. 2007. *Life and Words: Violence and the Descent into the Ordinary.* Oakland, CA: University of California Press.

——— (ed.). 2000. *Violence and Subjectivity.* Berkeley: University of California Press.

Davidson, A. I. (ed.). 2007. *Security, Territory, Population.* London: Palgrave Macmillan.

Davis, K. 2008. 'Intersectionality as Buzzword: A Sociology of Science Perspective on What Makes a Feminist Theory Successful'. *Feminist Theory* 9(1): 67–85.

Dean, M. 2010. *Governmentality: Power and Rule in Modern Society.* London: SAGE Publications.

Donaldson, M. 1993. 'What Is Hegemonic Masculinity?' *Theory and Society* 22(5): 643–657.

Edmonds, A. 2007. '"The Poor Have the Right to Be Beautiful": Cosmetic Surgery in Neoliberal Brazil'. *Journal of the Royal Anthropological Institute* 13(2): 363–381.

———. 2010. *Pretty Modern: Beauty, Sex and Plastic Surgery in Brazil.* Durham, NC: Duke University Press.

Elliston, D. 1995. 'Erotic Anthropology: Ritualised Homosexuality in Melanesia and Beyond'. *American Ethnologist* 22(4): 849–867.

Featherstone, M. 1995. *Undoing Culture: Globalization, Postmodernism and Identity*. London and New Delhi: SAGE Publications.

Foucault, M. 2010. *The Government of Self and Others: Lectures at the College de France*, edited by Frederic Gros. New York: Palgrave Macmillan.

Giddens, A. 1990. *The Consequences of Modernity*. London: Polity Press.

———. 1991. *Modernity and Self-identity: Self and Society in the Late Modern Age*. Redwood City, CA: Stanford University Press.

———. 2002. *Runaway World: How Globalization is Reshaping Our Lives*. London: Routledge.

Gledhill, J. 2005. 'Citizenship and the Social Geography of Deep Neo-Liberalization'. *Anthropoligica* 47(1): 81–100.

Gooptu, N. 2007. 'Economic Liberalization, Work and Democracy'. *Economic and Political Weekly* 42(21): 1922–1933.

———. 2009. 'Neoliberal Subjectivity, Enterprise Culture and New Workplaces: Organised Retail and Shopping Malls in India'. *Economic and Political Weekly* 44(22): 45–54.

Gramsci, A. 1971. *Selections form the Prison Notebook*, edited and translated by Quintin Hoare and Geoffrey Nowell Smith. London: Lawrence and Wishart.

Gremillion, H. 2005. 'The Cultural Politics of Body Size'. *Annual Review of Anthropology* 34: 13–32.

Hakim, C. 2010. 'Erotic Capital'. *The European Sociological Review* 26(5): 499–518.

———. 2011. *Erotic Capital: The Power of Attraction in the Bedroom and the Boardroom*. New York: Basic Books.

Halberstam, J. 1998. *Female Masculinity*. Durham, NC: Duke University Press.

Hanson, J. 2007. 'Drag Kinging: Embodied Acts and Acts of Embodiment'. *Body and Society* 13(1): 61–71.

Haraway, D. 1991. *A Cyborg Manifesto: Science, Technology, and Socialist-feminism in the Late Twentieth Century*. New York: Routledge.

Hartman, J. 2003. 'Power and Resistance in Later Foucault'. In *Annual Meeting of the Foucault Circle: 28 February–2 March*, 1–11. Cleveland, OH: John Carroll University. https://philarchive.org/archive/HARPAR. Accessed in October 2018.

Harvey, D. 1985. *The Urbanization of Capital*. London: Basil Blackwell.

———. 1990. *The Conditions of Postmodernity: An Enquiry into the Origins of Cultural Change*. Cambridge, MA: Blackwell.

———. 2005. *A Brief History of Neoliberalism*. New York: Oxford University Press.

Haugaard, M. 2002. *Power: A Reader*. Manchester: Manchester University Press.

Hearn, J. 2004. 'From Hegemonic Masculinity to the Hegemony of Men'. *Feminist Theory* 5(1): 49–65.

Hearn, J. 2012. 'A Multi-faceted Power Analysis of Men's Violence to Know Women: From Hegemonic Masculinity to the Hegemony of Men'. *Sociological Review* 60(4): 589–610.

———. 2013. 'The Sociological Significance of Domestic Violence: Tensions, Paradoxes, and Implications'. *Current Sociology* 61(2): 152–170.

Heller, K. J. 1996. 'Subjectification and Resistance in Foucault'. *Substance* 25(1): 78–110.

Hirst, P., and G. Thompson. 1996. *Globalization in Question: The International Economy and the Possibilities of Governance*. London: Polity Press.

Hogle, F. L. 2005. 'Enhancement Technologies and the Body'. *Annual Review of Anthropology* 34: 695–716.

Hoy, D. C. 1999. *Critical Resistance: Foucault and Bourdieu*. Oxford and London: Routledge.

Jeganathan, P., and P. Chatterjee (eds.). 2000. *Community, Gender and Violence* (Subaltern Series, part 2). New York: Columbia University Press.

Jenkins, J. H. 1998. 'The Medical Anthropology of Political Violence: A Cultural and Feminist Agenda'. *Medical Anthropology Quarterly* 12(1): 122–131.

Kordvani, A. H. 2002. 'Hegemonic Masculinity, Domination and Violence Against Women'. Conference Paper for 'Expanding Our Horizons: Understanding the Complexities of Violence Against Women: Meaning, Cultures and Difference'. http://www.adfvc.unsw.edu.au/Conference%20 papers/Exp-horiz/Kordvani.pdf. Accessed in August 2018.

Kotiswaran, P. 2010. 'Labours in Vice or Virtue? Neo-liberalism, Sexual Commerce, and the Case of Indian Bar Dancing'. *Journal of Law and Society* 37(1): 105–124.

Krohn-Hasen, C. 1994. 'The Anthropology of Violent Interaction'. *Journal of Anthropological Research* 50(4): 367–381.

Levi-Strauss, C. 1978. *Myth and Meaning*. Oxford: Routledge.

Mauss, M. 1947. *Manuel d'ethnographie*. Paris: Payot.

———. 1969. *The Gift: Forms and Functions of Exchange in Archaic Societies*. Translated by I. Cunnison with an introduction by E. E. Evans-Pritchard. London: Routledge.

———. 1977. *Structural Anthropology*. Translated by C. Jacobson and B. G. Schoepf. London: Allen Lane.

Merleau-Ponty, M. 1968. *The Visible and Invisible*. Evanston: North Western University Press.

Mertz, E. 1994. 'Legal Language: Pragmatics, Poetics, and Social Power'. *Annual Review of Anthropology* 23: 435–455.

Messerschmidt, J. W. 2003. *Flesh and Blood: Adolescent Gender Diversity and Violence.* New York: Rowman & Littlefield.

Morcom, A. 2013. *Illicit Worlds of Indian Dance: Cultures of Exclusion.* London: Hurst & Co.

Moser, C. 1998. 'The Asset Vulnerability Framework: Reassessing Urban Poverty Reduction Strategies'. *World Development* 26(1): 1–19.

Nagengast, N. 1994. 'Violence, Terror and the Crisis of the State'. *Annual Review of Anthropology* 23: 109–136.

Parker, R. 1989. 'Youth, Identity, and Homosexuality: The Changing Shape of Sexual Life in Contemporary Brazil'. *Journal of Homosexuality* 17(3–4): 269–289.

————. 1999. *Beneath the Equator: The Culture of Desire, Male Homosexuality, and Emerging Gay Communities in Brazil.* New York and London: Routledge.

Petersen, A. 1997. 'Risk Governance and the New Public Health'. In *Foucault, Health and Medicine,* edited by A. Petersen and R. Bunton, 189–206. London and New York: Routledge.

Plummer, K. 1995. *Telling Sexual Stories: Power, Change and Social Worlds.* London: Routledge.

Quinn, B. A. 2002. 'Sexual Harassment and Masculinity'. *Gender and Society* 16(3): 386–402.

Rajan, N. 2007. 'Dance Bar Girls and the Feminist's Dilemma'. *Economic and Political Weekly* 42(6): 471–474.

Rendell, J. 1999. The Clubs of St. James's: Places of Public Patriarchy – Exclusivity, Domesticity and Secrecy'. *Journal of Architecture* 4(2): 167–189.

Riches, D. (ed.). 1986. *The Anthropology of Violence.* London: Blackwell.

Sanders, T. 2008. 'Male Sexual Scripts: Intimacy, Sexuality and Pleasure in the Purchase of Commercial Sex'. *Sociology* 42(3): 400–417.

Sanford, V. D. L. 2006. 'Review: Anthropologies of Violence and Resistance'. *American Anthropologist* 108(3): 534–537.

Sanyal, K. K. 2007. *Rethinking Capitalist Development: Primitive Accumulation, Governmentality and Post-colonial Capitalism.* New Delhi and London: Routledge.

Scarry, E. 1985. *The Body in Pain.* New York: Oxford University Press.

Scheper-Hughes, N. 1992. *Death Without Weeping: The Violence of Everyday Life in Brazil.* Berkeley: University of California Press.

Scheper-Huges, N., and P. Bourgois (eds.). 2004. *Violence in War and Peace: An Anthology.* Hoboken, NJ: Blackwell.

Schippers, M. 'Recovering the Feminine Other: Masculinity, Femininity, and Gender Hegemony'. *Theory and Society* 36(1): 85–102.

Sen, K. and M. Stivens (eds.). 1998. *Gender and Power in Affluent Asia*. London and New York: Routledge.

Sharma, R. N. 2010. 'Transformation of Mumbai: Deepening Enclave Urbanism'. *Sociological Bulletin* 59(1): 69–91.

Sluka, J. K. 1992. 'The Anthropology of Conflict'. In *The Path to Domination, Resistance and Terror*, edited by C. Nordstorm and J. Martins, 190–218. Berkeley: University of California Press.

Spencer, J. 2007. *Anthropology, Politics and the State: Democracy and Violence in South Asia*. New Delhi: Cambridge University Press.

Staudigl, M. 2007. 'Towards a Phenomenological Theory of Violence: Reflections following Merleau-Ponty and Schutz'. *Human Studies* 30(3): 233–253.

Stoltzfus, M. J. 2003. 'Alfred Schutz: Transcendence, Symbolic Intersubjectivity, and Moral Value'. *Human Studies* 26: 183–201.

Thompson, K. 2003. 'Forms of Resistance: Foucault on Tactical Reversal and Self-formation'. *Continental Philosophy Review* 36: 113–138.

Trautner, M. N. 2005. 'Doing Gender, Doing Class: The Performance of Sexuality in Exotic Dance Clubs'. *Gender and Society* 19(6): 771–788.

Walker, G. W. 2006. 'Disciplining Protest Masculinity'. *Men and Masculinities* 9(1): 5–22.

Warren, M. E. 2004. 'What Does Corruption Mean in a Democracy?' *American Journal of Political Science* 48(2): 327–342.

Whitehead, N. L. 2004. 'Rethinking Anthropology of Violence'. *Anthropology Today* 20(5): 1–2.

Young, N. T. 2012. '"Uses of Erotic" for Teaching Queer Studies'. *Women's Studies Quarterly* 40(3–4): 301–305.

Zaidi, H. 2012. *Dongri to Dubai: Six Decades of the Mumbai Mafia*. New Delhi: Roli Books.

4

Festival, Spectacle, Eroticism

The *hijra*s in Bombay are quite particular about attending some religious festivals of Sufi saints at *dargah*s (shrines or tombs at which people worship). These annual festivals are popularly called Urs, indicating mass gatherings of people at the shrine to celebrate. The festival continues for some days. It is often believed within the *hijra* community that Islam is more welcoming and respectful of them, and during these festivals they are given greater importance. *Hijra*s from Bombay and other parts of the state of Maharashtra visit Haji Malang,[1] a Sufi shrine located at the urban fringes of the city, in a place called Kalyan, to attend the Urs every year. The shrine is located at the top of a hill, and pilgrims must come by train, car or bus to the base, and thereafter proceed on foot, a nearly two-hour climb. During the Urs, many Muslim families, and especially men in groups, visit the shrine to offer worship. There are small and medium-sized rest houses with shared toilets and bathrooms for visitors to stay; both *hijra*s and other visitors use such facilities. During the four or five days that the Urs is held, the *dargah* and its entire surroundings are decorated with multiple coloured lights; there are funfairs, music and worship. Remarkably, *hijra*s are not discriminated against at the *dargah*. Rather, they are given special respect and greeted enthusiastically by the Sufi sheikhs, visitors to the *dargah* and the local population.

In a similar fashion, but on a much larger scale, *hijra*s from Bombay also attend the Urs every year without fail. Popularly known as Ajmer Sharif, the *dargah* is the mausoleum of Hazrat Khawaja Moinuddin Chishti, who was a Sufi saint. Moinuddin Chishti, also called Khwaja Sahib or Khwaja Garib Nawaz, was a scholar of great repute and is believed to have been a direct descendant of Prophet Muhammad. According to his believers, he advocated universal love and peace for all mankind and preached the Quranic philosophy of the unity of religions. He is popularly called Garib Nawaz (*garib*: poor; *nawaz*: person who soothes) as he strictly followed a mission of kindness to the poor and destitute all his life. It is also believed that Garib Nawaz had blessed *hijra*s during his time, which is why the latter traditionally participate and pay homage at the shrine during the Urs. *Hijra*s from across India and even other parts of South Asia visit the shrine for the festival. The shrine and its people warmly and without discrimination welcome and accept all pilgrims, including *hijra*s.[2]

The Urs is held at the Ajmer Dargah in the summer months (Figure 4.1). The date is set according to the Islamic calendar; as popularly understood, it is celebrated during the first six days in the month of Rajab.[3] In the preceding months, the *hijra*s of Bombay are quite excited about the Urs festival. They shop for clothes, like *sari*s and *salwar kameez*es, jewellery, shoes, handbags, make-up and other things – coordinating clothes and accessories and planning their outfits for the six days they would stay in Ajmer. I accompanied Leela and her *chela*s to the to the festival in Ajmer. The journey started on a Wednesday morning in early June from the Bombay Central railway station. Special trains are deployed for travellers from Bombay to Ajmer city, which is an overnight journey. Once, Leela mentioned to me that there are special flights from Pakistan, Bangladesh and various places in the Middle East to bring pilgrims to Ajmer for the Urs festival. Also, special railway services run from different parts of India to Ajmer, to make it easy for visitors to attend the festival. She mentioned that the visit to the Ajmer Dargah is regarded as second only to the Hajj pilgrimage in the Islamic belief. The train in itself had a Sufi environment, with travellers singing Sufi songs, reciting Urdu poems and verses and chanting the name of Khwaja Garib Nawaz – creating an environment of *sufiyana*, a feeling of religiosity, divinity and festivity. The *hijra*s carried *dholak*s, or traditional drums, that they play to accompany their dances. They were beating the drums and singing songs. Men from other parts of the train peeped into the compartments in which the *hijra*s were travelling. Others enjoyed the *hijra*s' song and dance performances and took part in the festivities.

Every year during her visit to Ajmer Sharif, Leela stays at Shabbo Mian's house. Ajmer city and the vicinity of the railway station are congested, as is typical of old overcrowded smaller cities or towns in India. Hand-pulled rickshaws and autorickshaws fill the street adjacent to the station. Drivers try to attract commuters to their rickshaws and make quick bargains with passengers. Across from the station is the bus depot, with long-distance overnight buses to cities like Jodhpur, Delhi, Ahmedabad, Lucknow, Kanpur and Jaipur. The drivers calling every year, out for passengers and blowing bus horns to seek attention, add to the commotion. Roadside shops range from medical stores to garment shops, wine shops, tea stalls and food stalls. The city exemplifies a non-metropolitan city in post-Independence India, reflecting a post-colonial developing nation lacking urban planning.

AJMER SHARIF AND THE URS FESTIVAL

Yunus came to receive us at the Ajmer station. Yunus, who is an effeminate homosexual man, associates with the *hijra*s and is a *chela* to Leela. His sense of *hijra* identity vacillates between a man and a *hijra*, in the sense that he is a *hijra* (non-castrated) when he is with other members of the community – wearing *sari*s, jewellery and make-up. Again, he is a man when he is outside the community and lives with his family and runs a garment shop. Many effeminate men like Yunus live as he does; to fulfil their female desires, they affiliate with the *hijra* community while they also continue their lives in the 'outside world', as Leela once observed.

Yunus was wearing a white *kurta* (tunic) with a white pyjama (trousers) when he came to receive us at the station. The *kurta* was so long that it nearly fell to his toes, resembling a *kameez* often worn by women – thus an androgynous attire he was more comfortable wearing. He also carried a long, red *dupatta* (scarf or stole, part of women's dress that is draped around the shoulders) around his neck. Yunus has a familial relationship with one of the *khadim*s (Islamic priests) at the Ajmer Dargah, Shabbo Mian, who is his cousin. Shabbo Mian and Yunus jointly run a garment business in Bombay. Leela and her *chela*s stay at Shabbo Mian's home every year.

Shabbo Mian, who is in his late thirties, is fair skinned, tall and moderately built. Like Yunus, he associates with the *hijra* community in Bombay and identifies as an effeminate homosexual man. The latter is married to a local Muslim girl from Ajmer, who still lives in Ajmer. Shabbo Mian's wife is aware of her husband's sexuality, but they have a two-year-old son. Shabbo Mian once remarked that they cannot escape marriage, and giving birth to a child is a familial compulsion and a deliberate act to carry on the family lineage. Once men fulfil their obligations towards their *parampara* or *khandan* (tradition or family), their families do not interfere with how they live.

To reach Shabbo's place, several autorickshaws were hired from the Ajmer railway station. The areas we passed were congested and seemed to be lower-middle-class neighbourhoods, with heavy road traffic and domestic animals such as cows and goats freely roaming the streets and grazing on the roadside grass. The arrangement of buildings was such that houses were attached to each other on both sides, without any boundary walls in-between. As the autorickshaw moved on, the houses we passed were of a typical Rajput architecture, signifying the land of kings and queens. This style was prevalent to such an extent that even ordinary houses had hanging balconies, carved in the traditional style. These traditional patterns in the Rajasthani style of building and construction demonstrated adherence to tradition and heritage. As the rickshaw moved towards the *dargah*, it climbed a hilly path and passed through narrow roads. On either side of the street, freshly prepared snacks were drying in the front courtyard of each home. Women were chatting with each other in groups, while children were playing in the streets.

Shabbo's father, the head of the family, is addressed by all as Abbu (a respectful term for father). Their three-storied house has been built on the hillside near the *dargah*, of which its open-air courtyard has an unhindered view. The neighbourhood is famous for the *dargah bazaar*, or the traditional market, with shops on either side of the thoroughfare leading up to the main courtyard of the *dargah*. The *dargah bazaar* abounds with various stalls and shops – from flowers and sweets for offerings at the shrine, to garment shops, restaurants, hotels and rest houses, mobile phone shops, jewellery and accessory shops and many more. On the right side, the lane adjacent to the *dargah* boundary goes uphill, and it is here that *khadims*' houses are located. Shabbo mentioned that the *khadims* are believed to be direct descendants of Khawaja Garib Nawaz. Shabbo's father is a *khadim* too. They have a *khandani khadim parampara* (family *khadim* tradition). The priest, or *khadim*,[4] is a traditional occupation at the Ajmer Dargah, dating back to the time of Khwaja Mohinuddin Chishti.

Leela was warmly welcomed by Abbu to their house. They greeted each other with 'Salaam' (in the Islamic way), and Abbu expressed a sense of pride, calling Leela his *beti* (daughter). Abbu's pride related to the fame she has been acquiring as an icon in films and the media. The day of our arrival was the first day of the festival. Mutton (goat) biriyani, the traditional food during the Urs, was served to guests. The house was overflowing with people. For festival days, food was cooked by professional cooks in giant vessels, in amounts that could feed hundreds of guests. Before food was served, everyone residing in the house offered *namaaz* (prayers) in the courtyard that overlooked the *dargah*.

Leela has her associates and *chelas*. Among them is Yunus, who had come to receive us. Yunus is often seen in Leela's home in Bombay as a visitor with his other male friends. He is a fair complexioned, heavy but effeminate young man. He is in his mid-twenties and always has a smile on his face. As mentioned earlier, Yunus has a garment business in the Crawford Market area of South Bombay, which he runs with his cousin, Shabbo. Yunus is deeply associated with and plays an active role during the Urs in Ajmer.

The ancestral lineage of the *khadims* now extends to many families, and every male child in these families has to become a *khadim*. However, every *khadim* has other occupations too. Traditionally, they had flower shops or sweet shops around the *dargah*. But these days, younger *khadim*s also engage in other occupations like business in garments, electronic goods, food and beverages, and so on. In Ajmer, the *khadim*s' houses are located in the hills surrounding the *dargah*. These houses, while established since the time of Khawaja Garib Nawaz, have been refurbished from time to time. The *khadim*s live in large joint families; and as the families grow, rooms (that is, additional floors) are added to accommodate everyone.

Homosexual identity and relationships are subtle within the *khadim* community. Shabbo, as noted, is married to a woman and has a two-year-old son. But he also has a romantic relationship with a male friend in Bombay. He divides his time between Bombay and Ajmer. Romantic and sexual intimacies between *hijra*s and *khadim*s are prevalent. The elderly *hijra*s mentioned long-term male partners who are *khadim*s. Their relationships are romantic, and at times of financial hardship faced by either party they support each other. But it is also often the case that *khadim*s extort money from the *hijra*s, and the latter, in love, give away all. There is a story frequently heard of a *khadim* having manipulated a *hijra* in love with him to get money. The reason given was of the *khadim* wanting to start his own business and being short of money; the *khadim* promised to repay the *hijra* once he started making a profit. The *hijra*, in love, sold her belongings and jewellery and also handed over her savings to the *khadim*. The *khadim*, however, later forsook the *hijra* and failed to return any money. Thus bankrupted, her *hijra-guru* also abandoned her, and she was asked to leave the house. The *hijra* later begged on the streets, slept on the roadside and finally committed suicide by throwing herself on a railway track. This story is used as a warning to young *hijra*s who visit Ajmer. They caution each other against getting romantically involved with any *khadim*. The *hijra*s therefore socialize and flirt with casual visitors to Ajmer like themselves. They ramble around the *dargah bazaar*, hand-in-hand with their new-found love, visit the various stalls – those of food, jewellery, clothes and other items. Some even leave the *dargah* premises to other places in Ajmer in search of space for intimacy.

DRESS TO IMPRESS: BEAUTIFICATION, FASHION AND THE CULTURE OF FESTIVITY

Extravagant dress and beautification are a point of focus at the time of Urs for both women and *hijra*s. Both make every attempt to be beautifully dressed and look as attractive and feminine as they can. Visitors are centred around the *dargah* premises and enjoy themselves visiting the various shops, like those selling bangles, snacks and sweets, clothes, jewellery, pickles, utensils, religious (Islamic) objects and many more. Hotels and guest houses in the vicinity of the *dargah* are fully occupied at this time of the year. Women are dressed in traditional attire: *salwar kameez* with *dupatta*, *sari* or *ghagra-choli* with *dupatta*.[5] *Hijra*s also dress in the same way. They enhance their beauty by wearing beautiful clothes, jewellery and loud make-up, the degree of beauty being linked with the extent of embellishment. Besides these adornments, for the *hijra*s, beautification also relates to the enhancement of their breasts. As they do for their sex work in Bombay, here too the hijras place pieces of cloth beneath their newly formed breasts to enhance their shape and create cleavage.

Breasts are their sexual economy which they highlight as an important facet of their beautification. They usually ensure that their cleavage is visible. The *hijra* community is a relatively close-knit one where every *hijra*, if not known by name or face, is certainly know by their *gharana*, or hijra lineage, to which they belong. During the Urs, they mostly stay in the area around the *dargah* and socialize with each other. They chat and gossip, the main focus of their conversation being two themes: the size of their breasts, and men, boyfriends or their romance with those they believe would become their new *panthi*s. Breasts are an important topic of discussion for the *hijra*s: breast size, consumption of female hormones and the names of the medical drugs that

Figure 4.1   The Ajmer Dargah in Ajmer, Rajasthan
Source: Photograph by the author.

they either consume orally or inject in themselves to develop breasts. Further, they sit together and discuss as to which city *hijra*s having the most beautiful breasts belong, referring to the female hormonal tablets they take as *jaadu ki goli* (magic pill). The hijras candidly and proudly show each other their newly formed breasts. This embodiment allows them to achieve a form of femininity by which they feel confident and happy. In addition, there exists a rivalry between them as to who has bigger breasts. For them, the bigger the size, the more beautiful she is. Such internal contests often lead to a certain degree of resentment when comparing breasts in the context of region: *kalkatey ki hijre* (*hijra*s from Calcutta*)*, Dilli *ke hijre* (*hijra*s from Delhi), South *ke hijre* (*hijra*s from Southern India) and Mumbai *ki hijre* (*hijra*s from Bombay).

During the Urs festival, the *dargah* and its surroundings glitter with light in the evenings. Visitors pour in all through the day, but perhaps more so during the evening when it becomes immensely crowded. *Hijra* visitors usually wear heavy and loud make-up. They believe that painting their face with strong foundation and concealers adds an additional glow, or *jhalak*, to their face. Their eyes are always highlighted with shades of eye make-up coordinated with their clothes. Lips are made up with glossy red or dark shades and lined to help the lips look plump and big. The end result is a flamboyant look which would stand out in the public gaze. Dressed extravagantly, they roam around the *dargah* premises, the *dargah bazaar* and its surroundings. They usually go about in groups, either shopping or attending various cultural events (music and dance performances) in the vicinity of the *dargah*.

BEAUTY, EROTICISM, SYMBOLIC BODY

These images of feminine embodiment and beautification reflect ideals of beauty, which are an index and expression of popular cultural perceptions of beauty, desirability and body (Balsamo 1996; Bordo 1993; Davis 2002; Grosz 1994; Gremillion 2005; Negrin 2002; Turner 2008; Green2008 a, 2008b). The alternative conceptualization highlights the fundamental importance of the body, recognizing the capacity of embodied processes and the articulation and negotiation of 'symbolic' and 'agentic' possibilities to construct beauty and bodily performances (Reischer and Koo 2004). In this instance, the symbolic significance of the body marks the increasing complexity of the representation of cultural aesthetic ideals. Extending the argument of the body in relation to consumer culture (Bordo 1993), capitalist ideology serves as the site for material representation of consuming desires (Green 2008b; Featherstone 2007; Kong 2002; Yang 2011). This serves the analyses of 'corporeality' and 'embodiment' that deliver meanings of bodily experiences and further constitute the meaningful form of differential embodied practices.

Hijra beautification at the Urs festival in Ajmer actively recalls the new body – the boundaries and the different ways of corporeal experiences by which the *hijra* modes of sexual expression are deployed. Their beautification further brings out culturally marked notions of embodiment via means of their bodily display – highlighting their breasts, dress, loud make-up and other aspects – signifying an image on the ontological domain of desires and bodily representation. Elizabeth Grosz (1994: 55) suggests the corporeal significance of the body is linked to the network of meanings connected to the perspectives of desires and identifications. As Grosz contends, embodiment represents the possibilities of bodily experiences articulating the materiality and material forces that construct the body, so as to form the likeliness of its corporeal expressions and its significations (see also Barad 2003). The practice of materiality builds an active agent in the process of its materialization, with a mutual relationship between the 'matters' of the body and its meanings. Again, the dynamics of embodiment mark the importance of dress and bodily adornment, further installing the boundaries and fixities in identity and subject formation (Hanson 2007).

Dress contributes to the site of bodily embodiment that 'frames' the body in the 'cultural image of a signifier' – acting as an artefact to cast the body within the dominant cultural landscape (Evas, Cavallaro and Warwick 1998: 5). It further reinforces the corporeal (re-)inscription, providing a dimension of the body's behaviour, feelings, beliefs and sense of self (Evas, Cavallaro and Warwick 1998: 42; Hoogland 2002). Dress is not merely a piece of cloth, but a far more complex and meaningful object that inherently bears the ability to provide a 'signifying' power to re-determine a bodily being in its ability to uphold the body's desires, fantasies and identifications. It therefore bears an important relation to the sense of being, wherein 'dress' invokes the centrality of the subject's identity that genuinely enunciates the sensuous metaphor of shaping the flesh to its inner sense of desire. Dress, in this instance, is an active agent of the body's dynamism that connects the internal psychic interplay of the body to its surface reality and flesh.

Besides dress, attractiveness further recalls the elements of overall appearance that capture the aesthetic and visual stylization of the body. Sexual attractiveness invokes the culture of the erotic display of the various manifestations of material embodiment and bodily display that further upholds the physical veracity of the body. As Catherine Hakim (2010, 2011) observes, the meaning of 'erotic capital' of the body is essentially attributed to the expanding culturally specific meanings of beauty, which are largely constituted by the elements of the market-driven approach in the form of a 'capital' framework. Hakim's further assertion of the 'feminine' body, its performances and (re-)representation poses the appropriation of the corporeal dynamics in the context of which the disposition of the body meets the market demand for beauty and eroticism, in a way catering to the sexual and libidinal needs of patriarchy, evolving a meaning of masculinist illusion.

Furthermore, the explanations on eroticism are linked to 'eroticized schemas' – the locations, space and logic of the 'systematic stratification' of class, gender and race (Green 2008b; see also Morris 1995; Hanson 2007). The 'scripting' of eroticism features designated spatial locations, the impact of sexual interactions and the forms of relationships that are created. Borrowing from Bourdieu (1980) and Martin and George (2006), modern erotic context focuses on the situational metaphor of sexual desires and sexual fantasies that are met in a particular cultural and social framework. This particular framework is largely premised on the imagination of the patterning of the socio-sexual interaction that illuminates the thematic organization of space, producing desires, and the persistent representational character of the actors who negotiate that space.

Borrowing from Bourdieu (1977), 'erotic habitus' like habitus, is the socially constituted understanding of the ways in which eroticism is configured. It further adds to the implications of social structures and the stratifications of race, gender, class, sex and similar categories, which constitute the force and imagination of the collective and its historical representation. Based on this interpretation, Levine (1998) observes that the structure of desire is linked to erotic sensibilities establishing the ways in which a sexual subculture fashions its somatic display, practices, identity, and such. The sexual currency that prevails in this context makes a particular reference to a particular site, which shapes the social organization of the logic to its sexual fantasy, projecting a unique significance of the dynamics of power, body, objectification and an inherent sense of subjective construction.

Adding to this argument, Martin and George (2006) contend that the 'market' metaphor of the erotic world, considering the implications and logic of the 'market analysis' of the 'price' or 'utility' of an object, offers an exchange-value to the product as purchased (see also Green 2008a, 2008b; Laumann and Gagnon 1995). The market is further characterized by a given set of actors who structure the pattern of socio-sexual interaction. Bourdieu's theory of 'practice', in this context, highlights the social and structural backdrop, referring to the 'signs' that represent the micro-level interaction, corresponding to the systematic articulation of desires and desirability (Bourdieu 1980, 1986). The sexual-field character adds to the understanding of the actor and their negotiation, and features the politics of representation in terms of how the fantasies are structured, desires are met and relationships are materialized.

These theoretical analyses add to the evidence of the *hijras* in Ajmer, locating the importance of the argument in the context of the Urs festival and the erotic schema that is formed within the community. Dress, ornaments and other bodily accoutrements add value to their sense of beautification, with emphasis far beyond the notion of their body and sexual economy. The 'erotic habitus' is constructed in line with the features of a carnival, festivity, and the like, adding to the notion of men and *hijra* desirability. The 'market' in this context intersects with the Bourdieusian notion of (erotic) 'field' in which the relations materialize, and which projects the desirability of both the actors – the *hijras* and their *panthis* – further conceptualizing the reflexive relationship to the practices and their 'hexis' and the corresponding erotic capital they provide. This sexual-field framework brings into evidence a strategic reflexivity of the structures of desire and collective eroticized representation that are equally projected via the hegemonic currency of erotic capital, adding to the 'market' dimension of desirability and the libidinal economy.

Moreover, the *dargah bazaar* provides the spatial nodes of the sexual field, where the *hijras* meet their men. In these spaces, the erotic disposition seeks out and inhabits specialized sexual niches that project the significance of the order of the *hijras'* and Muslim men's eroticism. Furthermore, the 'field' in this context illuminates the erotic habitus of these actors, projecting the socio-sexual interactions – the signs and the symbolic management by which they befriend each other. This corresponds to the negotiation of their sexual practices in every micro-level interaction that compounds their specialized fantasy-structure and their structure of desire in a particular symbolic setting of their sexual sociability.

ROMANCING: SUFISM, *QAWWALI*, DANCE

Once when we spoke in Bombay, Leela reckoned that the *hijras* usually visit the Urs festival in Ajmer to find men. Indulging in sexual intimacy is very common for them. They believe that Muslim men are *ariyaal chissa* (very handsome and erotic, in the *hijra* language) and sexually potent. Further, they are interested in the fact that many Pakistani men visit the festival; the *hijras* find them even more fascinating and try to befriend them.[6]

Unlike their sex work which is part of their profession, during the Urs, the *hijras* are more interested in developing friendships with men. They often fall in love and engage in intimacy but rarely ask for money in return. Also, in many cases, men secretly develop relationships with multiple *hijras*. But when the *hijras* find out, they fight, accusing each other of snatching their men saying, 'Tu neye mera panthi chheen liya' (You have snatched my man).

The men who visit the Ajmer Dargah for the Urs also stay in the neighbourhood of the *dargah* during their visit. The *khadims* of the *dargah* and the local residents usually rent out their extra rooms at the time of the festival. These Muslim men commonly visit in groups, with their friends from various parts of India and South Asia. Abbu and Shabbo Mian also host Pakistani male guests in their house. Besides the home where they live, Abbu also rents out his additional house in the vicinity. He has a fixed set of guests from Pakistan who visit every year. Abbu once said that this has been almost like a ritual or practice he has been following like his father and grandfather – to host a fixed set of Pakistani friends from Lahore and Multan.

The *hijra*s usually enjoy wandering in the *dargah bazaar*. They find it an important and special zone where they can befriend men. Usually, they use an approach similar to that used for their sex work, making constant eye contact with the man they find attractive. Either they follow the man till they receive his full attention or they approach the man directly and seek friendship. Rarely does the man refuse.

Leela's *chela*s, Komal, Rajni, Nitu and Sara, usually roam about in a group. One afternoon, they were discussing the men they had befriended the previous year in Ajmer. The *hijra*s were talking about the *panthi*s whom they had met and who had promised to visit the following year too. But while praising their sexual encounters, the *hijra*s also started to curse these men. Speaking derogatorily, the *hijra*s cursed one such man, Saleem, as he had promised love to Sara and given her his contact details. He had even said that he would visit Sara from Delhi where he lives, share the news of his love affair with his parents, and marry Sara and take her to Delhi. But Saleem never contacted Sara. And the phone number he had given her was fake.

Nitu too was furious and in tears. Her *hijra* friends who were nearby tried to console her. Nitu also shared her story, remarking, 'Saab saley chor hain. Khwaja sa'ab keye paas aa kar dhokeybaazi aur chori karte hain' (All these bastards are thieves. They [the men] visit a holy shrine but indulge in betrayal and theft). Nitu had fallen in love with a young man named Abdul. The man seemed to be quite promising, and she mentioned they had had an intense love affair. But the night before they were to leave the city, Nitu realized that Abdul had fled with her gold chain kept beside her bed when she was asleep. Nitu was emotionally attached to her chain as she had bought it with her first earnings, and it was precious to her. Moreover, gold is an important possession for the *hijra*s.

The *hijra*s somehow feel that the cultural environment in Ajmer is extremely *hijra*-friendly, but not emotionally welcoming. The men befriend the *hijra*s for *masti* (fun) but leave them heartbroken in the end. In this visit, they realized this and said, 'Pyar ko goli maro' (Forget love). They shared this message with their *hijra* friends, warning each other, 'Pyar mein mat par idhar' (Do not fall in love here). They made plans to roam in the *dargah bazaar* or the *dargah* courtyard and enjoy the evening. In the evening, Leela's *chela*s met different men. Their usual practice was to walk around in groups, but as soon any of them found a man, they would go away with him. They would look for a place to engage in intimacy. Or, if they did not have their own space, they might climb a nearby hill or go to a secluded place in the open air. Sometimes, they rent a room in a nearby hotel. In some cases, if privacy becomes problematic, the *panthi* takes his *hijra* partner to Ajmer city and rents a room. However, this is not usual; men are afraid to be seen with *hijra*s as it is a taboo to have a *hijra* as a sexual partner. The next day, the *hijra*s wake up in the late morning hours or early afternoon, after which they sit together and chat. Each of them shares their stories of the previous night. While narrating their stories, the hijras laugh loudly, calling the man derogatory names before moving on to a new conversation and plans for that evening.

On the fifth day, Leela mentioned the ritual of *chaadar chadhana* (offering a piece of holy cloth) [7] at the shrine of Garib Nawaz. This is a conventional practice at the shrine. Every visitor during the Urs offers a *chaadar* (holy cloth) to Garib Nawaz along with red roses, incense sticks and sweets. The *chaadar* varies in cost from low prices to very high. Like other visitors, the *hijra*s also offer *chaadar*s to Garib Nawaz. Leela offered her *chaadar* on the last day of the festival, representing the *hijra*s of Bombay. The ceremony of making the offering is elaborate, where the offeror places the *chaadar* in an open casket and carries it on his or her head, walking all the way barefoot through the *dargah bazaar* and thereafter across the *dargah* courtyard to reach the shrine. The *chaadar* is placed neatly on the tomb and prayers are offered. Many visitors participated in Leela's *chaadar* ceremony. It resembled a procession with the *hijra*s dancing to the beats of the *dholak* – a two-hour long procession accompanied by dancing before ultimately reaching the shrine.

Leela mentioned that later that evening Abbu had organized a *jalsa* (celebration), [8] where professional *qawwali* singers would come and sing divine Sufi songs. After the *chaadar* ceremony, the *hijra*s went back to their rooms, dressed up and gathered in Abbu's courtyard for the occasion. Many *hijra*s, whom Leela had invited, joined the *jalsa*. That evening, Leela dressed in a silk *ghagra-choli* (Figure 4.2). The *dupatta* was draped so as to cover her head. Her *ghagra* fell to her toes and had multiple pleats, enhancing her beauty and femininity. She was also wearing heavy gold jewellery that included several necklaces, bangles, a nose ring, dangling earrings and a pair of anklets. *Qawwali* is an integral part of the Urs festival. *Qawwali* songs are sung in groups by professional singers in the *dargah* courtyard during the festival. These songs are an essential part of Sufi culture. Besides their *namaz* (prayers), *qawwali* is another way by which devotees connect with God.

Figure 4.2   Leela dressed up for a *jalsa* at the Urs festival in Ajmer, Rajasthan
Source: Photograph by the author.

The *qawwali* singers came in groups. The singers sat on a podium facing the shrine. Their songs were a gesture of thanksgiving and reverence to Garib Nawaz. Besides the songs, dance was an important part of the evening. The performances were so intensely emotional that the performers themselves were teary eyed as though offering their deepest selves to God. Beginning with the rhythm of musical instruments, the songs were soon accompanied by the audience clapping their hands.

CARNIVAL RHETORIC AND THE SUBVERSIVE METAPHOR

A number of factors place the Urs festival of Ajmer and *hijra* participation in the context of carnival culture. David Murray (2000) recounts the carnival culture in Brazil, as representing a festival in which the 'tradition' is maintained, and the 'carnival performances' emerge as a symbolic structure of 'inversion' or 'transgression' of the cultural politics of the people and the community (see also Bristol 1985; Baumann and Briggs 1990; Cowan 1990; Green 2008a, 2008b). Carnival articulates an expression of protest and subversion through a culture of festival, further conveyed via means of sentiments and emotions (Cohen 1980; Gilmore 1993; Bigenho 1999; Riggio 1988). Abner Cohen (1980) enunciates the relationship between 'culture' and 'politics', attempting to analyse the carnival movement in a symbolic form. The symbolic metaphor is further shaped through the constellation of the body that appears in a popular festive order, in terms of dress, mannerisms and performances, underlying the complicity and character of resistance. Felicia F. McMahon (2000) recounts the idea of the 'female body' as representing the 'carnivalesque', rendering the meanings and interpretation of festivity, laughter, delight, and impulse, associated with a new shape and ethos; women and the feminine representing 'softness' as the potential allegory of resistance and subversion (see also Taylor 1982; de Freitas 1999; Gilmore 1998). The 'soft' in this context, or the female and the feminine, holds a tenuous grip on their sensuality and seduction, so as to create a sense of self-eroticism at the time of carnival. The production of difference in the lines of performativity and resistance, lies in the analysis and the implication of a certain form of agency construction that is created through the means of act and interactions. The performance of the bodily display defines a situation that creates a subjective experience, interprets a social event and builds a meaning, producing a counter-imaginary to the dominant gender and sexual metaphysics.

This theoretical evidence provides an explanation of the eroticized and valorized image of the *hijra*s in the Ajmer Urs, signalling a perceived efficacy of the sites that centralize the fantastical or otherwise exotic display of the subculture. Reinforcing their images and performances, they open up their subjective positioning, locating themselves within the structurally ordained sociocultural context. Interrogating the conjuncture of culture and power, the Urs festival in Ajmer appropriates two important facets: first, the cultural mobilization of the dispersed (that is, the *hijra* subculture) that represents an essential element of the festival's integrity, historicity and the production of the festival's veracity. The spirit of the Urs is validated by the recognition of the gendered other, rooted in the festival's representation. This indicates the primacy of multitude, considering the rhetoric of cultural integrity with genuine experience within the demarcated sites of the festival's political space.

Second, the Urs in Ajmer Sharif provides a form of cultural hybridity that destabilizes the homogenized narrative of the nation state. As the ethnography notes, the Pakistani guests at Abbu's place, as well as several Bangladeshi, Burmese, Indonesian and Middle Eastern pilgrims, showcase a devout (Islamic) cultural order, regarding the Urs as next only to the Hajj. And the Urs clearly seems to offer a poignant emancipatory project that addresses a sign of equivalence in the matter of cultural or religious consumption.

Butler and Goffman on Subversive Performance

Judith Butler's (1990, 1993) and Ervin Goffman's (1969) scholarship on gender and performance draws attention to the symbolic meanings of performance, opening up new possibilities and newer meanings of sexuality in the context of carnival. The theoretical overview of performance by Butler and Goffman adds meaning to 'subversive' performances that challenge the power relations in popular gender dynamics. Butler's anti-essentialist understanding of performance and performativity poses a query in the order of sex, gender and meaning. Butler's notion of gender as a 'subject' category involves the order of performative action through ontological positions as shaped by language, repetition of acts and performances, the 'stylization' of the body and the 'copy' of heterosexuality. As Butler (1996) adds, a 'subject' becomes a subject by the very articulation of the 'regulatory' regimes that create the preconditions and the invested meanings of the gendered 'regulatory' illusions. On the other hand, Goffman's (1969) interpretation of performance offers a useful insight on the importance of 'self' and social interaction that involves the 'presentation' or the performance of self to exert influence on others. Goffman's presentation and performance of 'self' employs the metaphor of theatre – a dramaturgical one, analogous to the relationship between 'front stage' and 'back stage' like in the theatre that presents the actors' techniques and performances. In his later work, *Frame Analysis* (1974), Goffman proposes that performances are implicated in the form of 'frames' that are recognized as subjective experiences by which meanings are interpreted in the context of a particular social event or within a particular social framework.

Butler and Goffman analyse the subversion of a certain type of performance and the production of a new one. This analysis has implications for the importance of 'agency' that constitutes the production of difference and the subversive mechanism of a new form of performative regime (Brickell 2005). Butler's idea of subversion charts the 'parodic' performances and the 'resignification' of the performative meanings that connect the political meaning of a subject to that of an agency construction – implying the context of gender and sexuality that is socially situated and subverting any such categorical trope, opening up the possibility for creating new meanings and understanding of the same (Butler 1990, 1993). On the other hand, Goffman refers to the 'reflexive self' – a subversive mechanism that involves the mediation of a new set of meanings in the context of interaction, and which further needs appropriate introspection and negotiation of the situation or the social framework (Goffman 1969: 10). Thus, subversion is the possibility of 'reframing' and reorganizing the meaning of interaction. Butler and Goffman both rely on the importance of symbolism, presenting new symbolic resources as the conditions of subversion. Subversion and a new set of performances entail the dynamics of power relations that are mediated in interaction, discourses and institutions further potentially producing the dialectics, knowledge and new possibility of the social context.

Butler's theorization of subversion elicits a key feature of the discursive production of gender(ed) intelligibility. Uncoupling the ethnographic allegory provides an incitement of the tropes of sexual imagery – the *hijra*s overturn the sign and build a discursive repositioning of their sexual or performative assertiveness. In doing so, their discursive enactment opens up a multiplicity of subject positions that dramatically reverse from the ambivalent situatedness of a sex worker or beggar, to the possibilities of resignification. A neat illustration of *hijra* respectability in Ajmer Sharif and the Urs festival suggests the extraordinary realization that gendered 'signs' are arbitrary.

The 'sign' referred to here is the semiotics of performances that represent free-floating signals. The *hijra*s visit Ajmer to take on a different social status within the logic of the festival's claim. Their representation is re-actualized from abject identification to respectability. And the seamless festivity repudiates the sorrow and distress associated with their body, while their performances become a medium for otherwise implausible romantic accomplishment. What is evident from this embodied performance is the subversive approach to symbolically crucify their subjected identity and an invocation of an embodied performance. Revisiting this terrain demonstrates a striking detour from the popular clause on nationalism – elaborating a context of cultural and hence national hybridity metonymically represented within a cultural space. This leads to a modern nostalgia of a unified (South) Asian within one cultural frame, a possible future to the contemporary model of nationhood that is culturally defined. Thus, the crucial claim here is social equality – the Urs in Ajmer particularly displaces the political ecology of nationalism – offering a complex lexicon of acculturalization and inter-culturation to re-read nationalism's monologue.

Viewing this stylized enactment engages a significant notion of multiplicity that points to the locus of 'doing', or performance. Goffman's 'frame analysis' thus implicates a discussion of agency that follows the management of self-impression to the other in interaction. His approach to the presentation, or performance of the self, locates how *hijra* participation in the Urs implicates the subjective experience by providing meanings to social events. Indicating the social context of the festival-metaphor, *hijra* agency reinforces the negotiation of actions and interactions to express a newly formed self. Goffman's subversion in analysing *hijra* agency construction challenges the ongoing processes of the social world, with the possibilities it offers of the resignification of dominant meanings. That being said, the *hijra* parody and performances in the Urs festival offer a complex possibility to block the earlier frames of reference. Their new enactment suggests an embedded subjective fragility of interactions that set a new gendered presentation of desires and fantasies. Reframing subversion within the frame of reference of interactions, it perhaps grants subjective agency of the *hijra*s, refusing an essentialist view of the subject. This reflexive view is appealing because these 'structures' and 'contexts' determine the continuous disability of the subject's position. This subversive politics informs a non-foundational approach to a continual re-imagining of an individual or collective identity.

*HIJRA*S, THE AJMER URS AND BAKHTIN'S SUBVERSION

Mikhail Bakhtin (1984) recounts the subversive allegory of carnival culture in the context of folklore and the act of laughter. Bakhtin's interpretation of 'laughter' literally represents a sense of transgression and a shift from the hegemonic space, subverting any form of the present order. The act of laughter, which Bakhtin calls 'carnival laughter', expresses the reduction of its relative value and upholds the plurality of laughter and its broader consciousness, which is symbolic (Bakhtin 1984: 275). It transcends the objective reality of the carnival and brings forth the 'truth' of ambivalence and the negation of hierarchy and authority, ridiculing the prevailing dogmas through dramatic corporeal rhetoric (Bakhtin 1984: 229–231). The carnival and its semiotic meaning delve into the notion of bodily interplay that makes the transgression (and transition) from the dead to the living, reiterating the phenomenology of flesh and a new order of 'being'. Bakhtin imagines this bodily interplay and its ambivalence as the 'grotesque body' – revealing the ambivalence that lies in the 'death' of one 'being' and the 'birth' of the other (Bakhtin 1984: 365). Bakhtin's interpretation of the 'death' of the body is closely linked to the framework of ambivalence, rupture and the culture of dominance and repression. And 'birth' connotes his understanding of the new beginning of the dead, and the reappearance of the body with the politics of new meaning-formation, newer understanding and a claim for a fresh political consciousness. Bakhtin reinforces that the body is always in the process of 'becoming' that corresponds to the rhetoric of carnivalistic laughter, celebrating the complete withdrawal of oneself from the present state of authority and anarchy. Laughter involves the worldview of the transition from death to rebirth – affirming the profound impetus of a concrete truth of its denial and subversion (Bakhtin 1984: 127). Laughter, as Bakhtin adds, is a radicalized lexicon of symbols that opens the inside and outside of the body, and in a way, Bakhtin's carnivalesque culture becomes the literary representative of the culture of suffering, the emancipatory power of somatic semiotics.

The carnival metaphor adds to the understanding of the joy and celebration of the *hijra*s in the Urs festival in Ajmer. Moreover, the carnivalesque tradition of the Urs and *hijra* participation describe a kind of deep-seated ritualized practice with a concrete historical and cultural context, while also giving meaning to a world of eroticism and pleasure. The festival brings to light the symbolic representation of art, religion, multiculturalism and multiplicities of gendered identities that holds and incorporates an intrinsic relation to the semiotic dimension of performances – dance, *qawwali* songs, the festive ambience, dress and beautification and the act of romance and sexual intimacy. It further adds to the exotic and extravagant character of human experiences of joy, happiness, pleasure and laughter – to site a specific feature of sociality with a vibrant rigour of entertainment and participation. Further, the factors of adornment in the context of showcasing dress and make-up and the streetlights and decorations of the festival project the impetus of the festive display and the extravagant social environment.

Richard Parker (1991) in his study of carnival culture in Brazil recounts instances of how the carnivalesque tradition projects a sexual meaning in a symbolic form. Providing evidence of the display of breasts and buttocks, Parker locates the meaning of the sexual imagery of the festival, wherein body and bodily display provides the tenets of an open expression of sexuality, freedom and sensuality that reflect the transgressive logic and politics of repression. Thus, sex and eroticism become symbolic of a carnival metaphor that constitutes a particular cultural politics as mapping realities by means of cultural 'inversion' (Parker 1991; Lindahl 1996; Brophy 1997; McMahon 2000; de Freitas 1999). This particular cultural imagery provides an anthropological enterprise so as to locate the understanding of the fundamental inequality and the anarchy that are projected by certain representational means.

In a similar way, the Urs entails a festive aura, where the *hijra* participants shed their everyday struggles of life and immerse themselves in the joy and excitement of the festival. The festival exposes open expressions of the *hijra*s, situating excitement and their extravagant desires – a space in which they feel free to experience joy. Their seminal presence in the festival in rituals or otherwise, participating in dance and music and creating a spectacle for the larger audience in terms of visual entertainment, depicts the spatial and cultural resignification of the *hijra*s in a particular framework – the Ajmer Urs festival. Moreover, their performances of singing and dancing provide a distinct form of entertainment as a ritualized practice, in the case of which their presentation exhibits a symbolic reference to their culture, history and aesthetics with a sense of grandeur. Further, their performance presents the efficacy of their desired performative self-presentation, wherein the act of seeing by the audience frames the symbolic representation of the larger reality, in line with how the spectacle keeps the audience or observer entertained; accomplishing specific consumption that constitutes the whole essence of the bodily display and the community's ritualized presentation.

CONCLUSION

The subcultural representation here is related to the principles of desire and ambivalence. Their fantasies reveal romanticism and fear hand in hand, lifting the dramatic incontrollable consciousness to represent them and liberate them from ancient rigidities. As David Gilmore (1998) says, 'Carnival is the time for losing control, especially in crowds.' Gilmore (1993) asserts in another instance carnival's 'new danger' of 'rediscovering the polymorphous perverse self'. The underlying thread of the carnival from Rio (Parker 1991: 144) to the Urs in Ajmer is a ritualized space and gendered images engaging in parody, self-mimicry and obscenity – disassociating from defending the self-image. These anthropological accounts thus add meaning to the semiotic, symbolic and cultural meanings of a carnival metaphor that reflects affective democracy through discreet rebellion. The festival allows these participants to ventilate their hidden desires by means of highly ritualized and ceremonial practices, further adding the tonality of seductive charm, erotic sensuality, libidinal interplay, pleasure and bodily display. It brings to light an intelligible account of the community's free expression through the act of excitement, exhilaration and laughter. Sexual symbolism in the festival provides a new interpretation to the extravagant costumes and bodily display – breasts, stylized performances and exhibitionism create the structure of an erotic meaning that further focuses attention on the desires and the desirability of the *hijra*s. Therefore, the celebration as a whole recounts a cultural politics in itself, which nonetheless provides a uniquely inherent interpretation of the erotic and the sexual universe of the *hijra*s and their sociability in a carnival culture.

NOTES

1 Haji Malang, an Islamic shrine located at the urban fringes of Bombay, is a 300-year-old *dargah*, where Baba Abdul Rehman Malang, a Sufi saint, is buried. Malang came to India in the twelfth century from the Middle East. Haji Malang, in true syncretic tradition, is one of the few *dargahs* where a Hindu Vahivatdar (a traditional priest from the Hindu Karandekar family) and a Muslim Mutavalli (claiming to be the distant kin of the saint) both officiate at religious rituals. Situated at the border of Thane–Raigad district, the *dargah* is located halfway up a mountain. Today, the Haji Malang *dargah* in the Kalyan region is looked after by a Maharashtrian Brahmin family named Ketkar.

2 The association of the *hijras* with the Ajmer Dargah is linked to the story of Moinuddin Chishti, more popularly known as Garib Nawaz, who was regarded by the common people as the benefactor of the poor. It is believed by the *hijras* that he once met a *hijra* who asked him to endow her with the ability to bear a child. But the *hijra* failed to ask him to bless her with the ability to take the child out of her body after the nine months of pregnancy. In the tenth month her stomach was bloated with the child inside, and she felt extreme pain. The *hijra* took a dagger and slit her stomach open to release the child; both the *hijra* and the child died.

   At the annual festival of Urs, at the Ajmer Dargah, the *hijras* have a special role to play in worship and offerings. They come from across India, Pakistan and Bangladesh to visit the shrine and attend the festival. During this period, the *hijras* offer prayers to Garib Nawaz, and special prayers and rituals are performed in the name of the dead *hijra* and her child. It is also a common belief among the *hijras* that Garib Nawaz regarded them with the highest form of respect and deference as supreme human beings (Nanda 1990: 19–20; Reddy 2005). The *hijras* usually practise all the rituals of Islam like reciting the Quran; observing fasts during Muharram and Ramadan; the form of greeting, both inside and outside the community; Muslim burial practices and other conventions of Islamic law (Reddy 2005: 102). Sometimes, *hijras* also wear *burkhas*, especially when they have a *panthi* in their house, to retain their modesty and adopt the role of the 'wife' in the relationship. *Hijras* do not visit mosques for prayers; entrance is reserved for Muslim men only. However, after their religious pilgrimage to Mecca (Hajj), they start living like men, wearing a *lungi* (a type of sarong worn by Muslim men) and a shirt; they change their names to Muslim masculine ones and lead their lives as men (Reddy 2005: 104–106).

3 Rajab is the seventh month of the Islamic calendar. The lexical definition of the classical Arabic verb *rajaba* is 'to respect', which could also mean 'be in awe or be in fear'. This month is regarded as one of the four sacred months in Islam in which battles are prohibited. Rajab and Shaban precede the holy month of Ramadan.

4 *Khadim* or *khadem* is a Muslim community found in the state of Rajasthan, especially Ajmer. *Khadim*, in Urdu, literally means 'service' or 'care'. The *khadims* of Ajmer are converted Muslims from the Bheel region.

5   *Salwar kameez* is a South Asian dress comprising a tunic (the *kameez*) that falls below the knees, and stitched in different designs. The *salwar*, or the pants, are loose and taper down to the ankle. *Ghagra-choli* is regularly worn only in some parts of the country (and seen as a special or festive attire in cities). It comprises a skirt (*ghagra*) worn with a blouse (*choli*) and a scarf or stole (*dupatta*). All these dresses are elaborate and may be embellished with embroidery or beads and other such work.

6   The *hijra*s believe that Muslim men are physically attractive and sexually potent. In their community, 'Pakistan' symbolizes 'genuine Islam'. And during the Urs, if they meet 'Pakistani visitors' and befriend the 'most beautiful' men (*sabse chissa, pyara panthi*) from amongst them, their visit to the Ajmer Urs is seen as successful.

7   *Chaadar* is a piece of fabric hand-embroidered with glittering threads and decorated with lace.

8   *Jalsa* is a celebration or gathering of people which includes entertainment, food and drinks. *Qawwali* is a category of Sufi music.

BIBLIOGRAPHY

Bakhtin, M. 1984. *Rabelais and His World*. Translated by Helen Iswolsky. Bloomington: Indiana University Press.

Balsamo, A. 1996. *Technologies of the Gendered Body: Reading Cyborg Women*. Durham, NC, and London: Duke University Press.

Barad, K. 2003. 'Posthumanist Performativity: Toward an Understanding of How Matter Comes to Matter'. *Signs: Journal of Women in Culture and Society* 28(3): 801–831.

Bauman, R., and C. L. Briggs. 1990. 'Poetics and Performance as Critical Perspectives on Language and Social Life'. *Annual Review of Anthropology* 19: 59–88.

Beeman, W. O. 1993. 'The Anthropology of Theatre and Spectacle'. *Annual Review of Anthropology*. 22: 369–393.

Bigenho, M. 1999. 'Sensing Locality in Yura: Rituals of Carnival and of the Bolivian State'. *American Ethnologist* 26(4): 957–980.

Bordo, S. 1993. *Unbearable Weight: Feminism, Western Culture and the Body*. Berkeley, Los Angeles and London: University of California Press.

Bourdieu, P. 1977. *Outline of a Theory of Practice*. Cambridge: Cambridge University Press.

———. 1980. *The Logic of Practice*. Redwood City, CA: Stanford University Press.

———. 1986. 'The Forms of Capital'. In *Handbook of Theory and Research for the Sociology of Education*, edited by J. G. Richardson, 241–258. New York: Greenwood Press.

Brickell, C. 2005. 'Masculinities, Performativity and Subversion: A Sociological Reappraisal'. *Men and Masculinities* 8(1): 24–43.

Bristol, M. 1985. *Carnival and Theater: Plebeian Culture and the Structure of Authority in Renaissance England*. London: Routledge.

Brophy, J. M. 1997. 'Carnival and Citizenship: The Politics of Carnival Culture in the Prussian Rhineland'. *Journal of Social History* 30(4): 873–904.

Butler, J. 1990. *Gender Trouble: Feminism and the Subversion of Identity*. New York and London: Routledge.

———. 1996. 'Imitation and Gender Insubordination', In *Women, Knowledge and Reality, edited by A. Garry and M. Pearsall*, 371–387. London and New York: Routledge.

———. 1993. *Bodies That Matter: On the Discursive Limits of Sex*. New York and London: Routledge.

Cohen, A. 1980. 'Drama and Politics in the Development of a London Carnival'. *Man* (New Series) 15(1): 65–87.

Cowan, J. 1990. *Dance and the Body Politic in Northern Greece*. Bloomington: Indiana University Press.

Davis, K. 2002. '"A Dubious Equality": Men, Women and Cosmetic Surgery'. *Body and Society* 8(1): 49–65.

de Freitas, P. A. 1999. 'Disrupting the Nation: Gender Transformations in the Trinidad Carnival'. *New West Indian Guide* 73(1–2): 5–34.

Evas, M., D. Cavallaro and A. Warwick. 1998. *Fashioning the Frame: Boundaries, Dress and the Body*. Oxford: Berg.

Featherstone, M. 2007. *Consumer Culture and Post Modernism*, 2nd edition. Los Angeles, New Delhi, London and Singapore: SAGE Publications.

Gilmore, D. D. 1993. 'The Democratization of Ritual: Andalusian Carnival after Franco'. *Anthropological Quarterly* 66(1): 37–47.

———. 1998. *Carnival & Culture: Sex, Symbol and Status*. New Haven: Yale University Press.

Goffman, E. 1969. *The Presentation of Self in Everyday Life*. London: Penguin.

———. 1974. *Frame Analysis*. New York: Harper & Row.

Green, A. I. 2008a. 'Erotic Habitus: Toward a Sociology of Desire'. *Theory and Society* 37(6): 597–626.

———. 2008b. 'The Social Organization of Desire: The Sexual Fields Approach'. *Sociological Theory* 26(1): 25–50.

Gremillion, H. 2005. 'The Cultural Politics of Body Size'. *Annual Review of Anthropology* 34: 13–32.

Gremillion, H. 1994. *Volatile Bodies: Towards a Corporeal Feminism*. Bloomington: Indiana University Press.

Hakim, C. 2010. 'Erotic Capital'. *European Sociological Review* 26(5): 499–518.

———. 2011. *Erotic Capital: The Power of Attraction in the Boardroom and the Bedroom*. New York: Basic Books.

Hanson, J. 2007. 'Drag Kinging: Embodied Acts and Acts of Embodiment'. *Body and Society* 13(1): 61–106.

Hoogland, R. C. 2002. 'Fact and Fantasy: The Body of Desire in the Age of Posthumanism'. *Journal of Gender Studies* 11(3): 213–231.

Kong, T. S. K. (2002). 'The Seduction of the Golden Boy: The Body Politics of Hong Kong Gay Men'. *Body and Society* 8(1): 29–48.

Lachmann, R. 1988. 'Bakhtin and Carnival: Culture as Counter-Culture'. *Cultural Critique* 11(11): 115–152.

Laumann, E., and J. Gagnon. 1995. 'A Sociological Perspective on Sexual Action'. In *Conceiving Sexuality: Approaches to Sex Research in a Postmodern World*, edited by R. Parker and J. Gagnon, 183–213. New York: Routledge.

Levine, M. 1998. *Gay Macho*. New York: New York University Press.

Lindahl, C. 1996. 'Bakhtin's Carnival Laughter and the Cajun Mardi Gras'. *Folklore* 107(1–2): 55–70.

Martin, J. L., and M. George. 2006. 'Theories of Sexual Stratification: Towards an Analytics of the Sexual Field and a Theory of Sexual Capital'. *Sociological Theory* 24(2): 107–132.

McMahon, F. F. 2000. 'The Aesthetics of Play in Reunified Germany's Carnival'. *Journal of American Folklore* 113(450): 378–390.

Morris, R. C. 1995. 'All Made Up: Performance Theory and the New Anthropology of Sex and Gender'. *Annual Review of Anthropology* 24: 567–592.

Murray, D. 2000. 'Remapping Carnival: Gender, Sexuality and Power in a Martinican Festival'. *Social Analysis* 44(1): 103–112.

Nanda, S. 1990. *Neither Man Nor Woman: The Hijras of India*. Belmont, CA: Wadsworth Publishing.

Negrin, L. 2002. 'Cosmetic Surgery and the Eclipse of Identity'. *Body and Society* 8(4): 21–42.

Parker, R. 1991. *Bodies, Pleasures and Passions: Sexual Culture in Contemporary Brazil*. Nashville: Vanderbilt Press.

Reddy, G. 2005. *With Respect to Sex: Negotiating Hijra Identity in South India*. Chicago: University of Chicago Press.

Reischer, E., and K. S. Koo. 2004. 'The Body Beautiful: Symbolism and Agency in the Social World'. *Annual Review of Anthropology* 33: 297–317.

Riggio, M. C. 1998. 'Introduction: Resistance and Identity: Carnival in Trinidad and Tobago'. *TDR/The Drama Review* 42(3): 6–23.

Taylor, J. M. 1982. 'The Politics of Aesthetic Debate: The Case of Brazilian Carnival'. *Ethnology* 21(4): 301–311.

Turner, B. S. 2008. *The Body & Society: Explorations in Social Theory*, 3rd edition. London, Los Angeles, New Delhi and Singapore: SAGE Publications.

Yang, Z. 2011. 'Nennu and Shunu: Gender, Body Politics and the Beauty Economy in China'. *Signs* 36(2): 333–357.

5

Biopolitics and Biosocial Citizenship

Human sexuality is based on a range material and cultural forces organized on the pluralities and the multiplicities of social spaces, and the varied choices are emerging truths shaped in postmodern society (Featherstone 1991b, 2000; Giddens 1991; Plummer, 2003). Since the 1980s, there has been a major developmentf in the anthropological studies of body and embodiment (Grosz 1995b; Hird 2002, Shilling 2003; Turner 2008), which have indeed become a central feature of social life and its processes. The studies on body began to take seriously the important notions of symbolism and the practices of sex, as harbouring a host of meanings. One such important aspect is the new body-technologies of sexuality that are managed through medical intervention, conferring new modes of embodied sexuality (Bray 2007). Contemporary social theorists on the body have marked the increasing significance of the rise of individualism and consumerism that produce an unprecedented meaning of the body, bearing a symbolic value (Bourdieu 1989). Bourdieu's understanding of class and embodiment relates to the notion of the individual's social position and the formation of their 'habitus' and development of their 'tastes' – concerned with the management of their class and status in society. This posits a stark contrast to the formation of radical gender politics and transgressions in identity politics, bodies and embodiment and performances. This could be the starting point to talk about the new body technologies and the medical interventions that further act as a site of individual and aesthetic expression to create an identity that holds a bodily signification, visual image and corporeal stylization (Bolin 1994).

In relation to this argument, transsexuality and the medical establishment install an archetypical construction attributing reconstructive surgery and genital reassignment to the logic of mutilation of bodies, and bring about the change by means of curative genital surgeries. Surgical incursions into the transsexual body allow the bodily incorporation of the desired gender that is linked to the reality of their 'gender passing', and the shift from 'doing' to 'being' and from 'performative' to 'flesh' (Prosser 1998: 89).

The transsexual scholarship on embodying gender re-interrogates the understanding of agency and subjectivity that are deeply personal and profoundly political. The transsexual body delivers a meaning of a gendered body that further articulates a meaning of self, determining the legibility of the gender meanings that it derives through the processes of surgeries. The essential component of embodiment is emblematic to the signification of gender and the sexed body as a whole and further poses gendered performativity and gender norms as an expansive notion of embodied practices (Dellinger and Williams 1997; Gagne and McGaughey 2002; Rubin 2003; Negrin 2002).

Postmodern feminists like Judith Butler talk about transsexuality as an identity category that is based on the signification of imagination, desire and fantasy. This identity starts with the premise of the imaginary constellation of the body that is highly desired – and 'the strategy of desire' that is further manifested as the means to the end. Further, the imagination of the desired body is based on the fantasy of what is 'desired' and the claim to what is fantasized. The fantasy, as Butler says, is not 'real' but limits the 'real' – the 'desire' to believe in the reality of the desired genitalia which brings pleasure to the transsexual self and the body. This idea of the imagined state of the body is what Judith Butler terms 'melancholic heterosexuality' – the desired sex unites the anatomy to provide a 'natural identity' that is desired (Butler 1990: 90–91). Butler's further assertion is of the body as a malleable object that is spawned through its 'rearticulation' through a certain power dynamics and the creation of a new form of performative practices (Butler 1993). Her proposition rests on the idea of how 'sex' is related to a specific form of identification that defines the limits to the heterosexual matrix, and transsexuality as a category gains its social significance when the body is constructed by its material effect that ultimately brings 'stability', further culminating in a regime of sex, gender, subjectivity, gendered norms and some sort of bodily boundaries that propose its fixity to its re-identification. Although Butler conceives gender as the 'materiality of the signifier', her assertion on the body is too simplistic a generalization in her theorization of gender. In fact, her theorization on transsexuality shows the oversimplification of biological reductionism and the denial of the cultural discourse (Moi 1999: 74; Schrock, Reid and Boyd 2005).

Social science research sees transsexual embodiment as an embodied experience, a 'rhetoric of selfhood' that need not be equated with sex or gender distinction (Stoller 1968; Irvine 1990; Bornstein 1995). Transsexuality suggests more specifically the interactions between gender, the body and subjectivity – which propose deeper cultural meanings of the relationship of the 'sexed body' to the particular gender identity, further providing a view of that body in the construction of the gendered self (Rubin 2003; Stryker 2008). This form of embodiment specifically corroborates the understanding of how bodily transformation focuses on the essential ideals of the processes by which the body gains its subjectivity through specific needs, desires, the being-ness of the particular body, particular experiences, the narratives of gender passing, gender boundaries and their norms, and so on, thus further debating on the possibilities for transsexuality, discussing how sex, sex categories and gender are subverted or undermined to redo another gender (Connell 2010). The political implication of transsexual identity emerges in the effort of the interpretation of gendered performances, moving attention from 'undoing' to 'redoing' – taking into account the gender presentations of the self and the making of the subjectivity which passes through a rigid gender binary and certain accountability structures of gender norms (Deutsch 2007; Risman 2009; West and Zimmerman 2009).

Transsexuality and the fluidity of gender politics open up feminist interests and possibilities, delving into the experiences and the interactive practices of (re) doing gender. The deeper understanding of the interactions may suggest a site for change as well as stability that is always faced with the complex processes of discordance and negotiation to build a newly formed identity. Redoing gender thus particularly entails the exploration and addressing of structural changes and interactional patterns that enable new possibilities of interpreting the transsexual's gender transformation (see Garfinkel 1967). This forms a politics of visibility and, in a way, a strategic tool that allows the realization of the authenticity and rhetoric of embodied practices, and uncovers the remaking of the body with a certain sense of practical consciousness (Bolin 1996).

GLOBAL IDENTITY, LOCAL BEAUTY: THE JOURNEY TO BECOME A 'WOMAN'

I was introduced to Anita (Figure 5.1) by a friend of mine, who teaches gender and sexuality in a reputed university in Bombay. My first visit to Anita was in the beauty spa which she owns in suburban Bombay, in a place called Mulund. She holds a degree in Economics and was teaching in an undergraduate college. Anita and my friend were university mates as graduate students. Anita chose to leave her teaching profession. She was always motivated to take up a profession oriented to fashion, beauty and design, and started her own venture with a beauty therapy clinic, renting a space near her house.

Anita recounted her story as she sat in the lobby of her trendy beauty-treatment centre. She gave me some time between her work and attending clients. Anita has undergone gender reassignment surgery (GRS) and has assigned her new gender as female. Her story sheds light on her gender transition and the difficulties and challenges she faced during her gender passing, representing the experience of a transsexual person.

She was hesitant and nervous in narrating her life history, fearing that this might affect her married life. I was acquainted with her personal life through several informal meetings at her place. Anita took a long time before she agreed to meet me, and we had several telephonic conversations until she developed some trust. She is discreet with her past at her workplace and does not wish that people discuss it at all. Yet, finally developing a sense of comfort, after a long period of discussion on varied issues, Anita started to open up on the story of her life.

Figure 5.1   Anita in a coffee shop in Bombay after work
Source: Photograph by the author.

She narrated the anxieties and distresses she experienced in her childhood, specifically her discomfort with her body and gender identity during her junior school days. Anita used to wear female clothes behind closed doors when her mother was not at home. She wore her mother's *sari* and bangles and beautified herself with ornaments and make-up. This was a usual practice for her, and she looked for opportunities when she was alone at home so that she could dress up. However, one day her elder brother saw her in women's clothes and reported the matter to their parents. She was beaten badly by her father, and her parents thereafter began to keep a stern eye on her. In school, her classmates tormented her with derogatory words such as 'half-male', 'eunuch' and other such expressions, and by prodding her chest and buttocks. She was hesitant to report this to the school authorities and believed that if she did so, rather than supporting her, they would simply ask her to be 'more manly' and get a chance to call her parents, which would worsen her situation. Young Anita bore the brunt, graduated from school and went on to university to study Economics. Anita added that she developed emotional stress and depression as she was growing up, and gradually internalized the fact that she would have to face such ordeals every day. Anita became highly emotional when narrating this; she was resting her head on a cushion while lying on the sofa. She sat up and said that while growing up and in her teens, it pained her to see that her friends were into relationships with someone from the opposite sex, while as much as she desired to have a 'boyfriend', she was unable to. What she felt was 'lacking' was that she did not identify as a man and faced discomfort and anxieties being in a male body, the biological sex that she was born with. Anita added in tears that there were a couple of occasions when she tried to kill herself, but she failed. She asked, 'If a man or a woman who is comfortable with their gender and identity is asked to live, act and dress like the opposite sex, would they be able to do so? *That is so tough; so suicidal and suffocating.*'

Wiping her tears, Anita paused her narrative. There was silence in the room until she started to play some old Bollywood music on her newly bought gramophone. With a smile on her face, she offered me another cup of tea that I agreed to, and I followed her to the kitchen. While making the tea, she took a deep breath and her face gleamed with happiness. 'Very tough but possible,' she said and continued her story. She told me that soon after she finished her Masters in Economics, she got a job in an undergraduate college in Bombay University, where she worked for four years. Then she decided to undergo GRS. She had lost her father by then but her mother was traumatized on learning her decision – until Anita made her understand the situation. She also took her mother to the doctors with whom she had had clinical consultations and was somehow able to convince her mother to agree to her gender transition.

Her transition took place while she was teaching in college. She had to face bullying from her colleagues; her colleagues were unable to understand and were in fact not even aware that gender passing was possible. Anita was understanding of such remarks and agreed that the time when she transitioned was in the early years when such surgeries and clinical processes were not much known. It was not that she transitioned that long ago; it was in the early 2000s, but not many doctors in India were trained in these procedures. Our conversation led to discussions on the clinical procedures entailed in the transition. Anita was also hesitant to talk about her doctors and the initial diagnosis she had received from doctors in Bombay. She got nervous, perhaps wondering whether she should provide so much information. I too did not ask for more. But after another pause in our conversation, Anita mentioned that the doctors involved in her early diagnosis harassed her, and certain wrong treatments and diagnosis caused much damage to her health. She still faces nerve problems and sudden anxiety – the result of shock therapy administered by her psychiatrists in the early stages of her treatment. It was difficult to convince her doctors to agree to gender reassignment. Instead, the doctors somehow made Anita believe that a kind of shock therapy called 'electroconvulsive therapy' would reduce her depression and may also enable her to change her mind entirely about the gender transition procedure.

The doctor perceived transsexuality as a 'disorder', and his treatment was based on the idea of 'curing' Anita and preventing the transition. Repeated shock therapy for nearly ten sessions affected her health, causing her to develop a nerve disorder which is incurable. The damage led Anita to approach a different psychiatrist for treatment. Her new doctor, a lady therapist, was more understanding. Upon learning what her previous doctor had done, the latter became furious, and they both resolved to lodge a formal and legal complaint against the former doctor. But Anita stepped back from this plan due to the distress associated with legal processes and decided to focus on her therapies.

Anita laughed, patted my shoulder, and said to me, 'It is not so easy madam; a long process of two years.' Anita was glad to find a friendly and sensible psychiatrist who understood issues of transsexuality. Her transition thereafter was quite smooth, and her doctors ever since were helpful and cooperative. She further mentioned that the process runs through several clinical supervisions from multiple clinical specialists. Psychologists, psychiatrists, endocrinologists, urologists and plastic surgeons play a significant role in the process. Prior to any unalterable process being carried out, mental-health practitioners make a thorough analysis to understand and diagnose whether the person is the 'right' candidate for transition. For this, the 'patient' is asked to lead the life of the opposite sex, and hormonal therapy is administered simultaneously as a procedure for 'replacement'. During her psychiatric evaluation, her doctor referred her to an endocrinologist for hormone replacement therapy (HRT). Anita talked about certain emotional discomfort like mood swings and similar symptoms during the therapy. The HRT caused her to cry and feel quite emotionally low on some occasions, but she coped by undergoing counselling sessions with her psychiatrist. For the span of her treatment, Anita had to visit her doctors once every month for check-ups. After two years of treatments, she consulted a plastic surgeon and a urologist for the requisite surgery, which was actually the final phase of her transition. She said that her plastic surgeon and urologist formed a team with other surgeons for the procedures. Besides genital reconstruction, she underwent breast implants and other non-surgical procedures for facial feminization.

Anita is quite happy with her life. She does agree that she has undergone a lot of pain and agony, but all that was worthwhile when she thinks back to the kind of life she would have had to lead as a man. Her marriage was not that easy; it was rather an agreement between her and her husband, where they were married with full knowledge of her past, and her husband agreed to adopt a child after their marriage. Anita has been quite successful in achieving her dreams; she and her husband adopted a boy whom they named Suraj (meaning, the sun). Anita and Ajay's son is five years old and lives much of the time with Anita's mother. Anita is unable to provide fulltime care to the child since her busy professional schedule demands frequent travel; her son visits them during the weekends. She is absolutely adored by her in-laws, friends and relatives, and she feels that she does not need to share her story with anyone besides her husband. She calls her husband her 'best friend' with whom she shares her life, everyday work issues and other things, adding more value and positive energy to their relationship.

EMBODIMENT AND NARRATIVES OF TRANSGRESSION

Anita's story is one of her new life with gender conformity via surgical means of embodiment. Yet it was an upsetting experience, intrinsically associated with a series of upheavals undergone in her day-to-day life. For her, 'gender' is not a choice but a mandate of her being; the position is of affective promises to achieve gendered citizenship through bio-political means. Further, it illuminates the ways in which her embodiment provokes a mixture of fascination and hope, in relation to the moral and emotional force to gain aesthetic ideals of the bio-political locus that arguably assigns value to the body that emerges; scientific knowledge is central for the development of identity. Her story enables us to recognize the experience of science that benefits both her private and public interests as seen within the gendered purview of 'performativity'. To address these issues, Anita's identity reinforces the idea of gender as 'natural'; her naturalness is central to the political and personal construction of the corporeal. Further, we cannot neglect the role of embodiment within her gendered experiences and expressions.

I am particularly struck by the mention in Anita's story – or, for that matter, any gender transgressive narratives – of the continual mental whirlpool in the growing years as also of the social isolation. Her deep anxiety that reflected in our discussions added to the interpretation of the biomedical complexity correlated with the bodily and psychic changes. Grappling with this, Anita mentioned that the specific cultural circumstances of Indian society – the familial boundaries of restricted social space and strict gender legibility – made disclosure of her gender transgression an almost insurmountable barrier. Further, her narratives of womanhood have more to offer beyond the materiality of her sexed embodiment. The act of her 'becoming' is a constant performativity of its everydayness that substantiates a complex, ontological account of her struggles – the clinical and the psychological trials, personal tenacity, financial insecurity, social ostracism, loss of employment, and so on. The experience of her transition marks her speakability; more importantly, about two decades ago, when such radical gender transgressions were unheard of, she had to face serious social concern and criticism.

'Speakability' is not simply speaking, or, in the words of Jay Prosser (1999: 109), not just an oral narrative. Speakability constitutes the 'most unspeakable about the self'. Thus, Anita's life story grapples with a vast array of real-life experiences of gender crossing, which include the experiences of emotional and psychic pain, so as to achieve a new sense of self. Anita's conflict with her inner and outer self created a sense of discomfort, leading her to visit several psychotherapists. 'In those times, clinicians were insensitive to these facts,' she added. Tears rolled down her cheeks as she mentioned the shock (conversion) therapies and heavy doses of anti-psychotic medication that affected her neurologically in the long run.[1] She also mentioned how her family, neighbours and peers hurt her with spiteful names indicating a person with non-binary traits. Her account of the clinical process demonstrates the profound impact on her emotional and psychological well-being when her doctors raised false hopes of 'resolving' her dysphoria psychotherapeutically. She felt there was a grave lack of understanding of sex and gender in the medical establishment, at least when she underwent treatment. Unlike the Western system of diagnosis, in India even in the early years of this century, gender dysphoria was seen in terms of an illness. Anita also pointed to the practice of Indian clinicians who simply copy Western clinical gender dysphoric stances in the Indian context. She felt that the archetypical foreign import of (clinical) knowledge might be a hindrance to gender dysphoric patients in India, appearing as a complex domain where sex(ed) identity builds up into a biological bedrock to meet a universal effective criterion. Yet, despite having to go through various ordeals and upheavals, she managed to achieve her desired gender through HRT, GRS and other cosmetic procedures.

Thinking back over Anita's narratives, the invasive mechanisms of her gender transgression echoed pain as well as pleasure. Her persecution of her body-self and mind-self underscored the experience of paranoia and also coping through clinical strategies which involved scuttling from one doctor to the other. Yet in the midst of this persecutory anxiety, her surgery-led transgression brought a sense of euphoria and possibility, the realization of an impossible image of the self that she yearned to authenticate. The 'impossibility' is her physical transition, tearing the social semiotic within the regimes of signs: her transitioning physical appearance, genital reconstruction and somatic changes. This re-territorialization of signs points to a focus on her bodily signifiers that form the symbolic proof of sexual difference. Therein lies the binary logic of the real–impossible account of the corporeal markers that direct sexual difference. The point of course is the displacement – or what Jacques Lacan calls 'sexuation'– conceiving a sexualized cosmology that establishes a sexual identity within a symbolic norm imposed onto a 'polymorphous' body that never fits the ideal (Ragland 2004). This particular Lacanian impression relates to Anita's endless hysterical search for the genital or bodily signifier of the feminine, implying further a logic of relationship in the process of signification. Therefore, Lacan's re-ontologization of sexual difference involves a reference to a series of symbolic oppositions: the difference between the two sexes is not a direct opposing factor. Consequently, Lacanian 'sexuation' could philosophically problematize the discursive formation of gender identities that are undifferentiated within the 'being' of language (Lacan 1977; Ragland 2012).

Arguing further, the construction of 'gender' is performatively enacted, as grasped within the crucial distinction of the bodily signifier translocating and translating an entity encumbered with a political element – the sign value. Framing this bodily signification extends the Hobbsean model of 'name signification' (Baudrillard, Lovitt and Klopsch 1976). Crucial to this is corporeal materialism, naming and the utterance that Anita's account of embodied existence calls on us to view a host of signs. Significantly, these bodily signifiers assimilate into a regulative movement of the body – instancing a performative condensation that further transforms into a systematic practice of regulation, rule, norm and normalization. Again, the symbolic order tries to address an analogy with social class identity. In the case of Anita's sexed embodiment, her newly formed identity is a 'symbolic' class identity that translates into symbolic features within a benevolent class structure: a middle-class woman. Bringing together Lacanian 'sexuation' and the Hobbsean model of bodily signification, the space of contingent symbolization is the very constitution of her female embodiment. The subject is not just inherently sexualized, but also marks her mystical experiences in crossing the binary from one to the other. This further makes Lacan's 'phallic signifier' a more complex symbolic imaginary, conforming to the universal symbolic structure of the corporeal economy around trans[*2] embodiment. That is to say, the crucial unavoidability of Anita's sexed embodiment is coupled with class inscription that further determines her social construction of gender presupposing: 'woman' as a subject. Her 'sexuation' into the female gender(ed) space claims the point of reference of the quintessential 'real' – the corporeal and the behavioural intersubjective embodiment, accounting for the lived-through moment of her feminine being (McGrath 2010).

TRANSSEXUALITY AND THE MENTAL HEALTH DISCOURSE I: PRACTITIONERS AND PATIENTS

Mental health discourses on transsexual identity articulate the role of clinical technology in determining sexual identity. The clinical technology in this context is not only surgical but also technological as a 'discursive construction' that navigates globally and locally, based on the respective versions of clinical science. For example, transsexual diagnoses by mental health and medical practitioners in Bombay are based on the globally recognized criterion of the DSM-4.[3]

This language of mental health creates possibilities (and also constraints) that are related to the discourses and negotiations of a disease syndrome and the prospect of cure treatments. Based on that, the analysis would highlight the narratives and discussions of mental health practitioners in Bombay and their perceptions on transsexuality.

Dr Mahin and Dr Peck are prominent clinical psychiatrists at the Rasina Hospital in Bombay. They also hold professorial positions in this discipline at the University of Bombay. Their views on transsexuality are related to 'thought disorder'. Although both the doctors claim to diagnose 'transsexual patients', their understanding of this gender (and mental) syndrome is based on conventional outlooks. These doctors seemed to be unhappy with my questions and inquiries about their views on transsexuality but remarked that transsexuals have schizophrenic tendencies.

In a similar way, Dr. Banes, a middle-aged female doctor, recounted her views and experiences in diagnosing a transsexual child. The doctor, who is a specialized psychotherapist for children and adolescents, addresses non-heterosexual identities as 'abnormalities' and 'psychological disorders'. In her view, rigorous psychological testing such as 'MMP1'⁴ is the therapeutic route by which transsexuality and homosexuality can be 'cured'. The doctor also mentioned the need for accuracy and the sensitivity attached to this form of testing: she claimed any form of imprecision may lead to the patient developing schizophrenia.

Anita shared the experience of her treatment. She also did not escape diagnosis as a schizophrenic patient during her male-to-female gender transition. She recalled the acute distress and anguish she had undergone when she lived in Bombay and the insensitivity of her parents who initially did not recognise her gender identity disorder (GID). They took her to various psychotherapists in Bombay. The doctors treated her gender syndrome as an 'illness' which she refuted and vehemently opposed. However, Anita had to suffer and undergo certain unsuitable clinical treatments which affected her health. The doctor who initially diagnosed her addressed her mental condition as a state of 'pathology'. The doctor was of the view that Anita had been suffering from schizophrenia and was under a 'delusion' of having a different gender identity. The doctor also believed that Anita was lacking the sensibilities that are associated with the realities of life, as it is difficult for Indians to accept someone who has changed their 'sex'. Anita told me that she had read widely on transsexuality, visiting the central library in Bombay for many hours, and had gathered evidence to combat her family and doctor. Thus, she had enough facts to negotiate the clinical views of transsexuality. She discussed cases of Harry Benjamin, 'the chromosomal structure of transsexuals', rationalities of transsexual identity, the need for GRS, and so on, with her doctor. The doctor remained unconvinced by Anita's arguments and prescribed 'electroconvulsive therapy' – an intensive electrical shock treatment. The doctor rationalized that shock therapy would help Anita 'recover' from schizophrenia. Anita had to undergo the therapy because of her apparent agreement to accept the doctor's recommendations. If she adhered to her own opinion, her parents would ask her to leave the house. She went through eight sessions of shock therapy. Additionally, Anita had been prescribed heavy doses of sleeping pills to take at night, after the therapy sessions. The therapy caused her memory loss. She mentioned how she had become very forgetful, unmindful and careless due to the effects of the shock therapy, and how her sleep was disturbed by attacks of panic and terror.

Further, the understanding of mental health and therapeutic mechanisms amongst another set of transgender identities in Bombay – the *hijra* and the *kothi* – reveals a state of mental agony and despair relating to their gender identity, and a sense of vulnerability leading to everyday discrimination at home and in the workplace, and deceitful emotional relationships with their partners. Unlike the transsexual mental health discourse that prescribes an archetypical health imperative, regulating an identity category with a therapeutic decree that runs across the global–local context; *hijra* and *kothi* mental health is addressed with certain tents of counselling therapies, so as to deal with their health difficulties.

'We the People' is an LGBT community-based organization (CBO) in Bombay. It claims to be the first organization in the city that has mobilized these sexual minorities. It has been working on issues of human rights of these populations through various programmatic approaches to health and HIV/ AIDS prevention. The organization makes available a clinical psychologist and an HIV/AIDS medical practitioner at a drop-in-centre every Tuesday and Thursday. *Hijra*s and *kothi*s in the organization are aware of this facility and often consult the doctors for mental and physical health issues. They also encourage other *hijra*s and *kothi*s who are not directly connected with the association to utilize these services. The organization's aim is to 'target' (a programmatic term for health promotion) as many members of the community as possible, thus ultimately developing 'community health promotion'.

They counsel and provide mental health support to LGBT-identified individuals who suffer from depression and trauma in relation to their sexuality. The organization claims that their free clinical facilities are open to every LGBT individual in Bombay. The HIV/AIDS practitioner in the clinic examines them for illness related to HIV/AIDS and other sexually transmitted diseases, administering blood check-ups and medicine, and providing referrals to hospitals for those patients who need special care.

Dr Julie Patil is a young female doctor who is a clinical psychologist at the organization. She graduated in medicine from the University of Bombay. The doctor is sensitive to the needs of the *hijra* and *kothi* communities and recounted the everyday narratives and mental health discourses of persons from these populations. According to her, *kothi*s often undergo a sense of acute identity crisis. They represent themselves as genetically masculine but emotionally feminine and behave and conduct themselves in a feminine manner. Their inability to employ the accepted gendered cultural rules of society brings them ridicule and humiliation from their families and peers.

Dr Patil spoke about the root cause of GID in those children and young adults who suffer from identity crises during adolescence or puberty and are unable to locate or categorize their gender identity as either male or female. Their confusion arises from the distortion associated with their genital identity as male but mental identification as female. The doctor also mentioned that it is not necessary that these are simply traits of transsexuality. In her opinion, a patient identifying as a transsexual (woman) and seeking GRS is associated with various other psychological factors which will allow for the process of gender transition.

Dr Patil referred to many clinical cases arising from social ostracism, peer pressure and parents disowning their *kothi* or transgender-identified children.

She added that when transgender people recount their life histories to her, they often break down and ask her to provide them with an excessive dose of sleeping pills to end their life. In her clinical and social analysis of *hijra* and *kothi* mental health, she records the fact that *kothi*s and *hijra*s do not want to undergo gender transition; they prefer to be the way they are, and they mock and ridicule those who undergo GRS.

The doctor also records that there are roughly ten–fourteen cases every year in Bombay of *kothi* or *hijra* suicide. In addition to issues of identity, the rejection of love and emotion by their male partner is another cause of suffering. In certain cases, *kothi* men from villages are forced into marriages by their families, since the male child is expected to attract a dowry and gifts for the family. The doctor has seen cases of bridal suicides, female homicides or physical abuse of the bride by her in-laws and husband.

Dr Patil talked about the techniques of mental health therapy that she employs for her *kothi* and *hijra* patients. Her therapeutic approach consists mainly of counselling, in which she conducts three to four sessions with a particular patient. This allows a degree of comfort to develop between the patient and the doctor and creates a foundation for 'cognitive methods'. These methods include diagrammatic representation, handwriting and symbolic portrayals in which the patient is asked to represent, perform or create imagery. This, as she discusses, is broadly the method by which certain mental health practitioners acquire knowledge of the thinking process and psychological state of their patient. This process also allows the doctor to record behavioural patterns and allows the diagnosis and understanding of the phase or stage of the mental health trauma or distress the patient is undergoing. Additionally, it allows the doctor to evaluate and prescribe the pattern and degree of medicine and treatment.

The doctor explained that her clinic also provides counselling for the parents of a trans*-identified child. Various other doctors are also present to talk about homosexuality and transgender identities to parents, hoping to raise awareness of non-heterosexual characteristics. Dr Patil also said that through 'talk', the patient expresses their feelings and sufferings. It is through the means of conversation and allowing the patient to 'speak' that the patient communicates the sense of anguish and difficulty being suffered.

TRANSSEXUALITY AND THE MENTAL HEALTH DISCOURSE II: THE SCIENCE OF ELIMINATION OR EXCLUSION?

Health consciousness in modern society generates an understanding of meaningful practices of health and biomedicine with an expansive notion of disease, epidemic and cure – projecting a systematic articulation of the meanings and practices of the therapeutic ethos that regenerates a complex relationship of medicine, therapy and its processes (Cooter 2004; Crawford 2006). The modern medical system adds to the idea of the primacy of the patient, introducing certain elements of equality in the medical domain – rendering the idea of medicine as a social artefact and disciplining and installing a discourse through a certain cultural lens. The ontology of health in the twenty-first century broadly links to the growing urbanization and nuances of human problems in those spaces, leading to a different dimension in the understanding of health (McDonald et al. 2007).

Clinical psychologists and neurologists render an understanding of the sexual identity of a person from studies of the human brain. According to such studies, the chemical components of the brain give rise to the physiological, anatomical and sexual morphology of a person. In the beginning of the twentieth century, clinical scientists studied and experimented on mammals like rats and pigs. They tried to investigate the vital role of the brain in developing sexuality and sexual orientation. This was followed by research investigating brain composition and androgen reception by the brain (Cohen-Kettenis and Gooren 1999).[5]

The human brain is central in determining the sexual identity of a person. Diamond observes that biology and the environment together play a role in the comprehensive development of the human body. In the case of brain development and sexual orientation, testosterone determines the behavioural and biological construction of the male anatomy and physiology. If the testosterone level is high, it generates heterosexual men with 'manly' behavioural dispositions. The lack or discrepancy in the testosterone level leads to certain traits of non-masculine behaviour; neuroanatomy has a significant part in developing an individual's sexual orientation (Diamond 2002, 2009; Lunders and Sanchez 2009). In such cases, a person suffering from gender dysphoria is often regarded as an 'intersex identity' in the brain, with a confused sense of gender and sexuality. Diamond further notes that biological studies on transsexual brains show a 'female like sexual subdivision of the bed nucleus or the strata terminals with respect to the size and the number of neurons'. In clinical terms, there are 'female like volumes and neuronal densities of the interstitial nucleus of the anterior hypothalamus in male to female transsexuals' (Diamond 2009).

Medicalization of the body or a disease is linked to the politics of exclusion and segregation that could be re-interpreted as a certain classification of power in human society. In Foucauldian terms, bio-power forms a typical authoritative structure, where human subjects are labelled and categorized – conforming to certain hierarchies and segregations. The diseased person is viewed through certain lenses of power and authority and subjected to a form of clinical gaze, which Michel Foucault calls the 'anatomo-politics of the human body'. Foucault here considers the human body as a 'machine', subjected to different social, political and economic forces which result in it being changed, transformed and regularized through certain medical means of regulation and normalization (Conrad and Schneider 1980; Cadwallader 2007). Bio-power can also be reinterpreted in the modern medical field as the biological determinant of power often imposed with medical dominance and authority (Genal 2006; Lemke 2015; Peterson and Bunton 1997).

On the lines of this argument, the historical specificity of mental health issues has been broadly based on regulating and monitoring the structure of society through certain dominant disciplinary regimes. Based on the Foucauldian analysis of 'Bentham's Panapticon', mental health care involves distinctive clinical governance emphasizing power imposed on the human body with different ranges of 'visibility' (Foucault 1976: 201–204). Furthermore, clinical perceptions on transsexuality are linked to various disciplinary regimes – especially, as Foucault discusses, the ways in which modern medicine invests in various specialized clinical regimes to distribute set 'cures', whereby people are arranged in various favourable units (Foucault 1973 [1963]: 16). Disease and pathology are historically located and culturally positioned, rendering a technology of classification based on clinical regimes of power and surveillance in society (Norris and Armstrong 1997). This adds to Michel Foucault's idea on 'bio-power', concerning the biological determinant of power that is imposed with the technologies of medicine and clinical superiority. It further leads to his assertion of the 'anatomo-politics of the human body' whereby the human body as a 'machine' is transformed and regularized via certain medical means (Genal 2006; Cadwallader 2007; Luxon 2008).

Wen-Shing Tseng (2003) charts how international institutes on mental health use standards like those set out in ICD-10 and DSM-4[6] to evaluate the mental condition of a transsexual person with symptoms of gender dysphoria, manifested in characteristics of distress and conflict on being born in the wrong body. A transsexual individual's deepest desire is to become a member of the opposite sex and to lead the life of the desired sex. Psychotherapy is the path to 'gender reassignment' in the true sense (Gooren 1990, 2006). Mental health practitioners have investigated personality traits as the fundamental symptoms of gender identity. This further adds to the evidence of what they call 'peculiarities', corresponding to certain 'disorder' symptoms which are commonly diagnosed by clinical psychologists as 'schizophrenia' (Modestin, Herman and Endrass 2007). Schizophrenic tendencies amongst transsexual people relate to how doctors treat the desire for the other gender as a form of 'brain abnormality' and as indicating a sign of pathology of the brain. What they term as 'abnormalities' are certain confused traits of thought, delusions, some altered sense of self, emotional disruptions or severe psychological reactions (Doubt 1992; Pearlson and Marsh 1999; Cahill 2003).

Transsexuality and mental health governance showcase how psychiatry has been an explanation and a cause of the synergism of psycho-medical concepts related to gender dysphoria. In *Madness and Civilization*, Foucault (1973 [1963]) points to the historical undercurrents of how criminality and madness have been perceived through the lens of the complex processes and conjunctions of the law and psychiatry – the dense implications and proliferation of the psycho-medical conditions and categories that limit the freedom of the subject – and draws a critical understanding from an analysis of pathology (Deleuze 1994). By virtue of medicalizing techniques since the 19th century, 'psycho-pathology' becomes a moral panic, which is associated with criminal problems, rendering a focus on the techniques deployed in population management and the seemingly unambiguous distinction of moral insanity based on medical reasoning. In particular, moral insanity and moral imbecility related to transsexuality chart how identity is forged into desire, outlined within medico-cultural governance as attempting to suggest a particular form of knowledge within the domain of legal, psychiatric and social institutions which they manoeuvre – evoking a strange system of management focusing on the advancement of clinical essentialism to 'transform' and 'cure' these subjects (McCallum 1997: 68–70).

ENDOCRINOLOGY, HORMONES AND THE BODY

In the context of therapeutic approaches, the transformation of transsexual bodies is addressed from the perspectives of endocrinology and plastic surgery. Endocrinology is concerned with the hormonal structures of the body; the human body consists of a number of glands that produce and secrete hormones which control the body's metabolism, growth, development and sexual function. Hormonal action runs through the entire body, from the blood cells to the body tissues and every organ in the body.

Following the mental health diagnosis of GID, the patient is referred to an endocrinologist for hormonal therapy for a minimum of one to two years before GRS. The endocrinologist prescribes specific hormones to the patient, in doses determined by the clinical examination of their blood. For those patients who desire to attain the female gender through GRS, female hormones like oestrogens, progesterone and anti-androgen drugs are prescribed. The endocrinologist usually recommends oral consumption. This process of hormonal treatment is usually called hormone replacement therapy (HRT).

The discourses on endocrinology lead to clinical consumption and the reconstruction of the body. Internal change of the body through HRT creates its external identification. A reflexive mechanism affirms the visual dialectic, where the transsexual patient from male to female, recognizes her transformed body – the physical changes creating feminization. By this means, the social interpretation of the body continues in the dynamics of the observer and the observed. In this fashion, HRT creates the imagery of the body in relation to a female identity. In addition, the role of the endocrinologist in the therapeutic process is one of clinical vigilance, and the therapist is the source of assigning gender.

Sita Pandey is a prominent endocrinologist who has a private clinic in Worli, South Bombay. She is also associated with a prominent Bombay hospital as a senior consultant in endocrinology. She deals with patients from various social and economic backgrounds from Bombay and other parts of India, as well as a variety of age groups including school children, college students and adults of different ages. She shared with me her diagnostic experience of her former patients. One such instance was a case of genital deformity in which a woman had developed testes and a penis-like formation, slightly visible from the vagina. The doctor worked to correct the presence of both male and female organs in the body by means of hormone therapy. The individual was socialized as a female from birth, and further psychological, behavioural and endocrinological examinations reported her mental state as female. Dr Pandey was critical of any sexual categorization or of classifying a person as a hermaphrodite or transsexual. According to her, genital otherness and sexual categorization are social constructs. The act of classifying genders is linked to patriarchy, and the male–female gender binary is the symbolic representation by means of which the dominant gender forms in society are affirmed.

In relation to endocrinology and the treatment of transsexual bodies, Dr Pandey explained the role of hormones in determining a person's gender identity. The hormones that are secreted in the body and construct it also give it a definite gendered shape. Dr Pandey further explained that behavioural endocrinology records the effect of hormones on the nervous system and the effect of the nervous system on hormonal secretion. She has carried out HRT with several transsexual patients in Bombay. In the case of HRT for male-to-female transformation, the masculine features of the body are replaced and certain feminine traits are enhanced. The consumption of female hormones stimulates the formation of breasts, feminization in the texture of the skin, fat deposition in the buttocks and lower parts of the body and feminization of the voice. The side effects of the hormones are nausea, vomiting, hypertension and body ache, as well as weight gain.

HRT has the clinical power to transform one form of the body into the other, according to the person's desire. Based on the science of endocrinology, HRT treatment lays bare the power of medicine that is diagnosed, configured and deployed by the doctor. This power works to redefine the body through therapeutic construction, generating a new identity and a new self. Foucault points out how the language of clinical discourse is formalized and becomes strong enough to produce an objective categorization of the subject. This objectification is recognized in logic and becomes a particular scientific entity. In this fashion, a normative transsexual identity is formed based on Western clinical rationality and medical science. It becomes an intrinsic category for identification. The clinical rationality of transsexual identity is linked to the logic of neuroanatomy and endocrinological (hormonal) factors that give rise to the possibility of gender transformation through GRS.

THE VIOLENCE OF THE FLESH: HRT AND THE BODY-POLITIC

The production of biomedical knowledge and medicalization of bodies propagate social regulatory practices that have traditionally focused on controlling bodies (Monaghan 2003). The regulatory bodies are linked to the legitimization of biomedical knowledge of health care (Foucault 1973 [1963]; Lyotard 1984; Segal 2003) – a sort of governance in a neoliberal context intending to determine the body and its normativity. The new technologies of power integrate disciplinary technology by a sort of infiltration, embedding themselves with considerable importance in scientific knowledge of both biological and organic processes (Rose 2006; see also Franklin 2006).

Medicine becomes a 'political intervention' – a technique with specific power-effects that circulate between the 'disciplinary' and the 'regulatory' (Campbell and Sitze 2013: 72). Thus, medicinal consumption and HRT introduce technologies of bodily governance resulting in a form of embodiment and an experience of behaviour (Lock and Nguyen 2018 [2010]: 37). Following Foucault (1973 [1963]), 'technologies of bodily governance' chart the gradual emergence of and regularization within the bio-political body. Anthropological studies of the body and embodiment are influenced by the concept of 'body techniques' (Turner 2006) – body being understood as exclusively a system of cultural representation. Richard Shusterman (1992) has argued in *Pragmatist Aesthetics* that lived experience is vital in understanding performances in the study of the body. Underlying this theory, HRT and its anatomo-politics establishes the grid of political representation and its articulation of a sexual subculture, further suggesting medicinal governmentality as the analytics of new vital or political ambition in disciplining the populace. Further, HRT compliments the understanding of aspirations. In Anita's and similar such cases, medicinal consumption legitimizes a gendered landscape that transforms bodies with hope and aspiration.[7]

Anita's view on HRT and endocrinologists in Bombay is dismal. She believes very few in the city are actually sensitive about gender reconfirmation surgeries. Yet very few surgeons who perform such specialized surgeries in Bombay coordinate with endocrinologists, working as a team. One such doctor they rely on is Sita Pandey.

It is in this context of the governance of life that Foucault's genealogical account of sexuality is crucial for the management of society. As Sparke (2005) argues, the geography of governmentality has a 'micrological' focus. The bio-politics of HRT, as Sparke emphasizes, is 'messy actualities' and the intricacies of bio-political production. Thus, bio-politics as the analytical tool is imbued with the mechanics of life that focuses on individual bodies. The 'micrological' focus represents a linear movement of power as interpreted in the access of life and in the body, which Foucault calls 'disciplining the flesh' (Harcourt 2019). Further, micro-practices of disciplinary power exert the capacities of the life processes, which in turn transport the analytical focus from the individual body to broader issues of the bio-political management of life vis-à-vis macro-practices of bio-political power (Gagne and Tewksbury 1999; Jarrin 2017).

Discourses on Body Modification: Plastic Surgeons in Bombay

Anita mentioned to me that surgery is the last stage in the gender transition process: the mental health diagnosis followed by the HRT treatment is crucial, and the surgery comes at the end, completing the transition. According to Anita, GRS is new in India and not much spoken about in medical forums, especially by plastic surgeons. However, she undertook intense research to identify in which city she could possibly find an efficient surgeon. With the help of her friends, she gathered information about potential surgeons in Bombay. She received information of five surgeons whom she met personally, and after consultations for one full year, Anita came to a decision about her surgery. In one of our meetings, I noted that Anita was quite confident in her analysis of medicine and surgeries in relation to gender transition. When asked, she said that a transsexual person in the contemporary context would always have to be equipped with knowledge about the transition and read medical excerpts, accounts of other transsexual persons and the success-stories of these people. She also knew the methods by which the surgery is conducted, and in her clinical consultations with the doctor, Anita was able to discuss the procedure of the surgery and could even converse in clinical terms to identify which would suit her the best.

Anita narrated the story of her body modifications and of those instances that led to a sense of her gender appropriateness and reflected her identity as a woman – the path to becoming what she desired. Recounting the nuances of her bodily changes, Anita used the word 'magic' and said that her clinical consumption of female hormones resulted in a magical effect, like the feminization of the body and skin texture, development of breasts, rounded body parts and her hair becoming lighter and thinner – her overall appearance became feminine. This refashioning of the body induced in Anita a state of ecstasy during the phase of her transformation; her friends appreciated the changes that were taking place in her appearance. Anita also mentioned how much men started to like her and were enticed by her beauty. She talked about the occasions when she went for laser therapy for facial hair removal and the gradual disappearance of her facial hair; she felt she had taken a step forward towards her goal. The gradual loss of her facial hair augmented her beauty. Anita added that she used to board the local suburban trains to reach her clinic. For the initial sessions of her therapy, she was wary of getting into the train, thinking that men would bully her and her co-passengers would stare at her with curiosity. In those instances, she used to cover her face with a *dupatta*, and she wore women's clothes. But gradually, as her sessions proceeded, and her looks became more and more feminine, she could feel that people who had looked at her strangely now looked at her more pleasantly and amicably. Moreover, she added, male passengers felt that she is a woman, and she could sense some of them were looking at her quite admiringly.

Genital surgery (vagionoplasty) and breast implants were the final stage of Anita's gender passing. According to her, a person undergoing these sorts of surgeries gathers knowledge about the clinical and surgical techniques involved by reading from various sources. In another context, Anita had mentioned that 'knowledge is at our finger tips', by which she actually meant access through computers and the ways in which she could have gathered knowledge about sexuality, surgeries, doctors and transsexuality in India and the West.

Dr Neil is a qualified plastic surgeon, professionally attached to a prominent hospital in Bombay. He specializes in plastic surgery and holds a degree from the United States. He mentioned that in his early career as a surgeon in America, he had conducted GRS with a team of doctors. He explained his surgical techniques, stating that he conducts the entire process in two phases. In the first phase, the doctor surgically removes the testicles of the patient and constructs the labia-majora and labia-minora with the scrotal skin. In other words, he makes the use of the scrotal skin to construct the outer vertical layers of the vagina. He prefers to perform the second phrase after a gap of two weeks. In this phase, he constructs the vaginal cavity and urethra. The doctor usually performs the 'penile inversion technique' where the penis is dissected into layers and the flesh is folded inside to provide the actual shape and look of a vagina, both aesthetically and functionally.

When I asked the doctor about the failure of GRS in India, he said that patients are reluctant to perform dilations after the surgery which results in the closure of the vaginal cavity. Dilation is a method of inserting a penis-shaped glass-like object in the newly created vagina. Doctors encourage patients to perform this process after surgery to retain the vaginal cavity. Other similar patients, however, said that doctors do not allow patients to dilate until one or two weeks after the surgery, when the bandages from the operation are removed. They said they were asked by the doctors to dilate at that point in order to allow the wound to heal. But my transsexual friends from the United Kingdom mentioned that their doctors encouraged patients to perform dilation starting the day after surgery. They said the doctors believe that the vaginal cavity is newly made and the muscles there are weak and loose and do not contract. So, if patients start dilation at this early stage, then the cavity has a higher chance of retaining its functionality. In that case, the muscle in the vagina adapts to the required depth and retains the space. These doctors prefer their patients to dilate three times a day, a quarter of an hour each time for six months from the surgery. After that, the patient can reduce the dilation process, depending on the success of the procedure.

I further met an eminent doctor in Bombay, Dr Kelly, who also performs vaginoplasty. Dr Kelly is famous for having performed a similar surgery for a renowned businesswoman in India. Since then he has been interviewed in various national newspapers and has appeared on television shows. I met Dr Kelly in a private hospital in Bombay where he is a clinical consultant. The doctor mentioned quite philosophically that gender is based on 'vision'. He tried to explain his argument by saying that individuals make their own judgements based on what they see. What they perceive becomes the ideal depiction of gender and identity of the person that they see. By this act of seeing, the person constructs the gendered image of the person seen. Thus, he stated that GRS is necessary for confirming the identity of those who feel that they are caught in an inappropriate body; through this surgical procedure, an individual can achieve their desired gender.

With regard to vaginoplasty, the doctor mentioned the 'skin grafting method' as the appropriate mechanism. During this process, the doctor uses soft skin to construct the folds of the outer layers of the vagina. This extra skin is also laid into the inner spaces of the vagina, which allows some space within the newly formed vaginal cavity. The skin is lined up or stitched in such a way that even if the muscles contract at some point, there are possibilities that the cavity will have some space that has been surgically constructed. The doctor also explained that in the case of 'penile inversion', the penile and scrotal skin is not sufficient to construct a vagina; it needs additional skin to provide an aesthetic look and for its functionality.

These discourses are linked to ideas of 'truth' about transsexual women and the construction of female genitalia – essentially, which procedure will engender the most authentic, healthy and sustainable result. The 'truth' revolves around the method of surgery that can produce the aesthetic and functional authenticity of genital construction. Transsexual identity thus becomes a 'political' identity construct, which is discursively formed through the regimes of clinical and scientific knowledge, and their claims in terms of verifying people's new identities as a 'woman' (or man) – as a reassigned gender verified through genital alteration.

HORMONES, SURGERY, TECHNOLOGY

Endocrinology, regarded as part of 'internal medicine', diagnoses and treats diseases associated with internal glandular secretions or hormones. The endocrine system usually releases certain chemical components in the blood that develop the functioning of the organism. HRT treatment, which is based on the science of endocrinology, emphasizes the therapeutic (re) construction of the body, deploying biological processes of a clinical and disciplinary nature to regulate transsexual bodies (May 2002; Dellinger and Williams 1997; Williams 2002: 20). HRT restores the prevalence of androgen development and exposure, leading to a physiological change in terms of the feminization of the body and body parts in male-to-female transsexuals. The brain plays a significant role in the biological determination of gender identity; and more so, genetic and hormonal influences govern the gendered behaviour of the individual (Hird 2002). In relation to endocrinology and HRT amongst transsexual persons, the consumption of female hormones leads to the 'replacement' of male hormones from testosterone to oestrogen, leading to some visible impacts on the body, like the development of breasts, fat deposition in the hips and buttocks and softer texture of the skin.

Cosmetic surgeries, on the other hand, as Linda Hogle (2005) observes, are a form of 'bioengineering' that provide the technological capacity to enhance the body image. Such technologies appropriate the use of surgeries to solve the problem with the body through 'repair', so as to manifest a form of enhancement that will resolve the 'abnormality'. In a similar way, GRS provides a higher form of medical technology and new form of plastic surgery that defines sex and gender identity. As Joanne Meyerowitz notes, study of hormones and chromosomes has made possible the technological manoeuvring of 'trans' embodiment, and construction of subjects via surgical mechanisms (Meyerowitz 2002: 35–38). The medical narratives of the transsexual's bodily being chart how the materiality of the body imposes a reference to the discourse of signification through the institutional regimes of technologies and clinical superiority, which in a way broadly outline the root of analysis of power, technology and subjective discourses (Hausman 1995; Doan and Prosser 2001). Further, transsexuality and the politics of sex-change bring into the discourse emphasis of the malleable understanding of gender to a more gendered understanding of identity based on performance and the 'transgression' of the essentialist discourses on sex and gender (Hird 2002). This form of gender identity further focuses on the new vision of sex that makes a mark on the internal secretions of the body to emphasize the new idea of gender, transcending the morphology of genitalia by birth. On the basis of this varied understanding of sex, transsexual individuals undergo curative reconstructive surgery to assign a new gender to resolve their physical defect and achieve a 'healthy body' (Prosser 2002: 81). Georges Canguilhem (1978) suggested a conceptualization of diseases that constitutes health and health paradigms, further evoking the idea of the dominant notion of 'normalcy', recounting the bioethics and moral qualities of medicine to build new forms of sociality. Therefore, what counts as 'normalcy' here is the intricacies and nuances of therapy and enhancement that attempt to improve human life by means of clinical technology (see also Rabinow 1996). This aesthetic improvement of the body relates to reshaping and restructuring by means of surgical procedures that further mark the somatic incorporation of their gender(ed) embodiment. The politics of 'passing' takes into account the 'gender shift' as related to the materiality of the body and its performances, further recording the authenticity of the gendered being and the surface reality of the skin. The surgery constitutes the innate embodiment of the transsexual person as a legible subject that lays emphasis on the body-image, installing a profound subjective experience of embodiment.

SURGERIES AND THEORETICAL DEBATES

Anita's GRS, or what it is termed today as 'gender reconfirmation surgery', demonstrates the possibility of altering the physical manifestation of her body to a distinct ideal of bodily authenticity and approximation. That is to say, her genital reconstruction surgery, followed by other cosmetic or surgical manoeuvring, builds an archetype embodiment based on biological surgical construction to build on gender(ed) meanings (Epstein 2007). She recalled with relief her first breath on regaining her senses after anaesthesia. Anita and her sexed embodiment represent a new project of gendering identity, breaking through conventional binary ideals. The new biomedical and pharmacological systems of bodily transformation propose the reconfiguration of corporeal identities through 'molecular' and 'chemical interventions' (Halberstam 2018). Trans* embodiment thus, as Halberstam adds, is 'visualizable' and 'verifiable' – a gendered body within new forms of capitalism. In the age of genetics and biomedicine, and the 'molecularization of life', Nicholas Rose (2007) calls for a new 'ethopolitics' – the emergence of molecular self-management involving political axes on authoritative bio-political positions (Hannah 2011). Rose's 'ethopolitics' in relation to trans* embodiment reveals insights into the individual's life-engineering, premised on medical–moral technologies that possess the capacity to make individual subjects. This revolutionary technology reshapes the biological, cultural and social loci in identity construction (Andreescu 2016).

Anita's surgical story relates to her gender appropriateness. She pointed out that twenty years ago, these surgeries were not that prevalent in India and required seeking out very specialized plastic surgeons. Moreover, such surgeries are capital-intensive, time-intensive and quite perilous. There were stories of failed surgeries and records of surgeries that led to death. But given the complexity of the surgery, Anita chose a surgeon who was very experienced and had a clinic in Delhi as well as Bombay.

The emerging knowledge in medical anthropology is deeply embedded in sexual racialization and social or cultural disparity in trans* embodiment in India. Medicalization disciplines identity on the insights of how medicine and surgery materialize and is further embodied as a fundamental technology of exclusion and inclusion (Rapp 2019). This taxonomic enterprise of sexual racialization generates specific differences constituted within the political project of neoliberalism (Ferguson and Hong 2012). GRS, or 'gender conformity', is a raciologically valued neoliberal trans* identity surgery, and 'gender (re)confirmation' is a medically acceptable bio-political tool to manage 'the right to identity', eliminating identarian defects by a clinical project of bio-citizenship. Rethinking the discourse which has a deep-seated neoliberal logic of citizenship, governmentality, body and aesthetics, interlinks commodification and modernity of the medical market that has enormous potency to the market dynamics of aesthetics and health. In other words, modern sexual identity seeks to 'improve' the subject's 'defects'. The 'improvement' is symptomatic. That is to say, the conditions to objectify the defect could aesthetically 'cure' the suffering. Further, 'aesthetics' here is a social imagery of medicine that internalizes the visions of mental and sexual well-being that underline medicinal rationality vis-à-vis techno-medical enterprise.

Anita's womanhood after her surgery, and her marriage, family and adoption of a child, shape an extraordinary social prestige that translates to a form of 'value', a sign to structure and navigate her newly acquired gender identity. Her once precarious and unmoored, alienated identity transforms into a class-specific political project wherein transsexualism in India crystallizes into a new optimism of conviction. This optimism or hope of racial or sexual character is transnational in scope and shaped by international imageries, wherein the class dimension of the identity is a transnational practice. This identity adjoins different (inter)national borders with metropolitan body politics – what impels its movement is the bio-politics of the medicalized racial discourses that purport a claim to an acquired gendered body with a marked preferential treatment of its aesthetic evaluation. That is to say, there is implicit reaffirmation of beauty standards in the body's sexed significance and its aesthetic recognition.

This particular transnational bio-political discourse of the body politic is inextricably tied with two important attributes: first, the transnational logic of techno-medicines, and second, bio-political categories of identity and citizenship. As I argue, transsexualism is a political recognition – a political project, as Nicholas Rose (2006) terms it, of the material body and its social variables like health, vitality and complex processes of agency formation via varied technologies of resistance. Further, the legibility of the body, operates in a tactical way that might recall 'bioresistance' in Foucault's understanding (Siisiäinen 2018), or Michel de Certeau's 'military metaphor' (Frow 1991). I relate to this from the salience of the political management of health that defines sexual meanings of aesthetics, desire and a fatal consumption of techno-medicines. This attests to transsexualism and bio-citizenship, preferably a 'therapeutic citizenship (Lazar 2013) – the conceptual intersection of the 'bio' and the 'sexual' that plays a role in defining the governance of 'the self'.[8] Yet there is an intersecting resonance to the sovereign or decentralized political economy of hope (Happe, Jonson and Levina 2018: 235). The hope affiliates to the new informed ethics of the self to manage the conditions of the biological senses of identification – active economies of consumption within the structures of biopolitical-led capital. Thus, citizenship here prefigures an embodied pleasure and the risks associated with the embodying responsibilities (Epstein 1998: 22; Shilling 2005). This state of aggregating technologies complicates the assuredly neoliberalized formation of discourses through which this particular identity negotiates and engages in citizenship. This hopeful politics through biopolitical logic builds a utilitarian logic in claiming a typical image of womanhood. Thus, transsexuality becomes an inter(national) lexicon of neoliberal identarian project that is rooted in the politics of consumerism and capitalist enterprise.

Also, the capitalist-driven technological innovation relates the new market forces to new domains of experiences in body-related surgeries (Edmonds 2010: 246). The expansion of surgical mechanisms for transsexual women in Bombay paves the way for a beauty culture that is based on the desire of their sexualized body within the codes of surgical proposition. The transsexual desire for surgeries – namely breast augmentation and feminine facial reconstruction – builds a moment of affective authenticity that transports the self to a level of being. A claim for authenticity, 'passing' builds feminine appropriateness with a different kind of beauty. Further, their aesthetic enhancement echoes the logic of the organic world so as to align with social respectability. As Anita reckoned, her breast enhancement and facial surgeries are moments of her embodied perception that inhabit the space of *sacchhi aurat* (true woman). Her desires that she has fulfilled – for marriage to be respectable in society and her neighbourhood, and to adopt a child – are attuned to intersubjective processes of her embodied experience to 'become' a woman. This potentially redefines her beauty beyond the discourse of the erotic. A citizenship and a social identity that she claims as a woman transmutes her deep-seated (and painful) fairy tale. This celebratory claim emerges into a new middle-class identity in India that situates faith within the fetishization of radical desires, leading to a new material economy of identity. Therefore, the new possibility of self-determination in this sphere of womanhood serves a symbolic class, shaping one's life path. More significantly, the social and emotional site of these identities provides meaning to a sovereign appeal – a source of hope to meet the inner desires through the capital-led logic of biological and techno-sciences (Paley 2002).

SAMPURNA: CYBER CONNECTIONS, COMMUNITY FEELINGS AND ACTIVISM IN THE TRANSSEXUAL COMMUNITY

Sandip Roy (2003) has described gay activism via the internet as a form of democratic citizenship, where the 'voice' of the individual is a means of creating social change. This adds to Roy's concept of 'keyboard activism', which tries to mobilize homosexuals of South Asian lineage and connect them to the global homosexual community. The success of 'keyboard activism' is demonstrated by the internet's ability to strengthen communications related to gay activism worldwide as well. Roy charts how gay activism within India is further strengthened through ethnic solidarity, a solidarity that is linked through individuals' sexual identity and their race.

Sampurna (a Sanskrit and Hindi word which means 'complete') is a web-based network that attempts to connect trans*-identified South Asian people across South Asia and in the diaspora. There are informal meetings which enable members to interact and chat, but the larger goal is to provide each other moral and emotional support, besides exchanging information regarding gender transition and other issues. Suraj, a trans*-identified man, founded this organization based on his understanding of the immense psychological and familial turmoil that trans* people undergo to establish their true selves. Such networks and mutual support would ease the path to reach their goals and meet their innermost desires.

Suraj has worked immensely hard to become a successful cinematographer in the Bollywood film industry. He has won several accolades nationally and internationally for his work. He fervently believes that cinema is a strong medium to instil knowledge and communicate social issues and problems far and wide. Sampurna is a non-profit organization. The members connect via web networks and email. They can communicate and share information about topics such as gender-related surgeries, surgeons, clinics, mental health practitioners, HRT, beauty clinics, medical tourism, marriage, surrogacy, and so on. Further, Sampurna works to liaise with educational institutions, the government and corporates to raise awareness on transsexual identity, inclusive employability and related matters, through lectures and seminars. Suraj's goal is to develop a community of like-minded people to create cyber-activism across South Asia. Sampurna further helps new members with moral support during their process of gender transition.

Suraj conducts meetings once a month. One such meeting took place in the Barista coffee shop in Andheri in suburban Bombay. Suraj introduced to me to the members, including Kiran, Gazal, Shreya, Gauri and Rashmi who had undergone GRS from male to female. There were other members like Mohit, Akshay, Jay and Nikhil, who had different stories with regard to gender reassignment. The meeting was informal and there were discussions and narratives of their everyday life. In one such meeting, Suraj introduced a proposal to develop an association for doctors in Bombay that would excel in the various disciplines related to the needs of a transsexual person. His aim was to develop a high degree of clinical technology in Bombay, so that transsexual patients in India can access proper clinical treatment. As has often been reported by this group, GRS frequently results in failure because there are few Indian doctors who specialize in this treatment. Suraj's aim was to appoint doctors from overseas, mainly Thailand, the United States and western Europe, where these treatments are better understood. With their involvement and participation, Suraj proposes to create a committee in various hospitals in Bombay that will provide surgical knowledge to Indian doctors, which would eventually allow Indian transsexual patients to obtain appropriate surgery in India.

Suraj discussed his plan with a few Bombay businessmen whom he knew to be sympathetic. He realized that for this plan to come to fruition, it would take a long time, and the participation of Sampurna members was essential. Using the new 'public sphere' that the internet has made possible, Sampurna has created a space that transsexuals can use to gain an ordered sense of their identities, connect with each other and gain access to information and support. Another major part of Sampurna's contribution to trans communities in Bombay is to provide clinical information on medical tourism in Thailand. Many upper-middle-class transsexual patients from Bombay visit Thailand for surgery. Doctors in Thailand are technologically superior. Unlike the many unsuccessful stories of gender transition surgery in India commonly heard in Sampurna meetings, Thai doctors are quite experienced and professional in conducting these surgeries. Sampurna keeps records of relevant doctors in Thailand, in addition to information on hotels and places to stay based on detailed information they receive from any Sampurna member who has undergone such surgery. This information helps other members who wish to undergo similar procedures in Thailand, which seems to be the destination of choice for many. Sampurna members also decided to invite a surgeon and his team from Thailand to train Indian doctors in Bombay in GRS; for similar initiatives, they planned to take strategic action to raise money. Their main motive is that if Indian doctors learn to perform this surgery efficiently, then transsexual patients who are unable to bear the costs of surgery in Thailand would be able to seek treatment in India itself at relatively low costs.

WEB-ACTIVISM AND THE SOUTH ASIAN RHETORIC

Suraj is aware that surgical techniques for gender assignment are not well developed in India. Vulnerable patients suffer at the hands of these surgeons. Eventually, it is only a profit-making enterprise. Sampurna stands as an important medium to 'support', 'communicate' and 'share' information and related news far and wide within the community, so that they are warned against inadequate doctors. Besides mutual assistance and community-led solidarity, Suraj mentioned the community's initiatives in meeting with potential and experienced surgeons to discuss, counsel and develop empathy for successful surgery. This initiative has been beneficial for low-income persons who desire to undergo such surgical processes. Suraj makes it a point to actively engage with the team of doctors in the case of persons who are unable to pay for the surgery. In such instances, Sampurna advocates and liaises with the doctors and medical management for a subsidy in prices in government hospitals in Bombay. In India, medical treatment in government and government-funded hospitals is subsidized and could also be free. Additionally, Sampurna communicates with and delivers talks at various academic institutions, corporate organizations, government and private establishments to share and transmit ideas on the gender or sexual non-binary ethos, and to create perspectives of gender(ed) inclusivity in the professional space. Certain gender-inclusive and friendly corporates have been supportive of Sampurna's philosophy.

Sampurna's frame of reference is the web-based communication that runs in a secured space via email networks. Members residing in Bombay meet in-person. However, the network communicates via emails and related web-based platforms to build community sentiments and knowledge and to share information. Their wider axiom is to reach out to the wider population of gender non-conforming South Asians across the globe. This transnational movement by Sampurna indicates a perspective of network actions, diffused ideas and organizational visibility, mandating a supra-regional specificity with a solidarity of gender non-conforming South Asians. This web-network becomes a popular communication tool for the subculture – representing a local–global grid and informative platform of ongoing debate, dialogue and dissemination of gender-based knowledge.

To a meaningful extent, Sampurna evokes a revolutionary and democratic model that transforms capitalist consumer society and individualism. Drawing on the perception of online activism, Richard Kahn and Douglas Kellner (2003) in *New Media and Internet Activism* talk about the emergent technologies that enable the production of 'new social relations and forms of political possibility'. Therefore, Sampurna's solidarity is based on the premise of 'social justice'. Its political spectacle aims to deploy an emancipatory sexual subcultural citizenry so as to construct new social and political relations. The basis of this justice movement is an intense personal struggle: 'narratives' become political – a radical juxtaposition of the internet's free speech (hyer) textual architecture that steadily builds sensibility via digital magnificence across people and communities. This informs a diverse network of people coming together in a polyarchic state – a new politics of alliance and solidarity to overcome the limitations of hyper-capitalist consumerism (Kahn and Kellner 2003; Wellman and Gulia 1999; Markoff 2004).

Some scholars have argued that internet activism is 'post-bureaucratic democracy' describing participation within the culture of symbolism (Maravelias 2003; Attwood-Charles 2018). This sees the cultural tool of cyberspace communicative exchanges as facilitating a new site where value resides on the capabilities of the communicative potential to meet the political goal. As Dean (2003) suggests, internet activism is a form of 'communicative capitalism' – the democratic or consumer ideals are met by perceiving democracy with the 'intense circulation of content' (see Dean 2009: 24). Dean further envisions Jürgen Habermas's 'public sphere' within the interpretation of communicative capitalism. Saying this, these communications are goal-oriented messages devised within the circulation, visibility and recognizability of embodied communicative strategies that are capitalist in nature (Habermas 1996: 27). Essentially, these communications are based on economic exchange, generating economic and political revenues that further establish the 'symbolic capital network' (Bourdieu and Johnson 1993).

Sampurna's cultural and political processes in the symbolic capital network tangibly ensure the economies of community development and a stable currency of identarian value. Their political revenue is the construction of activism along the logic of democratizing access to health care needs. It is symbolic in the sense that the legitimacy cities the rights-claim of the sexual subculture – its proliferating artefact is the organic narrativization of life-history accounts that transforms with the power of symbolism, the visual or discursive representation of the South Asian transsexual community. Furthermore, the corporates in the activism network install a notion of civic engagement that pushes forward the representational labour of non-community subjects. They further expand the social cause and its adherence – a re-appropriation of the profound civic engagement that is created within the online civic space (Tatarchevskiy 2010). Also, establishing the impact on corporates of a particular online activism addresses a new civil society governance, exploring the framework of the potent mobilization of authoritarian regimes of power. This new form of participation contributes to corporate philanthropy as a social force of modern corporate response in building democratic ideals (Earl and Kimport 2011; Luo, Zhang and Marquis 2016).

Sampurna thus implicates a new global activism that creates a fresh frame of reference for this subculture and their political perspective. The new framing of this activism weighs identity-network relational ties that are patterned within digital configurations. This facilitates further a unique way of how weak identity ties organize and define their protest-politics within a transnational, digital platform. And finally, this particular web-based communication involves relationship-based practices and the evolution of a new democracy centring around collective identity frames of references. And through these political ties, individual identities are framed and constructed in a way Wellman calls 'networked individualism' (Wellman 2001; see also Bennett 2003).

Cyber Space, Cyber Networks and Medical Mobility

Sampurna evokes the idea of internet-based social movements, a form of cyber activism that holds certain democratic ideals – a movement of people that mobilizes certain minority populations for their sexual and cultural rights (Kahn and Kellner 2003; Wellman and Gulia 1999; Markoff 2008). This sort of electronic network provides a unique capacity to mediate participation, articulating a framework and a context wherein certain sensitive groups are mobilized, forming a new alliance and solidarity (Moghadam 2000). Cyberspace activism essentially addresses a new technique of 'virtual public sphere' that organizes and coordinates various strategies and tactics of 'resistance' – as in the case of Sampurna that generates a unique form of a 'network society' via electronic communication, projecting collective representation of certain identity categories through interactive processes, performative expressions of a specific group and a radical and progressive gender and sexual politics. This network system of the transsexual collective in Bombay renders characteristics of a new social movement that fosters emotions and acts, recognizing the transmission of information and ideas so as to establish certain democratic ideals that allow the subculture to build interpersonal networks. This act is further manifested through debates, discussions and shared knowledges that occupy a space for the constellation and the construction of identity, and recognition of certain personal and political goals. As Habermas (1996) puts it, modernity and cosmopolitanism reflect the ideals of democratic practices, participation and governance, adding to the social space with the aim of constructing a certain cultural objective; those thoughts that are mediated in the 'public spheres' through discourses leading to a form of communication practices that legitimates the mobilization of people and their ideas through a new kind of cultural model. Sampurna thus renders one such space – a 'virtual public sphere' (Langman 2005) – seeking to establish social justice and a humanistic ideal of citizenship rights that would attempt to imagine differently new systems of consciousness and the practical logic of their emancipatory potential: albeit an activism that is linked to new technologies formed in 'cyberspace' and cyber communication (Kellner 2002; see also Sassen 1991, 2000).

Medical Tourism and Gendered Enterprise

Sampurna also adds to the idea of the global commercialization of healthcare and its consumption practices, projecting the growing popularity of medical tourism (Hopkins et al. 2010). Transsexual activism in Bombay demonstrates how identity politics intersects with the neoliberalization of healthcare facilities, in the context of which identity and sexual politics are manifested with the infusion of medical consumption and social classification (Sengupta 2011). These individuals project a class category of growing capitalist upper-middle-class consumers seeking to (re)construct their identity based on their desiring self, with the ethics of globalization and expansion of market-driven healthcare. Affluent Sampurna members recorded how they have travelled overseas to Southeast Asian countries, Europe and even to the United States for their surgeries.

The Sampurna members visiting Southeast Asian nations for GRS and related procedures showcase gender(ed) spaces coupled with the political economy of medicine, surgery-led care and a radical/racialized transnational market of surgical supremacy and sexual politics (Aizura 2010; Arocostas 2009; Cook 2010; Mazzaschi 2011). Medical tourism marks an important trait of neoliberal India, enmeshed in identity-based politics and emerging consumer lifestyles, further providing evidence of the market-driven culture that in a way unveils the focus on the construction of a cosmopolitan identity, body-politics and a technique of an emancipatory project. In view of transsexual identities, this sort of transnational medical consumption not only renders an explosion of an increasing global healthcare system, but also induces the meaning of an 'identity-hub' that marks the proliferation of the commodified forms of medicine and surgeries that allow the formation of a desired gender identity. Medical tourism for reconstructive surgeries within Indian counterparts is an emerging issue. These techno-sciences intersecting with 'tourism' appropriate a new design of cultural knowledge further re-sexing identities within the configurations of the transnational formation of space and people (see Bray 2007; Wilson 2010, 2011).

EMERGING BIOSOCIAL CITIZENS

John Connell (2011) opines that medical-tourism-based practices have amplified across nations since the 1990s. Thompson (2011) describes 'medical tourists' as 'empowered biosocial citizens'. The persons seeking these sexed embodied surgeries build on an idea of surgical exoticism that seeks critical care abroad. This desired emancipation captures a feeling of hope and freedom (Connell 2006). As technological development has diffused with the growing commodification of healthcare and its consumption, the possibility of cosmetic procedure builds optimism amid savvy consumers. Amongst Indian consumers, Sampurna members primarily focus on reliability, authenticity and costs. The web-network allows experienced consumers to signpost news of experiences on the web-portal. These messages assist other members to choose surgeons.

Medical tourism and sexed embodiment are increasing gradually as a globalized consumption process with a social landscape unravelling sexed bodies as the social identifiers of aspirational consumption. The re-signification and gendering reflect an image of India's consumerist culture – the new middle class and its consumption strategies within a social position of subtle consumption-based hierarchies, as well as forms of exclusion which are continually reconstituted. This reconstitution is increasingly mediated by global economic integration – cross-border surgeries create a gendered hierarchy and authenticity, fulfilling an identity position in its widest corporeal symbolism. The desire for transnational tourism and surgery seeks skilled craftsmanship that could make possible corporeal refashioning. Such mutative practices carefully bring into focus the 'new India': a contemporary middle-class consumption of a certain subculture that is attracted by the new world of enterprise, techno-mobility and consumption (Kaur and Mazzarella 2009; Fernandes 2009). The 'new India', in other words, wants to see a rapidly pervading image of a consumer-oriented new middle class celebrating the capacity and desire for visible consumption (Brosius 2010; Saavala 2010; Nielson and Wilhite 2015). Further, the rising incomes and multiple global connections of this class dramatically transform into wide spatial mobility that culturally claims to be empowered, secular and remarkably class-conscious, further locating an international political economy of a representational (inter)national identarian syndrome. This relates to such gendered articulation as asserting 'respectability' that remains unmarked within the universal gender transgressive politics. Medical tourism and consumption in this case thus see a notable domestication of a radical sexed enterprise – markedly, these embodiments lead to a cultural appropriation of regulated practice determining an interpersonal recognition of the feminine being and womanhood. This clearly orientates to imagining underlying material intersubjective relations to establish a gender variant identity category within the global(ized) circulation to foster a new gender identity (Aizura 2010).

Exploring further, the anthropology of well-being comprises: '… an ongoing aspiration for something better that gives meaning to life's pursuit … striving for a good life involves the arduous work of becoming, of trying to live a life that one deems worthy, becoming the sort of person that one desires' (Fischer 2014: 17). In this context, I tried to link the crucial understanding of 'good life' by looking at the possibilities of the larger purpose for the commitment of life. It is an anti-erotic engagement – that is to say, 'surgeries' build the capacity of aspiration, an agency in itself, to realize and situate oneself within cultural ethics and the future. Again, the 'embodiment' is political – it is not 'just' beauty, but the virtue of embracing 'a subjective determination of value' (Fischer and Benson 2006; Nelson 2013).

This adds to the context of hyper-individualism that is structured beyond the mundane comprehension of individuality, far exceeding what Fischer (2014: 7) calls 'frustrated freedom'. Well-being here orients a measure of self-valuation, a conspicuous optimism and an embodied performative identity. The surgeries and the newly built gender substantiate the moral project of a deeply driven possibility of a transnational biopolitical logic with a complex interplay of class and race. This racialized body politic is an upper- or middle-class neoliberal project. 'The racialization of capital', as embodied with marked corporeal signifiers, is racialized to a global aesthetically and symbolically driven physiognomy and the body's marked raciology. In other words, the sexed embodiment calls for lived responses of a particular biopolitical mechanism of decisive identity formation.

I am encouraged by the similar thought of Satnam Virdee (2019) on the intimate relationship between race and capitalism. This hierarchical reordering is located within the civilized encounter of 'the West with the rest'. Explaining the structural force of racism implicates 'an emancipatory politics' to suggest racial ordering within the broader political economy of capitalism (Dantzler 2021). This understanding of race demonstrates how global capitalism has enabled development in the imaginary of embodiments – encouraging individuals to be 'flexible' and 'adaptable'. To regard this body-politic in contemporary times, Andreescu's (2016) 'human-machine assemblages', appropriating the changing global imaginary that shapes the body and its experiences, are relevant. In this embodied reality, 'commodity masquerades as living' – in other words, 'capital' renders an individual invisible, further intimating belonging. Further, capital's corrosive tendency as the very act of 'the invasion of markets', intensifying the speed of space and time, eventually leads modernity's sacred integrity to philosophize 'race' with new potentiality.

Conclusion

Gender is pervasive and fragile, and the norms of gender presentation draw an understanding of constant and rigorous gender surveillance. Such policing sees a definite pattern of gender norms that would reflect the normalization of the gender binary (Lorber 1994; Gagne and Tewksbury 1998). Jan Wickman (2003) draws evidence of the characterization of gender construction since the 1990s, taking into account the radical gender politics within varied sexed-embodiment-based networks. The radicalization entails showcasing the development of new identities through medical construction. Also, the 'sexualization' and 'commodification' that go deeper in the understanding of the embodiment-led manifestation of medical technologies emphasize the fluid and polymorphous character of identities, further opening up new ways to interrogate identity categories outside the traditional gender dichotomy (Brown 1998; Hale 1998).

The argument could be broadly conceptualized in line with the understanding of 'cultural citizenship' (Stevenson 1997) that effectively creates the possibility of the symbolic presence and visibility of a particular population in society from a relation of 'marginality' to 'assimilation'. Sexed bodies and their sense of assimilation broadly represent how their citizenship is related to consumerism – emphasizing varied neoliberal offerings and their consumption of cosmopolitan lifestyles that could meet their innermost desires. This tacit relationship of the body and the medical marketplace intersects to produce the newly formed subjectivity and agency. Or as Donna Haraway (1985, 1991) puts it, the positionality of the body is reconfigured through techno-science and capitalism producing a 'new world order'. The 'cyborg', as Haraway reckons, is a cultural artefact created through the means of technology and is the foci for the understanding of new dimensions of the relationship of the body to technology, so much so that there is a culture of 'perfectability' (Hogle 2003, 2005). Similarly, this new gendering order could be seen as the reference point for the understanding of the body, technology and the self, resting on the necessary conditions of desirability – bodies as cyborgs created by the technologization of identity, rendering a visible culturally endowed meaning to achieve 'gendered embodiment'; and further emphasizing the postmodern reference to the medico-corporeal discourse of the reification of a particular gender politics, an individual autonomy that is emblematic of the liberatory potential of the body and bodied representations (Prosser 1998; Stryker 1995, 2008; Meyerowitz 2002).

NOTES

1   Shock conversion therapy, popularly referred to as sexual orientation conversion therapy, was 'the treatment of choice' at the time homosexuality was thought to be an illness. This conversion theory, or in clinical terms 'sexual orientation change effort' (SOCE), had its roots in the nineteenth-century 'development of the science of sexuality'. This attempt 'to cure' homosexuality through psychiatric practices was eventually relied on by religious leaders to characterize homosexuality, male effeminacy or transgender-identity-based traits as 'abnormal' or an 'illness' (Ashworth 2018).

2   The term 'trans*', with an asterisk, is used within the LGBTQ+ community to refer to people who are transgender or self-identify with related terms and

concepts. The asterisk serves to cover a wide spectrum of identities that do not conform to 'traditional conceptions' of gender.

3   DSM, or the Diagnostic Statistical Manual of Mental Disorders, is the standard classification of mental disorders used by mental health practitioners in the United States. It is intended to be used in various clinical settings, beyond mental health practitioners, such as by social workers, nurses, occupational therapists, and so on. DSM-5 is the most recent edition of the DSM.

According to DSM-4, a person suffering from gender identity disorder (GID) could be either a male or a female who is uncomfortable with the biological sex that they are born with and has a strong sense of identification with the opposite sex. This sense of identification may or may not lead to gender reassignment via surgical mechanisms and HRT. The American Psychiatric Association (2000) defines GID as a psychological disorder, and to their understanding, transsexuality and the processes of gender reassigning are a more severe form.

4   Minnesota Personality Inventory (MMP1) is a psychological test that accesses personality traits and psychopathology. It is primarily intended to test people who are suspected of having mental health or other clinical issues. The test was developed by clinical psychologist Starke Hathaway and neuropsychiatrist J. C. McKinley when they were faculty of health sciences at the University of Minnesota.

5   Androgen is a hormone which configures the internal and external structures of the human body.

6   ICD, or the International Classification of Diseases, is the standard diagnostic tool for health management and clinical purposes. Like the DSM, the ICD is used across clinical disciplines. ICD-10 has been drafted by the World Health Organization (WHO) and contains the code of diseases and symptoms. The later version of the DSM, or the DSM-5, reflects the factor of 'distresses' instead of 'the 'identity', so as to chart the importance of the 'gender', as linking it to the desirability of the gender, and the distress that is associated with the gender.

7   Foucault's anatomo-politics of the human body centres on the idea of 'the body as a machine'. Its 'disciplining', 'the optimization of its capabilities', 'the extortion of its forces' and 'the parallel increase of its usefulness and its docility' signal Foucault's seventeenth-century 'population' as the main target of power. Further, what Foucault calls 'the biopolitics of the population' emphasizes 'the body' or 'the population' with special focus on births, deaths, health, and so on – with the purpose of regulation and control (Foucault 1976).

8   Here, 'the self' relates to Foucault's 'care of the self' which follows an 'ethical shift' – an idea that inspires 'freedom' and 'the aesthetics of existence'. The central idea of this is a way of life and a kind of 'self-care' that involves self-fashioning of individuals and designing a courage of the 'truth' of the 'self' with a point of resistance to disciplinary power. This 'ethics of the truth' that Foucault marks is designed to constitute 'truth discourse' in Foucault's later writings.

BIBLIOGRAPHY

Aizura, A. Z. 2006. 'Of Borders and Homes: The Imaginary Community of (Trans)Sexual Citizenship'. *Inter-Asia Cultural Studies* 7(2): 289–309.

———. 2010. 'Feminine Transformations: Gender Reassignment Surgical Tourism in Thailand'. *Medical Anthropology* 29(4): 424–443.

Andreescu, F. C. 2016. 'Embodied Subjects in Late Capitalism'. *Subjectivity* 9: 145–150.

Arocostas, J. 2009. 'Developing Nations Pour Cash Into Attracting Medical Tourism'. *BMJ: British Medical Journal* 339(20): 535–548.

Ashworth, S. 2018. 'The Pernicious Myth of Conversion Therapy: How Love in Action Perpetrated a Fraud on America'. Mattachine Society of Washington, DC. https://www.nclrights.org/wp-content/uploads/2018/11/Mattachine-Society-Conversion-Therapy-White-Paper-Redacted.pdf. Accessed in February 2017.

Attwood-Charles, W. 2018. 'Post-bureaucratic Organizations: Normative and Technical Dimensions'. https://core.ac.uk/download/pdf/199470465.pdf. Accessed in February 2017.

Baudrillard, J., C. R. Lovitt and D. Klopsch. 1976. 'Toward a Critique of the Political Economy of the Sign'. *Substance* 5(15): 111–116.

Bennett, W. 2003. 'Communicating Global Activism'. *Information, Communication and Society* 6(2): 143–168.

Bolin, A. 1994. 'Transcending and Transgendering: Male to Female, Dichotomy and Diversity'. In *Third Sex, Third Gender: Beyond Sexual Dimorphism in Culture and History*, edited by G. Herdt, 447–485. New York: Zone Books.

———. 1996. 'Traversing Gender, Cultural Context and Gender Practices'. In *Gender Reversals and Gender Cultures: Anthropological and Historical Perspectives*, edited by S. P. Ramet, 22–51. New York: Routledge.

Bornstein, K. 1995. *Gender Outlaw: On Men, Women and the Rest of Us*. New York: Vintage.

Bourdieu, P. 1989. 'Social Space and Symbolic Power'. *Sociological Theory* 7(1): 14–25.

Bourdieu, P., and R. Johnson. 1993. *The Field of Cultural Production: Essays on Art and Literature*. Cambridge: Polity Press.

Braunstein, N. 2003. 'Desire and Jouissance in the Teachings of Lacan'. In *The Cambridge Companion to Lacan*, edited by J-M. Rabaté, 102–115. Cambridge: Cambridge University Press.

Bray, F. 2007. 'Gender and Technology'. *Annual Review of Anthropology* 36: 37–53.

Brosius, C. 2010. *India's Middle Class: New Forms of Urban Leisure, Consumption and Prosperity*. London and New York: Routledge.

Brown, Lee A. 1998. 'Circling the Margins of Identity: Controversies in the Sydney Transgender Community'. Paper presented at the Third International Congress on Sex and Gender, An Interdisciplinary Conference: Transgender Agenda for the End of the Millennium, University of Oxford, 18–20 September.

Butler, J. 1990. *Gender Trouble: Feminism and the Subversion of Identity*. New York: Routledge.

———. 1993. *Bodies That Matter: On the Discursive Limits of Sex*. London: Routledge.

———. 2004. *Undoing Gender*. London. Routledge.

Cadwallader, J. 2007. 'Suffering Difference: Normalisation and Power'. *Social Semiotics* 17(3): 375–394.

Cahill, A. J. 2003. 'Feminist Pleasure and Feminine Beautification'. *Hypatia* 18(4): 42–64.

Campbell, T., and A. Sitze (eds.). 2013. *Biopolitics*. Durham, NC, and London: Duke University Press.

Canguilhem, G. 1978. *On the Normal and the Pathological*. Translated by C. R. Fawcett. Dordrecht, Boston and London: D. Reidel Publishing Company.

———. 1989. *The Normal and the Pathological*. New York: Zone Books.

Carver, T. and V. Mottier (eds.). 1998. *Politics of Sexuality: Identity, Gender, Citizenship*. London and New York: Routledge.

Cohen-Kettenis, P. T., and L. J. Gooren. 1999. 'Transsexualism: A Review of Etiology, Diagnosis and Treatment'. *Journal of Psychosomatic Research* 46(4): 315–333.

Connell, C. 2010. 'Doing, Undoing or Redoing Gender? Learning from the Workplace Experiences of Trans People'. *Gender and Society* 24(1): 31–55.

Connell, J. 2006. 'Medical Tourism: Sex, Sun, Sand and Surgery'. *Tourism Management* 27(6): 1093–1100.

———. 2011. *Medical Tourism*. Oxford and Cambridge, MA: CABI Publishing.

Conrad, P., and J. W. Schneider. 1980. 'Looking at Levels of Medicalization: A Comment on Strong's Critique of the Thesis of Medical Imperialism'. *Social Science and Medicine* 14A(1): 75–79.

Cook, P. S. 2010. 'Constructions and Experiences of Authenticity in Medical Tourism: The Performances of Places, Spaces, Practices, Objects and Bodies'. *Tourist Studies* 10(2): 135–153.

Cooter, R. 2004. '"Framing" the End of the Social History of Medicine'. In *Locating Medical History: The Stories and Their Meanings*, edited by F. Huisman and J. Harley, 309–327. Baltimore: Johns Hopkins University Press.

Crawford, R. 2006. 'Health as a Meaningful Social Practice'. *Journal of Health and Social Behaviour* 10(4): 401–420.

Dantzler, P. A. 2021. 'The Urban Process Under Racial Capitalism'. *Journal of Race, Ethnicity and the City* 2(2): 113–134.

Dean, J. 2003. 'Why the Net is Not a Public Sphere'. *Constellations* 10(1): 95–112.

———. 2009. *Democracy and Other Neoliberal Fantasies: Communicative Capitalism and Left Politics.* Durham, NC, and London: Duke University Press.

Deleuze, G. 1994. *Difference and Repetition.* Translated by Paul Patton. New York: Columbia University Press.

Dellinger, K., and C. Williams. 1997. 'Makeup at Work: Negotiating Appearance Rules in the Workplace'. *Gender and Society* 11(2): 151–177.

Deutsch, F. M. 2007. 'Undoing Gender'. *Gender and Society* 21(1): 106–127.

Diamond, M. 2002. 'Sex and Gender are Different: Sexual Identity and Gender Identity are Different'. *Clinical Child Psychology and Psychiatry* 7(3): 320–334.

———. 2009. 'Clinical Implications of the Organizational and Activational Effects of Hormones'. *Hormones and Behaviour* 55(5): 621–632.

Doan, L., and J. Prosser. 2001. *Palatable Poison: Critical Perspectives on the Well of Loneliness.* New York and London: Columbia University Press.

Doubt, K. 1992. 'Mead's Theory of Self and Schizophrenia'. *Social Science Journal* 29(3): 307–321.

Earl, J., and K. Kimport. 2011. *Digitally Enabled Social Change: Activism in the Internet Age.* Cambridge, MA, and London: MIT Press.

Edmonds, A. 2010. *Pretty Modern: Beauty, Sex, and Plastic Surgery in Brazil.* Durham, NC, and London: Duke University Press.

Epstein, S. 1998. *Impure Science: AIDS, Activism, and the Politics of Knowledge.* Berkeley: University of California Press.

———. 2007. *Inclusion: The Politics of Difference in Medical Research.* Chicago: University of Chicago Press.

Featherstone, M. 1991a. *Consumer Culture and Postmodernism.* London: SAGE Publications.

———. 1991b. 'The Body in Consumer Culture'. In *The Body: Social Process and Cultural Theory,* edited by M. Featherstone, M. Heapworth and B. Turner, 170–196. London: SAGE Publications.

———. 2000. 'Body Modification: An Introduction'. In *Body Modification,* edited by M. Featherstone, 1–14. Thousand Oaks, CA: SAGE Publications.

Featherstone, M. and R. Burrow, eds. 1995. *Cyberspace/Cyberbodies/Cyberpunk: Culture of Technological Embodiment.* London: SAGE Publications.

Ferguson, R. A., and G. K. Hong. 2012. 'The Sexual and Racial Contradiction of Neoliberalism'. *Journal of Homosexuality* 59(7): 1057–1064.

Fernandes, L. 2009. 'The Political Economy of Lifestyle: Consumption, India's New Middle Class and State-led Development'. In *The New Middle Classes*, edited by H. Lange and L. Meier, 219–236. Dorchester: Springer.

Fischer, E. F., and P. Benson. 2006. *Broccoli & Desire: Global Connections and Maya Struggles in Postwar Guatemala*. Redwood City, CA: Stanford University Press.

Fischer, M. 2014. *Anthropological Futures*. Durham, NC, and London: Duke University Press.

Foucault, M. 1973 (1963). *The Birth of the Clinic: An Archaeology of Medical Perception*. London: Tavistock Publications.

———. 1976. *The History of Sexuality*, vol. 1. Translated by Robert Hurley. New York: Vintage Books.

Franklin, S. 2006. 'The Cyborg Embryo: Our Path of Transbiology'. *Theory, Culture and Society* 23(7–8): 167–187.

Frow, J. 1991. 'Michel de Certeau and the Practice of Representation'. *Cultural Studies* 5(1): 52–60.

Gagne, P., and D. McGaughey. 2002. 'Designing Women: Cultural Hegemony and the Exercise of Power among Women Who Have Undergone Elective Mammoplasty'. *Gender and Society* 16(6): 814–838.

Gagne, P., and R. Tewksbury. 1998. 'Conformity Pressures and Gender Resistance Amongst Transgendered Individuals'. *Social Problem* 45(1): 81–101.

———. 1999. 'Knowledge and Power, Body and Self: An Analysis of Knowledge Systems and the Transgendered Self'. *Sociological Quarterly* 40(1): 59–83.

Gagne, P., R. Tewksbury and D. McGaughey. 1997. 'Coming Out and Crossing Over: Identity Formation and Proclamation in a Transgender Community'. *Gender and Society* 11(4): 478–508.

Garfinkel, H. 1967. *Studies in Ethnomethodology*. Englewood Cliffs, NJ: Prentice Hall.

Genal, K. 2006. 'The Questions of Biopower: Foucault and Agamben'. *Rethinking Marxism* 18(1): 43–62.

Giddens, A. 1991. *Modernity and Self-identity: Self and Society in the Late Modern Age*. Redwood City, CA: Stanford University Press.

Good, M. J. D. 2010. 'The Medical Imaginary and the Biotechnical Embrace: Subjective Experiences of Clinical Scientists and Patients'. In *A Reader in Medical Anthropology: Theoretical Trajectories, Emergent Realities*, edited by M. M. J. Fischer, S. Willen and M. J. D. Good, 272–280. Hoboken, NJ: Wiley-Blackwell.

Gooren, L. 1990. 'The Endocrinology of Transsexualism: A Review and Commentary'. *Psychoneuroendocrinology* 15(1): 3–14.

————. 2006. 'The Biology of Human Psychosexual Differentiation'. *Hormones and Behaviour* 50(4): 589–601.

Grosz, E. 1995a. *Space, Time and Perversion*. New York and London: Routledge.

————. 1995b. *Volatile Bodies: Towards a Corporeal Feminism*. Bloomington: Indiana University Press.

Habermas, J. 1996. *Between Facts and Norms: Contributions to a Discourse Theory of Law and Democracy*. Studies in Contemporary German Social Thought. Cambridge, MA: The MIT Press.

Halberstam, J. 2018. *Trans*: A Quick and Quirky Account of Gender Variability*. Berkeley: University of California Press.

Hale, J. C. 1998. 'Consuming the Living, Dis(Re)membering the Dead in the Butch/FTM Borderlands'. *GLQ: A Journal of Lesbian and Gay Studies* 4(2): 311–348.

Hannah, M. G. 2011. 'Biopower, Life and Left Politics'. *Antipode* 43(4): 1034–1055.

Happe, K. E., J. Johnson and M. Levina. 2018. *Biocitizenship: The Politics of Bodies, Governance, and Power*. New York: New York University Press.

Haraway, D. 1985. 'A Manifesto for Cyborgs: Science, Technology and Socialist Feminism in the 1980s'. *Socialist Review* 80: 65–108.

————. 1991. *Simians, Cyborgs and Women: The Reinvention of Nature*. New York: Routledge.

Harcourt, B. E. 2019. 'Foucault's Keystone: Confessions of the Flesh: How the Fourth and Final Volume of "The History of Sexuality" Completes Foucault's Critique of Modern Western Societies'. Columbia Public Law Research Paper No. 14-647, Minda de Gunzburg Center for European Studies, Harvard University.

Hausman, B. L. 1995. *Changing Sex: Transsexualism, Technology, and the Idea of Gender*. Durham, NC: Duke University Press.

Hird, M. J. 2002. 'For a Sociology of Transsexualism'. *Sociology* 36(3): 577–595.

Hogle, L. 2003. 'Life/Time Warranty: Rechargeable Cells and Extendable Lives'. In *Remaking Life and Death: Toward an Anthropology of the Biosciences*, edited by S. Franklin and M. Lock, 61–96. Santa Fe, NM: School for Advanced Research Press.

————. 2005. 'Enhancement Technologies and the Body'. *Annual Review of Anthropology* 34: 695–716.

Hopkins, L., R. Labonte, V. Runnels and C. Packer. 2010. 'Medical Tourism Today: What is the State of Existing Knowledge?' *Journal of Public Health Policy* 31(2): 185–198.

Irvine, J. 1990. *Disorder and Desire: Sex and Gender in Modern American Sexology*. Philadelphia: Temple University Press.

Jarrin, A. 2017. *The Biopolitics of Beauty: Cosmetic Citizenship and Affective Capital in Brazil.* Oakland: University of California Press.

Kahn, R., and K. Douglas. 2003. 'New Media and Internet Activism: "Battle of Seattle to Blogging"'. *New Media and Society* 6(1): 87–95.

Kaur, R., and W. Mazzarella (eds.). 2009. *Censorship in South Asia: Cultural Regulation from Sedition to Seduction.* Bloomington: Indiana University Press.

Kellner, Douglas. 2002. 'Theorizing Globalization'. *Sociological Theory* 20(3): 285–305.

Lacan, J., A. Sheridan and M Bowie. 2020 (1977). *The Signification of the Phallus.* London: Routledge.

Langman, L. 2005. 'From Virtual Public Spheres to Global Justice: A Critical Theory of Internetworked Social Movements'. *Sociological Theory* 23(1): 42–74.

Lazar, S. (ed.). 2013. *The Anthropology of Citizenship: A Reader.* Hoboken, NJ: Wiley-Blackwell.

Lemke, T. 2015. 'New Materialism: Foucault and the "Government of Things"'. *Theory, Culture and Society* 32(4): 3–25.

Lock, M., and V-K Nguyen. 2018 (2010). *An Anthropology of Biomedicine.* Oxford: Wiley-Blackwell.

Lorber, J. 1994. *Paradoxes of Gender.* New Haven and London: Yale University Press.

Lunders E., and F. J. Sanchez. 2009. 'Regional Grey Matter Variations in Male to Female Transsexualism'. *NeuroImage* 46(4): 904–907.

Luo, X. R., J. Zhang and C. Marquis. 2016. 'Mobilization in the Internet Age: Internet Activism and Corporate Response'. *Academy of Management Journal* 59(6): 2045–2068.

Luxon, N. 2008. 'Ethics and Subjectivity: Practices of Self-governance in the Late Lectures of Michel Foucault'. *Political Theory* 36(3): 377–402.

Lyotard, J. F. 1984. *The Postmodern Condition.* Minneapolis: University of Minnesota Press.

Maravelias, C. 2003. 'Post-bureaucracy: Control through Professional Freedom'. *Journal of Organizational Change Management* 16(5): 547–566.

Markoff, J. 2004. 'Who Will Construct the Global Order?' In *Transnational Democracy*, edited by B. William, 239–276. Ashgate: London.

———. 2008. 'Before the Gunfire, Cyberattacks'. *New York Times.* www.nytimes.com/2008/08/13/technology/13cyber.html_r=0. Accessed in February 2017.

May, K. 2002. 'Becoming Women: Transgendered Identities, Psychosexual Therapy and the Challenge of Metamorphosis'. *Sexualities* 5(4): 449–464.

Mazzaschi, A. 2011. 'Surgeon and Safari: Producing Valuable Bodies in Johannesburg'. *Signs* 36(2): 303–312.

McCallum, D. 1997. 'Mental Health, Criminality and the Human Sciences'. In *Foucault, Health and Medicine*, edited by R. Peterson and A. Burton, 53–73. London and New York: Routledge.

McDonald, R., N. Mead, S. Cheraghi-Sohi, P. Bower, D. Whaley and M. Roland. 2007. 'Governing the Ethical Consumer: Identity, Choice and the Primary Care Medical Encounter'. *Sociology of Health and Illness* 29(3): 430–456.

McGrath, S. J. 2010. 'Sexuation in Jung and Lacan'. *International Journal of Jungian Studies* 2(1): 1–20.

Meyerowitz, J. 2002. *How Sex Changed? A History of Transsexuality in the United States*. Cambridge, MA: Harvard University Press.

Modestin, J., S. Hermann and J. Endrass. 2007. 'Schizoidia in Schizophrenia Spectrum and Personality Disorders: The Role of Dissociation'. *Psychiatry Research* 153(2): 111–118.

Moghadam, V. M. 2000. 'Transnational Feminist Networks: Collective Action in an Era of Globalization'. *International Sociology* 15(1): 57–85.

Moi, T. 1999. *What is a Woman? And other Essays*. Oxford and New York: Oxford University Press.

Monaghan, L. F. 2003. 'Hormonal Bodies, Civilized Bodies: Incorporating the Biological into the Sociology of Health'. In *Debating Biology: Sociological Reflections on Health, Medicine, and Society*, edited by G. Bendelow, L. Birke and S. Williams, 110–133. London and New York: Routledge.

Negrin, L. 2002. 'Cosmetic Surgery and the Eclipse of Identity'. *Body and Society* 8(4): 21–42.

Nelson, J. 2003. *Embodiment: An Approach to Sexuality and Christian Theology*. Minneapolis: Fortress Press.

Nielson, K. B., and H. Wilhite. 2015. 'The Rise and the Fall of the "People's Car": Middle-class Aspirations, Status and Mobile Symbolism in "New India"'. *Contemporary South Asia* 23(4): 1–17.

Norris, C., and G. Armstrong. 1997. *The Unforgiving Eye: CCTV Surveillance in Public Space*. Hull: University of Hull.

Paley, J. 2002. 'Towards an Anthropology of Democracy'. *Annual Review of Anthropology* 31: 469–496.

Pearlson, G. D., and L. Marsh. 1999. 'Structural Brain Imaging in Schizophrenia: A Selective Review'. *Biological Psychiatry* 46(5): 627–649.

Peterson, A., and R. Bunton. 1997. *Foucault, Health and Medicine*. London and New York: Routledge.

Plummer, K. 2003. *Intimate Citizenships: Private Decisions and Public Dialogues.* Seattle and London: University of Washington Press.

Prosser, J. 1998. *Second Skins: The Body Narratives of Transsexuality.* New York and London: Columbia University Press.

Rabinow, P. 1996. *Making PCR: A Story of Biotechnology.* Chicago: University of Chicago Press.

Ragland, E. 2004. *The Logic of Sexuation: From Aristotle to Lacan.* Albany: State University of New York Press.

———. 2012. *The Logic of Sexuation: From Aristotle to Lacan.* Albany: State University of New York Press.

Rapp, R. 2019. 'Race & Reproduction: An Enduring Conversation'. *Medical Anthropology* 38(8): 725–732.

Risman, B. J. 2009. 'From Doing to Undoing: Gender as we Know It'. *Gender and Society* 23(1): 81–84.

Rose, N. 1999. *Powers and Freedom: Reframing Political Thought.* Cambridge: Cambridge University Press.

———. 2006. *The Politics of Life Itself: Biomedicine, Power and Subjectivity in the Twenty-first Century.* Princeton, NJ: Princeton University Press.

Roy, S. 2003. 'From Kush List to Gay Bombay: Virtual Webs of Real People'. In *Mobile Cultures: New Media in Queer Asia*, edited by C. Berry, F. Martin and A. Yue, 180–200. Durham, NC: Duke University Press.

Rubin, H. 2003. *Self-made Men: Identity and Embodiment Among Transsexual Men.* Nashville, TN: Vanderbilt University Press.

Saavala, M. 2010. *Middle Class Moralities: Everyday Struggle Over Belonging and Prestige in India.* New Delhi: Orient Blackswan.

Sassen, S. 1991. *The Global City: New York, London, Tokyo.* Princeton: Princeton University Press.

———. 2000. 'Spatialities and Temporalities of the Global: Elements for a Theorization'. *Public Culture* 12(1): 215–232.

Schrock, D., L. Reid and E. M. Boyd. 2005. 'Transsexuals' Embodiment of Womanhood'. *Gender and Society* 19(3): 317–335.

Segal, J. Z. 2003. 'Rhetoric of Health and Medicine'. In *The Sage Handbook of Rhetorical Studies*, edited by A. A. Lunsford, K. H. Wilson and R. A. Eberly, 227–246. London and New York: SAGE Publications.

Sengupta, A. 2011. 'Medical Tourism: Reverse Subsidy for the Elite'. *Signs* 36(2): 312–319.

Shilling, C. 2003. *The Body and Social Theory.* London: SAGE Publications.

———. 2005. *The Body in Culture, Technology & Society.* London: SAGE Publications.

Shusterman, R. 1992. *Pragmatic Aesthetics: Living Beauty, Rethinking Art*. Oxford and New York: Rowman & Littlefield.

Siisiäinen, L. 2018. *Foucault, Biopolitics and Resistance*. London and New York: Routledge.

Sparke, M. 2005. *In the Space of Theory: Postfoundational Geographies of the Nation-state*. Minneapolis: University of Minnesota Press.

Stevenson, N. 1997. 'Globalization, National Cultures and Cultural Citizenship'. *Sociological Quarterly* 38(1): 41–66.

Stoller, R. 1968. *Sex and Gender: On the Development of Masculinity and Femininity*. London: Hogarth Press.

Stryker, S. 1995. 'Transsexuality: The Postmodern Body and/as Technology'. *Exposure: The Journal of the Society for Photographic Education* 30: 38–50.

————. 2008. *Transgender History*. Berkeley: Seal Press.

Sullivan, N. 2003. *A Critical Introduction to Queer Theory*. Edinburgh: Edinburgh University Press.

Tatarchevskiy, T. 2010. 'The "Popular" Culture of Internet Activism'. *New Media and Society* 13(2): 297–313.

Thompson, N. 2011. *Medical Tourism*. New Delhi: Discovery Publishers.

Tseng, W-S. 2003. *Clinician's Guide to Cultural Psychiatry*. Amsterdam, Boston and London: Academic Press.

Turner, B. S. 2006. 'Body'. *Theory, Culture and Society* 23(2–3): 223–229.

————. 2008. *The Body & Society: Explorations in Social Theory*. London, New York and New Delhi: SAGE Publications.

Virdee, S. 2019. 'Racialized Capitalism: An Account of Its Contested Origins and Race Consolidations'. *Sociological Review* 67(1): 3–27.

Wellman, B. 2001. 'Little Boxes, Glocalization, and Networked Individualism'. Kyoto Workshop on Digital Cities. https://link.springer.com/content/pdf/10.1007%2F3-540-45636-8.pdf. Accessed in February 2017.

Wellman, B., and M Gulia. 1999. 'Net-surfers Don't Ride Alone: Virtual Communities as Communities.' In *Network in the Global Village: Life in Contemporary Communities*, edited by B. Wellman, 167–194. New York: Routledge.

West, C., and D. H. Zimmerman. 2009. 'Accounting for Doing Gender'. *Gender and Society* 23(1): 112–122.

Wickman, J. 2003. 'Masculinity and Female Bodies'. *NORA: Nordic Journal of Feminist and Gender Research* 11(1): 40–54.

Williams, S. J. 2002. 'Corporeal Reflections on Biology: Reductionism, Constructionism and Beyond'. In *Gender, Health and Healing: The Public/*

Private Divide, edited by G. Bendelow, G. M. Carpenter, M. C. Vautier and C. S. Williams, 3–29. London and New York: Routledge.

Wilson, A. 2010. 'Medical Tourism in Thailand'. In *Asian Biotech: Ethics and Communities of Fate*, edited by A. Ong and N. Cheng, 118–143. Durham, NC: Duke University Press.

———. 2011. 'Foreign Bodies and National Scales: Medical Tourism in Thailand'. *Body and Society* 17(2–3): 121–137.

6

Performative Participation, Sexual Health and Community Development

The chapter is based on the framework contextualizing 'participation as a development tool' for community engagement, inviting the possibility of 'self-organization' through mobilization, resistance and participation in governance and decision-making, claiming rights, and so on (Cornwall 2000; Cornwall and Eade 2010; Cornwall 2011a). Following this perspective, this ethnographic study draws evidence on the collective efficacies of gendered otherness, generating a form of 'protest participation' that focuses on facilitating 'citizen-to-citizen' deliberations. This emphasizes collective action to form a specific movement-based politics, or a radical political manoeuvring (Newman and Clarke 2009; Lee 2010; Cohen and Uphoff 2011: 35; White 2011: 59; Hilmer 2010). Andrea Cornwall (2011a) recalls 'invited participation' that foregrounds issues of 'power' and radical democratic tenets giving space to marginalized and 'subaltern voices' (Fraser 1997). This further determines the mobilization and articulation of citizens with a meaningful engagement of the marginalized to challenge the trajectories of 'usual' development politics on the one hand (Mohanty 2011: 268; White 2011: 58), and to claim participation by the community's self-construction of social networks, organizations and its competence on the other (Barnes and Mann 2011; Haque and Kusakabe 2011; Franklin 2014). In the wake of the economic restructuring around the globe and the so-called 'transformative project' of the North–South, donor-recipient dynamics since the 1960s and 1970s, followed by neoliberalism from the 1980s, a 'participatory development' agenda has emerged that strongly resembles the re-institutionalization of the colonial flavour and exclusionary mechanism, sidelining the 'local' political or cultural factors of the community's engagement (Leal 2011: xiv; Cornwall 2011a).

This chapter digs deep into the different dimensions of community development and participation so as to explore issues of shared experiences, knowledge, language, speech, acts and performances – a tool and a creative practice to identify the possibilities of social change (Butler 2010). This performative magic constitutes 'dialogue' which has again a performative dimension and a certain kind of speech which are necessary for actualizing politics, and delves into the 'performative lens' of the politics of interaction. The symbolic metaphor that is generated thus highlights a particular language of participation which in a way builds a specific form of cultural image for community mobilization, and strategies for self-empowerment and claiming rights and citizenship (Ibrahim and Alkire 2007; Niemi and Plante 2008; Dean 2009; Palacios 2015). Also, this chapter provides new thinking on the pedagogical tool and methodological apparatus that underpin the realization of technology as a means for effective 'local' participation, enabling the evolution of new ideas for a desirable community and public-health initiative (Bery and Stuart 2011: 152; Patel 2011: 133; Abah 2011: 142–144). Further, this brings to notice decentralization as a force of institutional change whereby local people articulate their interests, mediate their differences and exercise their rights (Tandon 2008). As decentralization of power and politics becomes an increasingly important debate in the new discourses on community health and the development paradigm, it becomes the prime focus in renegotiating the framework of power to build citizens' capacity with competencies and skills within the disenfranchised and the marginalized (Gaventa 1995; Eade 2007).

WORLD AIDS DAY IN BOMBAY

Leela pointed out that World AIDS Day is an important occasion, and *hijra*s participate in a rally coordinated by the Mumbai Districts AIDS Control Society (MDACS) – a state-led initiative to engage various civil society activists and non-governmental organizations (NGOs) in an AIDS-awareness solidarity-based programme. She further mentioned details as to the rally's route and plan. It comprised a march for a few kilometres, public demonstrations and street plays so as to create awareness and public visibility of sexual minorities. The rally started from an extensive green park and was followed by street theatre, public slogans and other performances to demonstrate solidarity. There was participation of multiple strands of people: from school and college students to various NGOs and community-based organizations (CBOs) in Bombay that work on community health, educators, film actors, media personnel, female sex workers' organizations, female sex workers, *hijra*s, *kothi*s and other sexual minorities. By visual means and public events like banners, hoardings, posters as well as speeches, it also tried to reduce stigma and discrimination against sexual minorities by communicating knowledge on sexual health and attempting to establish diversity and inclusivity of gendered representation in public culture.

The street plays were meant to showcase everyday realities in intra-personal relationships and patterns of intimacies and associations across genders. The main aim of the demonstration was to create a public understanding of safer sex practices and sex education related to contraceptive usage, human immunodeficiency virus (HIV) and acquired immunodeficiency syndrome (AIDS), antiretroviral therapy (ART), sexually transmitted infection (STI)-led contamination and other such issues. In other words, the plays attempted to build awareness on risk-related behaviours and practices that are likely to spread sexually transmitted diseases. These plays were based on research on sexual health by NGOs and international non-governmental organizations (INGOs) including analytical research on specific groups like truck drivers, female sex workers, *hijra*s, *kothi*s and HIV-infected heterosexual men. By means of theatrical presentation, the participants portrayed sexual and behavioural 'risks' and steps that could be taken to safeguard against those risks. These performances also had a political motive – that is, to prevent discrimination against sexual minorities, especially *kothi*s and hijras.[1]

There were three plays. The first depicted a man visiting a brothel and insisting on non-contraceptive sex. But the female sex worker is steadfast and encourages the man to use contraception. The man becomes violent and threatens the woman, saying that he has paid for 'the work', and if she refuses, he has the power to complain to her master and make her lose her job. The play depicts a heated debate between the man (the service seeker), the sex worker and the sex worker's master, demonstrating a vernacular consciousness within sex work practices: *bimari* (illness, referring to HIV and STIs) that they are warned against by the local team of doctors, activists and health workers.

The second play showcased a side lane along a highway, where long-distance truck drivers rest, eat food in *dhaba*s (food stalls) and often look for sex workers (female or *hijra*) for pleasure. A truck driver tries to sexually exploit a *hijra* sex worker, asking for anal sex without the use of condoms. The play depicts how the *hijra* has been trained to practice safe sex through sexual health programmes by the local NGO at the place where she lives. It shows her refusing to engage in sex without a condom. The truck driver abuses her and threatens to report her name to the local police. The man insists that she perform oral sex instead, and after she has complied, he refuses to pay her money. At that time, other *hijra*s who are present performing the same work with their respective clients come in support of their friend. Instantly, solidarity is formed and they approach the local police station, seeking justice against the abusive truck driver. The play coveys how *hijra*s are becoming well-informed about their rights and protocols even if there are instances of coercion or attempts to allure with extra money.

And finally, the third play exhibited a male same-sex relationship, highlighting two men who meet in a rights-based organization in Bombay. They fall in love with each other. One partner has been found HIV positive. The play depicts the emotional bond between these two men as lovers, further showcasing how this strong bond stands up to battle a taboo-prone stigmatized disease, like HIV/AIDS.

The plays demonstrate the active participation of female sex workers, *hijra*s and gay men in sexual health promotion, and their role in NGO activism and civil society initiatives. They underline the impact of local activism on HIV – depicting the degree of awareness of safer-sex practices when performing sex work. They further highlight the self-awareness of these groups on rights claims and in contesting abuses and harassment faced during sex work. Each of these plays establishes a strong political message, underlining the diversity

Figure 6.1   Street-theatre performance on World AIDS Day in Bombay
Source: Photograph by the author.

of identity-categories, an inclusive strategy and the ways in which they make democratic-rights-based claims. These plays also urge society to embrace differences, such that the minority population and stigma-laden identities build a democratic space for claiming their citizenship rights. It is also interesting to see the local–global interface in the rally, reinforcing further the programmatic approach depicted in the plays.

The World AIDS Day rally is funded by the MDACS and various other national and international NGOs. Local NGOs and CBOs attended the rally with their posters and placards, presenting different slogans and messages on AIDS, health and sexuality.

REVISITING PARTICIPATION: LANGUAGE, SPACE AND CITIZENSHIP

The World AIDS Day rally in Bombay (Figure 6.1) exhibits a form of community participation and a political efficacy of the cultural environment with democratic attributes of the movement's constituency (Wojcieszak, Baek and Carpini 2010). Further, it exhibits a model of citizen-centric deliberations that provide the importance of 'civility' and participation with a view to enhancing and promoting participatory goals by means of collective action (Read and Saphiro 2014). Francis Lee (2010) evokes the idea of 'collective action' in an analysis of social movement studies, saying that these sorts of movements create a specific social group of activists that expresses political sentiments, manoeuvred and manifested through a political mobilization and a representative politics that ultimately forms the fundamental dogma of the movement. In other words, the movement delivers an important insight into the citizens' role: an agency is formed to build sovereign claims in their collective efficacy, which respond to a culture of representation, further signifying a context in which these agents of change hold a certain political motive and seek certain political outcomes. Thus, the rally installs a collective efficacy, a form of protest participation, contributing a model of a movement-device that focuses on the ultimate goal of perceived social change (Lee and Chan 2008; Lubell 2002; Lee 2006, 2010).

The chief focus of such participation is upholding 'good governance' (Newman 2010; Cornwall 2011a). In relation to this, 'governance' is entangled with citizenship-claiming, constituting the enactment of a particular citizenry and their practices, eliciting and encouraging 'local' participation. Moreover, it sheds light on a certain progressive project of democratic renewal – a radical political and cultural discourse as a counter-hegemonic frame of reference, and a language to build a diverse edge to the analysis (Sharma 2008). Such framing of empowerment explains further the nuances of the provincial, local voices, and how the solidarity is self-driven as a movement's initiative from 'below' (Cornwall and Coelho 2007; Sharma 2008; Newman and Clarke 2009; Ackerman 2011).

Contextualizing the AIDS Day rally sheds light on two important attributes of participatory democracy. On the one hand, it marks a space for participation while reimagining and renegotiating the elements of democracy and space-construction within a certain set of power relations. On the other hand, the rally installs the meaning of a performative social movement, wherein activists display a form of agency that gives a symbolic meaning to their identity and a discursive possibility to establish a new self. Further, participation in such a spatial context reflects Habermas' notion of the 'public sphere' as 'political' – an effective action that subsequently establishes democratic politics (Habermas 1989). The space here identifies discursivity in decision-making, allowing critical debates to be addressed and negotiated. Further, discursivity opens up a new political project and a pedagogic constellation of a new form of claiming; this efficacious political action ultimately reveals a symbolic way to highlight the community's cultural disposition and the style of their inimical politics of life (Cornwall and Goetz 2005).

Deploying Judith Butler's (1997) 'speech act' in the context of movement politics establishes a performative element by means of 'verbal enunciation'. Borrowing the idea from John L. Austin, Butler talks about 'illocutionary' and 'perlocutionary' performatives, characterizing 'speech acts' and 'utterances' that articulate deeper realities beyond the act – symbolic and social.[2]

Butler (2010) further suggests a theoretical framework evoking the idea of how the performative is manifested to constitute a new form of the subject in a context of extraordinary tension or during a period of crisis. She proposes to dismantle the Marxist approach to explain and understand community formation. Instead, Butler draws evidence, borrowing from the Japanese social theorist Maruyama Masao in her 'historical' and 'hermeneutic' method in articulating the formation of new subjects, and also Hannah Arendt's theorization of the 'plurality' of individuals. Maruyama suggests an established framework in explaining subjects as a form of 'performative agency' by means of a 'speech act'. This act of enunciation enables a new form of representation that breaks the earlier framework. Maruyama further brings to her argument the importance of enunciation as a performative exercise by means of which a new subject is formed, with a newer articulation of the social organization. Arendt, on the other hand, instates an outline that interrogates the 'plurality of humans'. She offers an insight to address a dialogic relationship within the 'self', appropriating human thought as essential to address the 'actualization' of the person. She further proposes the importance of language and speech as part of 'interlocution' – as the power of language binds people together, cultivates a social condition for freedom and provides legitimacy to exercise rights (Youdell 2006).

In line with these thoughts, the World AIDS Day rally provides an intelligible account of the discourses around the potential and the putative non-normative sexual identities. Their expression and the politics of claim emerges in the engagement of contentious politics as what Butler calls 'critical subversion' and 'radical resignification' (Butler 2004: 334). The street plays by sexual minorities and activists showcase the metaphor and a form of discourse that hold a symbolic legitimacy in terms of their utterance and the performative representation by means of theatre. They thus propose the importance of language and bodily (re)presentation as a means to subvert a particular political dogma, and to claim the other. And, the importance of this weaving together builds the trajectories of this performative politics that engages in a particular political process to contest the overarching social and cultural dynamics, further asserting a new form (Webb 2019; Reisch and Jani 2012; Garrett 2013: 588–589).

ANAND TRUST: *HIJRA* PARTICIPATION IN SEXUAL HEALTH PROGRAMMES

I was very keen to gather evidence and conduct an ethnography on the CBOs in Bombay's urban fringes. This led to a journey of two hours on a suburban train from the city's core to a place called Kalyan. Anand Trust is a local organization in a slum settlement in Kalyan which is working on health programmes self-initiated by sex workers. Their aim is very similar to Sakhiyani in Malad, but the former is different in that it does not have a fixed office space. But Nita's house becomes one every evening after the young girls return from their sex work. Also, unlike Sakhiyani, Anand Trust welcomes both female sex workers and *hijra* sex workers in their community-based initiative. Quite noticeably, there is a deep association between these different strands of sex workers. And such close association would imply that they are jealous of and yet cordial to one another. If any sex worker, be it a female or *hijra*, is facing trouble, they all stand in solidarity with each other. Nita and Rajni initiated this programme in their slum. All the sex workers in the slum are migrants from various non-urban parts of India. The land occupied by the slum has a long history over the past forty years; initially barren, the slum came into being when sex workers in the Kalyan region were thrown out into the fringes of popular settlements. Nita reminisced over bygone years recalling how in her early twenties, she was a victim of trafficking from Bengal. Now in her late forties, she smiles indicating, 'All the rest is history.' But her early life was one of dread, when Nita came to stay with her 'master', an elderly woman who owned the slum; the woman welcomed the young girls, pushed them into sex work and extracted significant sums from each. The trafficking had a deep nexus and involved the elderly woman paying a significant amount of money to pimps who brought her girls from around India or even Bangladesh and Nepal. Also, the pimps had sub-pimps closely linked to local contacts in various towns, cities and villages.

Nita inherited her master's house. The inheritance was a result of her loyalty, trust and services. The slum where she stays is not a designated brothel. Like Malvani slum, where Sakhiyani is located, Nita's neighbourhood is a poor people's settlement with mixed dwellers. Perhaps this intermingling of the population is a unique trait of Bombay slums. But it happens to be the case that there are several women living in the slum who have the same profession as Nita. They perform sex work in their own houses and they also go out for 'work'.

Rajni has a story similar to Nita. Both of them realized the need for sexual health awareness within their community. Unlike in brothels like Kamathipura in Bombay, where sexual health initiatives are civil-society driven,[3] because their slum settlement is hidden from activists' eyes and various donor agencies, they realized the need to create awareness themselves. During the early years, the expenses were collectively raised within the community. Nita is treated with reverence in her slum. Other women in the same profession were convinced of the plan and contributed decisively. With Nita's serious efforts and hard work, the government AIDS organization, the MDACS, started to fund their project.

During formal meetings, the 'outreach workers' (field workers) in the community speak candidly about oral sex, anal sex, safe vaginal intercourse and contraceptive usage. They have undertaken a survey in various slums in Kalyan where sex workers reside, so as to develop a support system for the community. Anand Trust encourages local doctors in their slum to undergo regular clinical trainings on sexual health. In return, the Trust funds the doctors, bearing the expense of their meal and transport for the day of the training. In a way, the trust aims to create awareness of their deep commitment to sexual health and well-being (Figure 6.2). Most significantly, reports and regular updates are forwarded to the MDACS. Further, office space is rented for project-based work such as employee training with technical knowledge in computing and software skills, interactions with AIDS educators, as well as for organizing formal workshops on sexual health. With time, their diligence has led to more financial support, enabling them to establish their own clinic for HIV testing. This caters to the needs of sex workers, nearby vegetable vendors and other blue-collar workers in and around the Kalyan region. Doctors and pathologists visit the clinic every Wednesday for check-ups; blood-test samples are collected and sometimes referrals are made in instances of clinical need to the nearby hospital.

Nita reckons that she has grown older and has no urge to engage in sex work. She believes that she has a mission in life to empower her peers and build awareness around rights-claims and sexual health. By means of her organization, she has realized the essence of dignity in her life. While sex workers are looked down upon and disrespected, she has eventually made a mark as an activist, and her leadership is much-praised and respected by the community workers and the government – so much so that Nita is often invited to attend meetings and symposiums at various significant forums in the country.

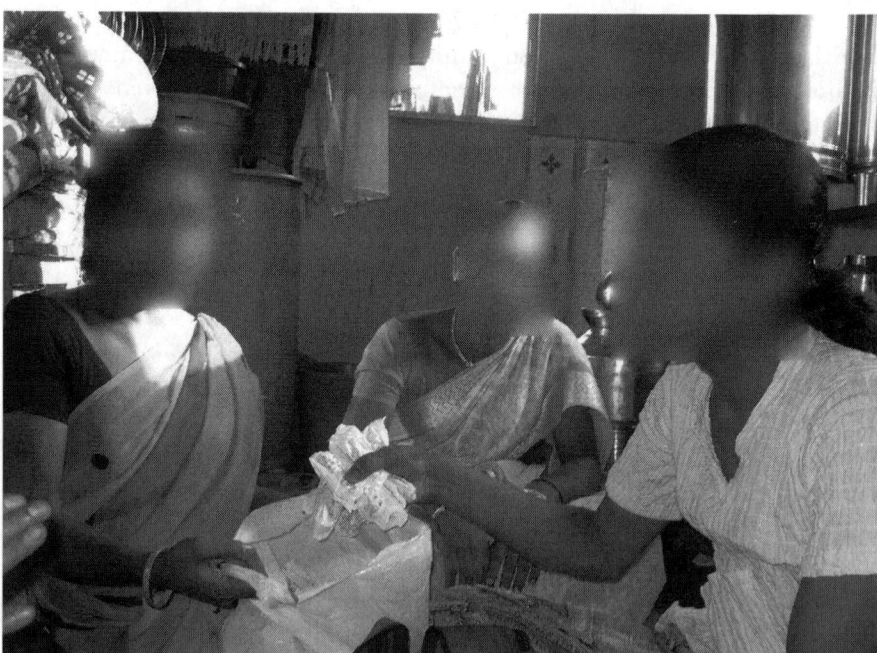

Figure 6.2   *Hijra* and *kothi* outreach workers from Anand Trust distributing condoms to other *hijra*s in their slum as part of sexual-health promotion activities
Source: Photograph by the author.

THE GEOGRAPHIES OF BELONGING: COMMUNITY PARTICIPATION AND THE EMPOWERMENT OF THE MARGINALIZED

Community participation is a strategic action that engages the marginalized population in political processes to create social change (Hilmer 2010; Saxena 2011; Franklin 2014). The main focus of these participatory practices is to cultivate and strengthen community relationships, so as to create community solidarity with the widespread involvement of its members. This ensures the central role of the population in addressing their problems and their self-representation (Patel 2011: 131–132).

Nita and Rajni's activism signifies the importance of 'local participation' (Chambers 2011: 165). This justifies the objective reality of community involvement in sexual and public health upliftment. Further, these measures generate ideas of 'development' that would build knowledge and skills as part of mutual support and strengthen solidarity. Robert Chambers foresees this sort of participation with higher degrees of 'equity' and 'democratic values' as likely to generate increasing capability for self-management and create self-reliance (Chambers 2011: 167–168; see also Leal 2011: 73–74; Tandon 2011: 90).

The mobilization of the marginalized population characterizes decentralized governance and an empowering strategy enabling the local people to engage in the complexities of their social conditions, critically examine their own struggles and make efforts to overcome them (Newman 2010; Eeva 2012; Franklin 2014). This particular instance represents empowerment of the marginalized population as a strategy of livelihood, further enabling the 'decentralization' of development programming (Tandon and Ranjita 2002; Edwards 2004; Tandon 2008). Decentralization also posits the establishment of the politics of skills and capacities, enhancing people's abilities, mobility and the subversion of social barriers in the 'redistribution of power' within and outside the community (Oakley 1995; Eeva 2012). In particular, Anand Trust and the shifting roles and identities of the *hijra*s from sex work to activism recognize the ways in which civil society articulates and mobilizes these populations to understand and determine their self-worth and public recognition (Correa and Jolly 2006; Eade 2007; see also Smith 1996). In other words, the act of self-empowerment with capacity-building initiatives attempts to equalize the 'interrelationships' between donor and recipient, and state and NGO, with focus on the role of the 'local' people with localized knowledge (Eade and Williams 1995: 19).

Invoking the relationship of 'partnership' may lead to 'bad governance', but capacitating or 'redefining' roles and responsibilities with further training and education of the local population leads to balanced competing claims within a good governance paradigm (Eade 2007). Furthermore, these sorts of governance claims with mutual accountability, professional responsibility and the distribution of power across stakeholders and partners gives rise to the possibility of dismantling hierarchies and oppression, repudiating injustice and building a governance based on respect, mutual sharing of knowledge and solidarity (Eyben 2006: 48; Seligson 1980). Anand Trust and the activists also showcase leadership development via means of civic education and technical skills. John Gaventa (1995) brings to notice how these forms of 'community action' through multiple forms of learning build skills and knowledge within the disenfranchised population, ultimately enhancing a social movement that leads to empowerment. It further adds to the useful understanding of the politics of citizenship as a method of 'political efficacy' and 'advocacy skills' (Gaventa 1995; see also van Houten and Jacobs 2005). The process involves the relationship between the social movement and the citizenry to build effectiveness, skills and competencies, illuminating empowerment through participation. Arguably, what Bryan Turner (2011) refers to as 'active citizenship' develops through means of meaningful participation in one's own community with an increased sense of community belonging (Milner and Kelly 2009).

This further echoes the notion of empowerment as an essential tenet of 'freedom' so as to bring change and to effectively gain more power from a situation of powerlessness (Rose 1996; Eeva 2012). The explanation thus far sums up the understanding of enhancing people's capabilities to participate in, negotiate, influence and advocate a significant institutional and organizational capacity allowing effective agency-formation. In other words, as Chambers (1994) argues, 'empowerment' that entails a bottom–up process – involving the marginalized population in social, political and territorial programmatic actions – enables full participation and a sense of self-enhancement and community building. Therefore, the emergence of these forms of governance are deemed particularly instrumental to a situation that enables (re)balancing the structures of power, strengthening firm accountability and collective action within civil society, the state and people.

Raastha: HIV Intervention in Malvani Slum

Malvani slum has a mixed population of various strands of people. A usual characteristic of Bombay slums is the deep sense of sociability between households.[4] And it also seems – unlike the social discrimination that we observe in middle-class neighbourhoods, or read about in the Indian media, newspapers and tabloids – the slum seems to be an exceptional version of society. To put it differently, people of different religions, caste identities and varied sex-based/sex(ed) identifications reside together in harmony. Illustrating instances of this, Geeta mentions how she often invites her female neighbours during Diwali. And during Eid celebrations, there are feasts in the slum where Muslim and non-Muslim families gather, eat and celebrate.

This spirit informs the various sexual health programmes implemented by CBOs in Malvani slum, charting an inclusive approach. Raastha, an NGO in the slum, works on sexual health and sex education. Raastha (meaning road or journey in Hindi and Urdu) believes in a positive spirit to awaken the population into awareness of sexual health and well-being. The men residing in the slum are vegetable vendors or owners of various shops including of meat shops. But many work in factories as labourers or in the Bombay dock and commute to their workplace by the suburban railway. Women stay at home and look after the children. Some assist their husbands in their shops, while a few women work as domestic help in the nearby middle-class neighbourhood.

Anand Trust is located in *saat numbar gali* (lane number 7) in Kalyan. The lane is close to the police station and is a two-minute walk from the main road. Raastha, another CBO in Malvani slum in Malad, Bombay, provides a community space for the slum population. The organization attempts to strengthen a community feeling within the slum dwellers through informal interactions, like chats, games and group-discussions, which ultimately seek to build sexual health awareness. These sorts of interactive mechanisms are referred to by Raastha as *khel khel mein* (in fun and games).[5] By means of 'games', the slum population are invited to attend workshops, health-based talks and informal schooling. These workshops are conducted in gender-stratified categories. Multiple forms of 'games' are played paralleling everyday gender roles of men, women and *hijras*.

The *hijras* were asked to attend meetings every Tuesday evening; Thursday afternoons were allotted to women, while men attended on Sunday afternoons. The games were supervised by a team of healthcare professionals who have been trained by the state initiative for sexual health promotion. *Hijras* were thrilled to attend the *khel khel mein* sessions on Tuesdays. A major reason that encourages them to attend is that Raastha serves refreshments at the end of every meeting. Shinde, the head of the organization, believes that refreshments are a good way to attract more attendees. Maintaining the theme of the workshop as the informal *khel khel mein*, the meeting started with laughter and amusement. The *hijras* happily exchanged information about their *pan*, or sex work. They amused each other with stories of their *panthis* (boyfriends or clients). Those dissatisfied with their clients criticized them using derogatory words. The supervisors taught them using demonstrations –

for example, the effective usage of contraceptives (using a model) or safe practices of oral sex (with the help of an ice-cream lollypop).

The oral sex demonstrations sought to convey safe practices so as to avoid STIs. The *hijra*s broke out in laughter. This allowed them to vent their own stories around sex, their different experiences of oral sex, and so on. The workshop also used other visual modes of communication like short films and documentaries about health and safe sex practices.

In the case of women's participation, Shinde recounted the difficulties and obstacles in encouraging women from the slum to take part in the workshops. He said that the Muslim population in the slum is significantly higher, and women's involvement in *khel khel mein* becomes a challenge. But the local government near the slum makes an effort to persuade the families and the male head of the household to give permission to them to attend. Sex education for them was strictly restricted to women trainers. It also covered contraceptive usage and safe practices around oral sex. The trainings were narrative-based, instancing cases from their personal life. But to reach this stage, it took several sessions to convey the significance of these workshops and to understand the momentum of sexual health and community health. During the workshops, female and male genitals were explained through diagrammatic representations. Further, they were made aware of safe sex practices, STI, HIV and AIDS. They were also taught about refusing unsafe sex and encouraging partners and husbands for HIV testing in nearby hospitals and clinics.

For men too the workshops were quite similar to the others. Films on sex education were shown, trainers conducted in-person demonstrations and community development practitioners delivered speeches on sex education, safer-sex practices, health-related detriments of having multiple sexual partners, and so on. The men were further familiarized with warning symptoms and encouraged to consult slum-based physicians and HIV-testing centres in the nearby government clinics for STI-related tests and blood and swab tests for AIDS detection. A few workshops were conducted by community health experts from the MDACS around sexual health, community development, hygiene and sanitation, slum development, domestic cleanliness and related issues.

CLINICS AND THE *HIJRA*S: PERCEPTIONS ON AIDS

Sruti and Madhu from Sakhiyani quite often visit a slum-based clinic in Malvani. Dr Patil owns the clinic and shares the workspace with his wife who is also a doctor. During the day, the doctor works in a nearby hospital as a physician, and from the evening till 9 p.m., he attends to patients in his private clinic in the slum. Sruti reckons that the slum dwellers trust the doctors' diagnosis, and both doctors are highly revered. Moreover, the traditional Muslim women in the slum have complete faith in the doctor and visit the clinic by themselves when suffering ill health. Their *aadmi* (literally, man; colloquially, husband) allow their wives to visit the doctor unaccompanied. His patients trust his medicine and approach the doctor for any healthcare need. At the same time, the doctors have high regard for all their patients – more so, their *hijra* patients. Sruti said that unlike other doctors she knows, both these doctors are decent and respect *hijras*. When treating his patients, the doctor prefers to administer injections in the arm unlike the 'other doctor' who often touched them inappropriately under the pretext of administering injections.

According to the hijras in Malvani, 'Dr Patil *bhagwaan hain*' (Dr Patil is god). Sruti and Madhu have been tested positive for HIV. Madhu visits Dr Patil for her monthly treatment (Figure 6.3). The doctor also provides her with vitamin tablets for free. He encouraged Madhu to adopt a healthy diet. Sruti and Madhu often visit government hospitals for ART. Sruti performs her job as an outreach worker in Sakhiyani very seriously. Her work is to make door-to-door visits in the slum and raise mass consciousness around sexual health. In addition, she distributes contraceptives, encourages HIV patients to undergo ART,[6] encourages sex workers to take blood tests and performs many other related tasks. She claimed that she has gathered vast knowledge about sexual health by means of Sakhiyani-led workshops. Her knowledge has enabled her to represent herself as a '*hijra* HIV-positive activist' and to share narratives to create awareness on safe sex practices. She pointed out that the *hijras* in the slum are yet to consider sexual health seriously. Many of the *hijras* in the slum neglect their treatment thinking that they would soon be cured by the local doctor. Some of them suffer deeply and die unaware of their condition.

Madhu and Sruti are, however, unhappy with the neglect of health which, they feel, is detrimental across genders. They approve the role of Sakhiyani and Raastha in cultivating sexual health awareness in the slum. Women from the slum discuss these issues with each other. As they sit on their front porches every afternoon after finishing their household chores, they talk over what they have learnt from Raastha workshops. Usually, mature girls and newly married women discuss these matters in whispers, even share giggles. But if news of the training passes on to their overbearing mothers or mothers-in-law, their visits to the workshops are discontinued for a while. Raastha health workers have negotiated with each family member, and even persuaded elderly women members to attend a special workshop so as to make them aware of the significance of these programmes. Gradually, Raastha-led health workshops have become established in Malvani. Girls and women visit Raastha or clinics to seek information or gain clarity when suffering unusual symptoms.

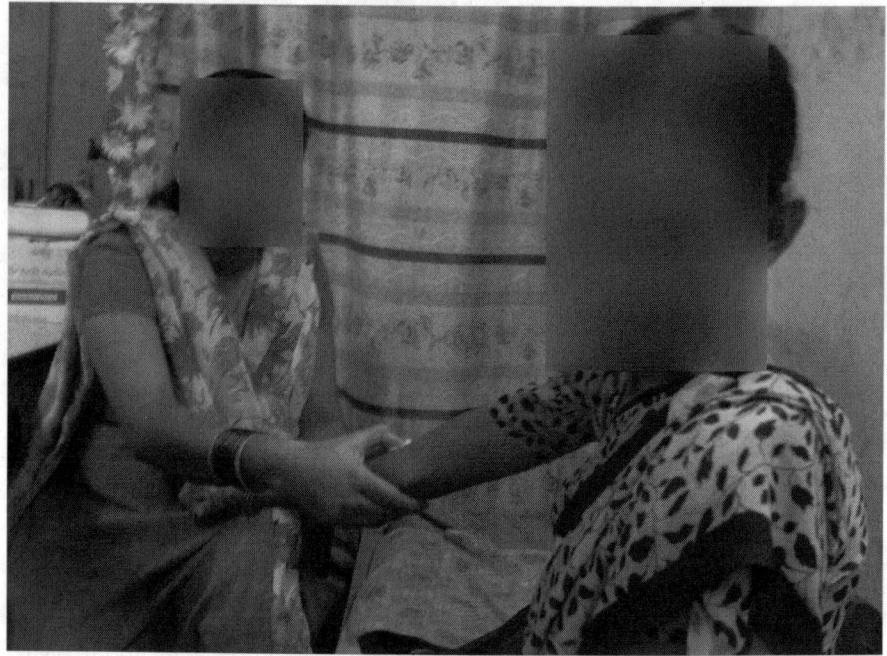

Figure 6.3 Madhu being treated by Dr Patil
Source: Photograph by the author.

PARODY, PERFORMANCE AND PEDAGOGY OF COMMUNITY HEALTH

The lessons based on the films and sexual-health demonstrations establish a form of 'community learning' as a provincial technique for the disenfranchised (Anderson and Zuiker 2010). This technique provides a frame of reference with a different way of imparting knowledge and community consciousness. Jean Trumbo (2000) suggests that 'learning' and 'communication' through visual representation depicts a form of symbolic rationality, leading to broader understanding and participation. Relevant in this context is Stacy Leigh Pigg's (2001) study of AIDS awareness creation in Nepal by the government and civil society, deploying sex education in a developing country through 'performative participation'. In her analysis, she specifies how AIDS organizations use multiple communicative methods in sex education so as to communicate national as well as global standards on community health. She further focuses on 'local' and 'social' understandings in the context of communicable diseases such as AIDS and STIs. Describing this situation as a 'contextual reality', Pigg explains the 'local' initiative of the NGOs in Nepal through demonstrative and diagrammatic representations of the male and the female body. This way of communicating biology and human physiognomy are referred to by Pigg as 'another' form of an 'effective participatory method', creating space for open discussions on sex, pleasure, as well as discontent around intimacy. Similarly, Renuka Bery and Sara Stuart's (2011: 151–153) study of women in rural Bangladesh highlights the importance of 'participatory communication' through the means of participatory videos that involve dialogue, group discussions, decision-making, awareness initiatives and the mobilization of the community. This sort of communicative practice aims to create change and to strengthen women's social and economic positions (Bartlett and Holland 2002; Gurtoo 2011; Kulynych 1997).

Khel khel mein echoes a similar method of participatory community development, reflecting the approach of the Global South. Films, parody and conversations as part of these development paradigms build a 'sensitive solidarity' to a particular programmatic approach in knowledge-making. Further, featuring parody reinforces 'political change': laughter enables the comic imitation of the 'original' deploying the critical function of utterances that are generally not allowed to be stated (Parker 2002; Borgerson and Schroeder 2005; Kenny 2009; Santone 2014; Collinson 2002). Parody thus exposes the original yet regulates its duplication. What appears to be serious is shown as ludicrous: 'the powerful is shown to be vulnerable, the unchangeable contingent, the enchanting dangerous' (Hariman 2008: 251). Butler's *Gender Trouble* (1990) posits the role of parody in the understanding of the power politics that plays out within gender binaries. This draws upon the observation of performances, interrogating the understanding of the 'real' vis-à-vis that of the 'unreal' – further negotiating the categories that one sees (Butler 1990: xxii). This act of 'radical contingency' via parody subverts the political meaning of authoritarianism, and in this case, the key role of the visuals and enactments is to democratize a public culture which once limited discursive public speech. These images decentre public morality, transforming a discursive demand and setting a counter morality for a larger project, that is, sexual health. Further, these expressions are a form of 'dissent' in the parodic performances, attempting to mobilize these imagined alternatives to act as a critical function for a particular political change (see O'Doherty 2007: 1999; Kavanagh and O'Sullivan 2007; Pullen and Rhodes 2013). Underlying *khel khel mein* is a framework that reveals the deeper truth, punctuated with 'laughter', which is essentially comical. But 'the laughter' constitutes a critical political reason that discloses a democratic renewal of rational–critical rhetoric mobilizing the disenfranchised for their health and rights claims. This act is perhaps a practice of cultural citizenship that employs an order of political participation with subversive potential through vernacular forms contributing to rethinking citizenship, political participation and civic engagement in a culturally-oriented perspective.

CONCLUSION

What can be concluded here is the need to revisit the beliefs and ideas of community participation that address the themes of gender, sexuality and participatory development from the standpoint of 'inclusion' (Cornwall 2011a: xvii). Viewing the idea of re-politicizing participatory development, this chapter fundamentally explores the changing relations of power and the increasing role of the community and the 'local people' who engage in change and transformation through various means of capacity-building (Gaventa 2011; Bradley 2012). David Moose's (2013) critique on the international development sector sees the donor–recipient matrix as detrimental to the non-West. Thus, the culturally specific community development in the non-West maps a performative participatory development that addresses reflexive practice-based research, strategizing 'symbolism' as a material form of practice. Films, performances, enactments and visual demonstrations install a form of knowledge-making, representing a micro-engagement and allowing the identification of dialogic processes to raise the critical consciousness of the actors. This further addresses a vantage point to establish a strategy for social change that is embedded in performative discursivity to enhance community development. Showing clear signs of reflexive reality and an increasing impact of community-led action, the chapter highlights social and class-based inclusive goals to promote (sexual) health, well-being, empowerment, upholding critical voices, and so on. However, there are internal struggles and moral ambiguities; this ethnography builds evidence of critical participatory or performative action research as offering a promising insight into the act of social change. Thus, the work holds together a context of 'difference' that deals with diversities in interactions and performances. As Chantal Mouffe suggests, 'Identities are always contingent and depend on specific forms of identification' (Mouffe cited in Cornwall 2011b: 218). Recognizing and reconceptualizing an 'effective participatory approach' could address the diversity of voices and concerns of minorities and 'strategize' power in a way that would essentially 'enable' and 'reconfigure' those unheard voices, further allowing the creation of a democratic and inclusive social environment.

NOTES

1   Besides *kothi* identities, who are effeminate lower-economic-and-social-status homosexual men, the MSM (male-sex-with-men) as a sexual category has been brought to the surface by the initiative of gay activists, health practitioners and similar advocates on the realization that male-to-male sexual activities are not only based on *kothi*, *hijra*, gay or other queer identities. MSM covers all male-to-male sexualities that are not only determined by earlier evidence on homosexuality but encompasses all sexual acts between two men. The advocacy around the MSM category further addresses 'un-notified' male same-sex relations that may or may not view or identify their sexual identity as gay or homosexual. It thus brings to light those unidentified male-to-male relationships that are hidden, and which policy practitioners have realized the need to identify for sexual health promotion.

These policy practitioners noticed that the lack of self-recognition or unidentified homosexual practices undermined sexual health interventions. Thus, MSM as a sexual category emerged in the HIV/AIDS programme and embraces the entire category of homosexuality: men who are effeminate (*kothis*), gay, *panthi*s, transvestites and the general male (masculine) population who practise same-sex acts, such as truck drivers, massage *walla*s (massage-giving men) and other unidentified men. Furthermore, the idea of MSM was reached by considering circumstances beyond the locations where homosexuality is commonly seen: public toilets, parks, prisons or the army. Several epidemiological research studies on truck drivers and sexual health have noted that truck drivers could be a vulnerable population for HIV/AIDS and STI contamination, given the fact that they run long-distance trucks and look for quick sexual intimacies in *dhaba*s or food joints beside highways. There are female and *hijra* sex workers who cater to their sexual needs.

2   Butler borrows from Austin the idea of 'speech act', or illocutionary performance, that significantly relates to the pronouncement of the state or law (Butler 1997). But, in this context, the movement or the rally evokes certain tenets of both speech acts (as affirmative) and perlocutionary speech as utterances.

3   Kamathipura is a neighbourhood in Bombay with a history of brothel workers who came to the city from eastern Europe in 1869. Kamathipura's initial residents – artisans, sweepers and construction workers – leased rooms or living spaces to brothel workers at low rates. It eventually became the largest brothel in India and is in fact today often regarded as Asia's largest red-light area – a low-income zone with tiny rooms separated from each another by thin curtains.

4   Malvani slum is organized on the basis of lanes. The slum is divided into lanes numbered one to ten. The lanes start from the Malvani police *chowki* (station) and subsequent lanes extend towards the beach. Some of these lanes – from *numbar ek* (number 1) to *numbar paanch* (number 5) run parallel to each other, while the rest criss-cross the former. There are raised drains that run through the *gali*s (lanes) and common toilets for residents; the toilets are assigned and used by designated households. These common toilets are *kachha* (non-bricked),

made with bamboo placed over the raised drains, enabling the refuse to be carried by the drain flowing beneath.

5   *Khel* is a Hindi word which means 'game'. *Mein* means 'within'. Hence, Raastha names to meetings as *khel khel mein*, conveying the meaning of promoting sexual health through games and play.

6   ART, or antiretroviral therapy, is the usual treatment for HIV. Biomedical research states that ART 'controls' HIV. The treatment involves two injections that are administered every month. ART doses and intensities vary from patient to patient. They on the medical condition the patient has and how the immune system works in each case. The medication has side effects too like diarrhoea, fatigue, dizziness, skin rashes, and so on.

BIBLIOGRAPHY

Abah, O. S. 2011. 'Voices Aloud: Making Community and Change'. In *The Participation Reader*, edited by Andrea Cornwall, 140–149. London: Zed Books.

Ackerman, J. 2011. 'Co-governance for Accountability: Beyond "Exit" and "Voice"'. In *The Participation Reader*, edited by Andrea Cornwall, 322–344. London: Zed Books.

Anderson, K. T., and S. J. Zuiker. 2010. 'Performative Identity as a Resource for Classroom Participation: Scientific Shane Vs. Jimmy Neutron'. *Journal of Language, Identity and Education* 9(5): 291–309.

Barnes, W., and B. C. Mann. 2011. *Making Local Democracy Work: Municipal Officials' Views about Public Engagement*. Washington, DC: National League of Cities, Centre for Research and Innovation. https://publicpolicy.pepperdine. edu/davenport-institute/content/researchreportmakinglocaldemocracywork. pdf. Accessed in July 2018.

Bartlett, L., and D. Holland. 2002. 'Theorizing the Space of Literacy Practices'. *Ways of Knowing Journal* 2(1): 10–22.

Bery, R., and S. Stuart. 2011. 'Powerful Grassroots Women Communicators: Participatory Video in Bangladesh'. In *The Participation Reader*, edited by Andrea Cornwall, 150–164. London: Zed Books.

Borgerson, J. L. 2005. 'Judith Butler: On Organizing Subjectivities'. *Sociological Review* 53(1): 63–79.

Borgerson, J. L., and J. E. Schroeder. 2005. 'Identity in Marketing Communications'. In Marketing Communication: New Approaches, Technologies, and Styles, edited by A J Kimmel, 256–277. Oxford: Oxford University Press.

Bradley, Q. 2012. 'A "Performative" Social Movement: The Emergence of Collective Contentions within Collaborative Governance'. *Space and Polity* 16(2): 215–232.

Butler, J. 1990. *Gender Trouble: Feminism and the Subversion of Identity*. London: Routledge.

———. 1997. *Excitable Speech: A Politics of the Performative*. New York and London: Routledge.

———. 2004. *Undoing Gender*. London and New York: Routledge.

———. 2010. 'Performative Agency'. *Journal of Cultural Economy* 3(2): 147–161.

Chambers, R. 1994. 'Participatory Rural Appraisal (PRA): Analysis of Experience'. World Development 22(7): 953–969.

———. 2011. 'Managing Local Participation: Rhetoric and Reality'. In *The Participation Reader*, edited by Andrea Cornwall, 165–171. London: Zed Books.

Cohen, J., and N. Uphoff. 2011. 'Participation's Place in Rural Development: Seeking Clarity Through Specificity'. In *The Participation Reader*, edited by Andrea Cornwall, 34–56. London: Zed Books.

Collinson, D. 2002. 'Managing Humor'. *Journal of Management Studies* 29(3): 269–289.

Cornwall, A. 2000. *Beneficiary, Citizen, Consumer: Perspectives on Participation for Poverty Reduction*. Stockholm: Sida.

——— (ed.). 2011a. *The Participation Reader*. London: Zed Books.

———. 2011b. 'Whose Voices? Whose Choices? Reflections on Gender and Participatory Development'. In *The Participation Reader*, edited by Andrea Cornwall, 203–223. London: Zed Books.

Cornwall, A., and A. M. Goetz. 2005. 'Democratizing Democracy: Feminist Perspectives'. *Democratization* 12(5): 783–800.

Cornwall, A., and D. Eade (eds.). 2010. 'Deconstructing Development Discourse: Buzzwords and Fuzzwords'. Warwickshire, UK: Oxfam.

Cornwall, A., and V. Coelho (eds.). 2007. *Spaces for Change: The Politics of Citizen Participation in New Democratic Arenas*. London: Zed Books.

Correa, S., and S. Jolly. 2006. *Sexuality, Development and Human Rights*. Stockholm: Swedish Ministry of Foreign Affairs.

Dean, J. 2009. *Democracy and Other Neoliberal Fantasies: Communicative Capitalism and Left Politics*. Durham, NC: Duke University Press.

Eade, D. 2007. 'Capacity Building: Who Builds Whose Capacity?' *Development in Practice* 17(4–5): 630–639.

Eade, D., and S. Williams. 1995. *The Oxfam handbook of Development and Relief*, vol. 1. Oxford: Oxfam.

Edwards, M. 2004. *Civil Society*. Cambridge: Polity Press.

Eeva, L. 2012. *Practicing Democracy: Local Activism and Politics in France and Finland*. London: Palgrave Macmillan.

Eyben, R. 2006. 'Making Relationships Matter for Aid Bureaucracies'. In *Relationships for Aid*, edited by R. Eyben, 41–56. London: Routledge.

Franklin, S. 2014. 'Race, Class and Community Organizing in Support of Economic Justice Initiatives in the Twenty-first Century'. *Community Development Journal* 49(2): 181–197.

Frazer, N. 1997. *Justice Interruptus*. London: Routledge.

Garrett, B. L. 2013. *Exploring Everything: Place-hacking the City*. London and New York: Verso.

Gaventa, J. 1995. 'Citizen Knowledge, Citizen Competence and Democracy Building'. *Good Society* 5(3): 28–35.

———. 2011. 'Towards Participatory Local Governance: Six Propositions for Discussion'. In *The Participation Reader*, edited by Andrea Cornwall, 253–264. London: Zed Books.

Gurtoo, A. 2011. 'Public Participation in Formal Deliberative Forums in India: Who Participates and Why?' *Journal of Asian Public Policy* 4(2): 201–220.

Habermas, J. 1989. *Structural Transformation of the Public Sphere*. Boston: Beacon Press.

Hariman, R. 2008. 'Political Parody and Public Culture'. *Quarterly Journal of Speech* 94(3): 247–272.

Haque, M. M., and K. Kusakabe. 2005. 'Retrenched Men Workers in Bangladesh: A Crisis of Masculinity'. *Gender, Technology and Development* 9(2): 185–208.

Hilmer, J. D. 2010. 'The State of Participatory Democratic Theory'. *Political Science* 32(1): 43–63.

Ibrahim, S., and S. Alkire. 2007. 'Agency and Empowerment: A Proposal for Internationally Comparable Indicators'. *Oxford Development Studies* 35(4): 379–403.

Kavanagh, D., and D. O'Sullivan. 2007. 'Advertising: The Organizational Production of Humour'. In *Humour, Work and Organization*, edited by R. Westwood and C. Rhodes, 235–249. Abingdon: Routledge.

Kenny, K. 2009. '"The Performative Surprise": Parody, Documentary and Critique'. *Culture and Organization* 15(2): 221–235.

Kulynych, J. 1997. 'Performing Politics: Foucault, Habermas, and Postmodern Participation'. *Polity* 30(2): 315–346.

Leal, P. A. 2011. 'Participation: The Ascendancy of a Buzzword in the Neo-liberal Era'. In *The Participation Reader*, edited by Andrea Cornwall, 70–84. London: Zed Books.

Lee, F. 2006. 'Collective Efficacy, Support for Democratization, and Political Participation in Hong Kong'. *International Journal of Public Opinion Research* 18(3): 297–317.

———. 2010. 'The Perpetual Bases of Collective Efficacy and Protest Participation: The Case of Pro-Democracy Protests in Hong Kong'. *International Journal of Public Opinion Research* 22(3): 392–412.

Lee, F., and J. M. Chan. 2008. 'Making Sense of Participation: The Political Culture of Pro-democracy Demonstrators in Hong Kong'. *China Quarterly* 193: 84–101.

Lubell, M. 2002. 'Environmental Activism as Collective Action'. *Environment and Behaviour* 34(4): 431–454.

Milner, P., and B. Kelly. 2009. 'Community Participation and Inclusion: People with Disabilities Defining Their Place'. *Disability and Society* 24(1): 47–62.

Mohanty, R. 2011. 'The Politics of Domesticating Participation in Rural India'. In *The Participation Reader*, edited by Andrea Cornwall, 265–280. London: Zed Books.

Moose, D. 2011. 'The Making and Marketing of Participatory Development'. In *The Participation Reader*, edited by Andrea Cornwall, 182–202. London: Zed Books.

———. 2013. 'The Anthropology of International Development'. *Annual Review of Anthropology* 42: 227–246.

Niemi, W., and D. J. Plante. 2008. 'Democratic Movements, Self- Education and Economic Democracy: Chartists, Populists, and Wobblies'. *Radical History Review* 102: 185–200.

Newman, J. 2010. 'Towards a Pedagogical State? Summoning the "Empowered" Citizen'. *Citizenship Studies* 14(6): 711–723.

Newman, J., and J. Clarke. 2009. 'Narrating Subversion, Assembling Citizenship'. In *The Subversive Citizen*, edited by M. Barnes and D. Prior, 67–82. Bristol: Policy Press.

O'Doherty, D. P. 2007. 'Heidegger's Unfunny and the Academic Text: Organization Analysis on the Blink'. In *Humour, Work and Organization*, edited by R. Westwood and C. Rhodes, 180–204. Abingdon: Routledge.

Oakley, P. 1995. 'People's Participation in Development Projects: A Critical Review of Current Theory and Practice'. Occasional Paper Series. Institute of Development Studies, University of Sussex, Brighton. https://www.participatorymethods.org/sites/participatorymethods.org/files/people%27s%20particiaption%20in%20development%20projects_Oakley.pdf. Accessed in July 2017.

Palacios, J. M. 2015. 'The Sex of Participatory Democracy: An Analysis of the Theoretical Approaches and Experiences of Participatory Democracy from a Feminist Viewpoint'. *Democratization* 23(5): 940–959.

Parker, M. 2002. 'Queering Management and Organization'. *Gender, Work and Organization* 9(2): 146–166.

Patel, S. 2011. 'Tools for Empowerment: Community Exchanges'. In *The Participation Reader*, edited by Andrea Cornwall, 131–133. London: Zed Books.

Pigg, S. L. 2001. 'Language of Sex and AIDS in Nepal: Notes on the Social Production of Commensurability'. *Cultural Anthropology* 16(4): 481–541.

Pullen, A., and C. Rhodes. 2013. 'Parody, Subversion and the Politics of Gender at Work: The Case of Futurama's "Raging Bender"'. *Organization* 20(4): 512–533.

Read, J. H., and I. Shapiro. 2014. 'Transforming Power Relationships: Leadership, Risk, and Hope'. *American Political Science Review* 108(1): 40–54.

Reisch, M., and J. Jani. 2012. 'The New Politics of Social Work Practice: Understanding Context to Promote Change'. *British Journal of Social Work* 42(6): 1132–1150.

Rose, N. 1996. 'The Death of the Social? Refiguring the Territory of Government'. *Economy and Society* 25(3): 327–356.

Santone, J. 2014. 'The Economics of the Performative Audience'. *Performative Research* 19(6): 30–36.

Saxena, N. C. 2011. 'What Is Meant by People's Participation?' In *The Participation Reader*, edited by Andrea Cornwall, 31–33. London: Zed Books.

Scoones, I. 2011. 'Ten Myths About PRA'. In *The Participation Reader*, edited by Andrea Cornwall, 122–124. London: Zed Books.

Seligson, M. A. 1980. 'Trust, Efficacy and Modes of Political Participation: A Study of Costa Rican Peasants'. *British Journal of Political Science* 10(1): 75–98.

Sharma, B. 2008. *Voice, Accountability and Civic Engagement: A Conceptual Overview.* Commissioned by Oslo Governance Centre, Bureau for Development Policy, United Nations Development Programme. London: Overseas Development Institute. https://www.undp.org/sites/g/files/zskgke326/files/publications/2008_UNDP_Voice-Accountability-and-Civic-Engagement_EN.pdf. Accessed in August 2017.

Smith, B. C. 1996. 'Sustainable Local Democracy'. *Public Administration and Development* 16(2): 163–178.

Tandon, R. 2008. 'Participation, Citizenship and Democracy: Reflections on 25 Years of PRIA'. *Community Development Journal* 43(3): 284–296.

———. 2011. 'The Historical Roots and Contemporary Urges in Participatory Research'. In *The Participation Reader*, edited by Andrea Cornwall, 88–91. London: Zed Books.

Tandon, R., and M. Ranjita. 2002. *Civil Society and Governance*. New Delhi: Samskriti.

Trumbo, J. 2000. 'Seeing Science: Research Opportunities in the Visual Communication of Science'. *Science Communication* 21(4): 379–391.

Turner, B. S. 2011. 'The Short History of Human Rights'. *Contemporary Sociology: A Journal of Reviews* 40(6): 678–680.

van Houten, D., and G. Jacobs. 2005. 'The Empowerment of Marginals: Strategic Paradoxes'. *Disability and Society* 20(6): 641–654.

Webb, R. 2019. '"Being Yourself": Everyday Ways of "Doing" and "Being" Gender in a "Rights-Respecting" Primary School'. *Gender and Education* 31(2): 258–273.

White, S. 2011. 'Depoliticizing Development: The Uses and Abuses of Participation'. In *The Participation Reader*, edited by Andrea Cornwall, 57–69. London: Zed Books.

Wojcieszak, M. E., Y. M. Baek and M. X. Delli Carpini. 2010. 'Deliberative and Participatory Democracy? Ideological Strength and the Processes Leading from Deliberation to Political Engagement'. *International Journal of Public Opinion Research* 22(2): 154–180.

Youdell, D. 2006. 'Subjectivation and Performative Politics – Butler Thinking Althusser and Foucault: Intelligibility, Agency and the Raced–Nationed–Religioned Subjects of Education'. *British Journal of Sociology of Education* 27(4): 511–528.

7

Cosmopolitanism

Rights, Citizenry and the Culture of Representation

INTRODUCING BOMBAY ALTERNATIVE SEXUALITIES

One evening, Sophie and Berry, two friends who work as make-up artists in Bollywood and the Bombay fashion industry, mentioned a gay community-based organization (CBO) in Bombay. Sophie and Berry are biologically male but effeminate in personality and dress androgynously. Kuldeep, my friend who is a fashion designer and make-up artist from Bollywood, initially introduced me to Sophie and Berry. Kuldeep often hosts dinner parties and get-togethers at his place to which I was invited on several occasions. Sophie and Berry spoke of an informal organization of gay men in Bombay, which provides a system of support. Sophie and her (she preferred to be referred to with she/her pronouns) friends are actively involved in this community. With the help of Sophie, I was introduced to one of her friends, Rohan, who is a member of this community. The organization is called the Bombay Alternative Sexualities, or BAS.[1] Rohan is of South Indian Tamil origin, belongs to the Brahmin caste and is a gynaecologist by profession. He is six-feet tall, dark and masculine in appearance.[2] I was invited by Rohan to attend their 'Saturday meeting'.[3]

The monthly meetings are held in Santa Cruz, a suburb of Bombay. The most popular way to reach the area is to take a suburban train to the Santa Cruz station. Rohan provided me with directions. He told me to go along the Western side of the station until I reach a place called the 'Main Avenue'. After arriving at the station, I took an autorickshaw which drove me through the famous S. V. Road, took a right turn to follow the Juhu Tara Road straight along until the third turning on the left, past the 'German Bakery Shop' until I came out close to Rizvi Gardens. The meeting was taking place at the home of Nilesh, a member of the BAS group. A fashion designer by profession, Nilesh seemed to be in his early forties and lived with his boyfriend.

The BAS's aim is to develop community acceptance and strengthen community identity by creating a forum in which relevant issues can be discussed. Meetings are also used as a sounding board for the interpersonal relationships of members. Most BAS members are from the middle- and upper-middle classes. They are well-educated and fluent in English. The membership includes not only Bombay natives but also a fair number of non-resident Indians. Members have encouraged the participation of vernacular-speaking gay men in Bombay as well. Among those included are speakers of Hindi, Marathi and Gujarati.

Rohan greeted me as I arrived at the meeting. He introduced me to Nilesh, the host of the event. His house was on the tenth floor of a multi-storey residential complex, a two-bedroom apartment with an extensive, rectangular living room. Both ends of his living room had an open space with glass windows, with a cool sea breeze flowing in, creating the perfect atmosphere with the twilight. Nilesh had also made a perfect choice of music – Jagjit Singh's *ghazals*[4] at a low volume. Four low-voltage electric lamps lit the room from each corner. Rohan added that they were expecting fifty members accompanied by their partners for the meeting that evening. The meeting was moderated by Rohan.

On that occasion, the discussion was about members' everyday experiences. They spoke about their relationships, emotions and love. Social possibilities were explored, as were techniques in overcoming social constraints related to their identity. The meeting was followed by a question-and-answer session. Questions were asked by various participants and answered by members based on age, seniority, occupation and their affiliation to the community.

QUEER COSMOPOLITANISM IN BOMBAY

This chapter broadly identifies and describes the qualities and characteristics of cosmopolitanism, including the discursive and material process of consumption, city and city-spaces, culture, identity, citizenship and politics. The chapter, in a way, attempts to recognize the geographies of the transnational locality with a new configuration of relationships within a specific subculture. The new form of cultural articulation and the public life that Bombay generates strongly resemble what Binnie et al. (2016: 8) call 'cosmopolitan urbanism' – reflecting a neoliberal cultural trait and a kind of urban life with a specific form of consumption, lifestyle and cultural sensibilities (see also Burns and Davies 2009).

Ulrich Beck's (2002: 17) understanding of cosmopolitanism reflects a radical constellation of flows of capital, people, images, identities, ideologies and structures, fundamentally developing a new form of consciousness. Beck reveals that cosmopolitanism brings into evidence a new situation of the world that fundamentally identifies a new form of modernity, triggering the conflation of varied projects of the capitalist framework – corporate reorganization, new transfer of labour and people, free trade – leading to a situation of cultural progress that transcends political boundaries to the domain of an interlocking institutional framework of people, region, space and context (Bell and Binnie 2004; Rantanen 2005; Leahy 2013; Mythen 2013).

Arjun Appadurai's (1996, 2001) anthropological study of transnationality, with special reference to Bombay, identifies an interesting trope of the logic of 'disjuncture'. In his essay 'Disjuncture and Difference in the Global Cultural Economy', Appadurai emphasizes the analytics of 'disjuncture', relating to the constant flow and movement of people in the new global cultural economy (Appadurai 1996: 32–33). It further adds to the idea of a radical shift to a larger transnational imagery that materially shapes the meaning of human action (Appadurai 1996: 44–45). Also, Appadurai's specificities in his analysis on 'flows' and mobilities in shaping relations profoundly conceptualize the importance of the concept of 'deterritorialization', breaking with the past, and a critical anthropological notion in his analysis of the 'new order', which is formed with the convergence of cultural styles, creates a global cultural uniformity (Appadurai 1996: 47). Further, the homogenization of Western practices develops certain ethics of transnational politics at the local level, where the rubric of modern life is significantly driven by market consumer choices (Inda and Rosaldo 2002: 22).

The growing cosmopolitanism of the city of Bombay is bounded by the post-colonial analysis of the city to its growing economy, characterizing a city with a sign of modernity that appeals to nativist contours of the image of the land, religion, politics, migration, business and trade on the one hand, and the growing presence of a multinational space that emphasizes the capitalist production and cultural representation of the city on the other (Hansen 2001; Dossal 2007; Vicziany and Bapat 2009; Ashcroft 2011). As Swapna Banerjee-Guha (2002, 2009) importantly articulates on the metropolises in the Global South in a time of 'neoliberal urbanism', it is the notion of 'market ethics' and the emergence of enterprise culture that notably comprise their neoliberal character as 'sovereign consumers' (see also Gooptu 2009).

This chapter has made an attempt to foster the new wave of scholarship on transnational politics and images of gay identities in Bombay, with newer visibilities and identity formations within the discourses of varied spaces, like protest movements, activism, fashion and the gay club culture. Svati Shah (2015) considers evidence of queer politics in India in the 21st century and the era of neoliberalism in charting her analysis of economic liberalization that forms the fundamental organizing rubric determining and shaping these identities and subjectivities. In her analysis, the sexual politics of neoliberalism in the Global South marks an era of emphasizing the intersection of identity and wealth, constituting a notion of 'privacy' and transmitting cultural dynamics from the West to the non-West. What she refers to here is the newness in the formation of sexual identity that reifies the class-based sexual politics in the analytical formation of urban queer subjects. Hence, the wealthy gay subjects in the Global South follow certain normative social forms that condition their 'aestheticization' of identity – forming a brand new kind of cosmopolitan connoisseur, reflecting the neoliberal agendas of hyper-consumerized material geographies and spaces (King 2007; Kong 2002; see also Binnie et al. 2016: 225).

Gay clubs, bars and other gay entertainment spaces frame the emotional geographies of gay space, charting the boundary and fixity of the apparent consumption rituals of these identity categories (Brewis and Jack 2010; Brickell 2000; Cattan and Vanolo 2014). The space becomes sociable with the complex performances of fun, dance, intimacy and pleasure – displaying a network of individuals who interact with a gendered class comprised of affluent, savvy, gay consumers who fundamentally construct a 'gay habitus' and are openly and comfortably gay.

Furthermore, the gay-solidarity movement and activism reveals what David Harvey (2005) calls 'cosmopolitan citizenship', adding to the evidence of the performative representation of certain political practices, either by means of street activism like gay parades or through the collective association of gay groups like community-based politics.

Valeria Cappellato and Tiziana Mangarella (2014) discuss the politics of movements, charting the importance of space and its negotiation in claiming 'sexual citizenship'. This occupies a particular space that conditions the expression of gay individuals and transgresses the hegemonic heteronormative domain. These movements further represent the politics of spectacle and visualization: a space that dominantly represents the heteronormative arena; the gay parade temporarily crosses the boundaries and destabilizes the 'normative' location of the public realm (Tan 2015; Ammaturo 2015). At the same time, community-based discussions add to the understanding of new participation in decision-making, a new ideology of equality that underscores the formal membership of individuals, adding to a form of collective sentiment (Field and Mattson 2016). Gay men's associations or parents and families of gay men meeting in solidarity provide evidence of organized groups, emphasizing democratic and sovereign tenets for empowerment and claiming rights (Burns and Davies 2009; Peck 2011). The dialogues of participants become a form of collective movement, a type of political participation that mobilizes gay individuals. It further deeply conditions the new movement politics and aids in a deeper understanding of citizenship – projecting a meaning of the transnational solidarity of the gay populace, where there is an overlapping imperative of the movements' ideology with gay citizenship rights.

CONTEXTUALIZING THE BAS

BAS meetings usually involve narrativized techniques in the sharing of experiences by members of how they negotiate their sexuality amongst family and friends. The political aim of the meetings is to bring the unspoken or repressed issues of gay sexuality to the forefront of public debate; these meetings represent a medium to uphold the implicit accounts of their sexuality, building solidarity, movement and support. On one such occasion, a meeting was primarily focused on sharing members' personal experiences of 'coming out' – a few members shared their experiences of how they came out about their sexuality to their family. They also mentioned how their families were initially apprehensive in understanding or accepting their sexuality and sexual choices. The families upheld the rationale of *bhartiya sanskar* (Indian tradition) which does not accept homosexuality. The initial confession of sexuality to the family remains hard; convincing and communicating with parents involve certain arguments borrowed from the West such as talking about activism, self-help groups, the media, film and television representations, literature, science, biology, and so on. But families argue about Indian values as not endorsing any male-to-male relationships or that a public disclosure would potentially bring *sharam* (shame) to the family. The concept of *bharatiya sanskar* in this context relates to the notion that Indian culture does not acknowledge gay identity. Societal norms within *bharatiya sanskar* utilize *sharam*, or shame, to maintain a strict sense of social protocols based on cultural demands. The reference to *sharam* reflects the society's conservative views and intolerance towards socio-sexual difference. Moreover, *sharam* attempts to maintain the status quo of the heterosexualized terrain – the hegemonic, procreative sexual choices which do not allow non-heterosexual choices as a way of being. *Sharam*, in other words, depicts a cultural tool and a nationalized apparatus to subdue the 'alternative', claiming to portray a form of prevailing cultural dogma which is popularly acclaimed and applauded. *Sharam* stands as the inverse code of cultural nationalism; gay sexuality in the context of Indian ideology is something non-Indian, obscene and not-to-be spoken of, something that does not ally with the cultural code of conduct and life of Indian(ness) (Sinha 1995; Gupta 2002; Bose and Bhattacharyya 2007).

'Coming out', on the other hand, generates a few important ideas on how the public discourse on homosexuality conflates with *sharam* and *bhartiya sanskar*, evoking the interplay of tradition and modernity in terms of cultural nodes, and highlighting a new form of discourse, so as to interrogate how the contemporary culture of Bombay is (un)receptive to same-sex sexual choices. It further builds evidence of how being gay in cosmopolitan Bombay is similar or different to that in the West, generating a view of the globalization of sexuality. Though the BAS projects the tenets of the Western metamorphosis of 'coming out' as a pattern of sexual confession, it also highlights how (local) Indian culture shapes self-confessed gay identity in the everyday context. And the emerging social class structure and the emerging new middle class in Indian cities bear evidence of the cultural conflation of the Western and the non-Western, generating a meaning of the gay subculture in the contemporary Indian context.

Furthermore, in many instances, families and friends of gay men attend BAS meetings as a form of support. Like 'coming out', the theme of another BAS meeting was 'parents and their voices'. The BAS also takes the initiative to bring families and friends together as a form of support and to communicate a broader understanding of homosexuality in terms of culture, biology and society. In this case, the involvement of parents resembles similar activist groups in the West, such as Parents, Families and Friends of Lesbians and Gays (PFLAG). This organization advocates social acceptance, a sense of empowerment and a culture of 'sexual' recognition and tolerance (Allen and Demo 1995; Patterson 2000; Broad, Crawley and Foley 2004). Understanding homosexuality in this particular social context echoes the development of homosexuality in a cosmopolitan space – that is to say, a space that allows and welcomes open discussion and dialogue on sexuality, sexual preferences and identity, and includes friends and family as a practice to 'mainstream' (homo)sexual choices and to break the notion of it as something repressed. Broad (2002) posits that family involvement in gay activism reinforces the broader social movement. Forums like the BAS therefore encourage a sort of participation and dialogic communication, generating inclusivity and increase in legitimacy of a pluralist cultural metaphor, further echoing the cosmopolitan traits of a city's space.

THE NEW MIDDLE CLASS

The emergence of the new middle class in India is based on the production of a distinctive social and political identity that lays emphasis on economic liberalization, consequent mass consumption and a change in lifestyle patterns (Varma 1998; Gupta 2001; Baviskar and Ray 2011; Fernandes 2006: 69). These sorts of class patterns feature a consumerist group related to a certain class formation, a perception and position of a social group based on capital and thus a structure of identity that critically articulates a new dominant ideology of a new India with new ways of seeing themselves and others (Chatterjee 2004; Fadaee 2014; Schindler 2013). As Leela Fernandes (2018: 29–31) contends, the actual material effect of liberalization leads to new opportunities for consumer choice and projects a restructuring of the labour market that has only benefitted with newer employment possibilities and rising salaries at multinational firms. This, in a way, has led to a sharp disparity in the class structure that has benefitted the 'new rich' and marginalized traditional public-sector employees (Goodman and Robinson 2013; Fadaee 2014).

The 'new rich' symbolize stylized middle-class spaces that identify with a cosmopolitan Indianized version of modernity. Their economic transformation and the socio-cultural transit from an indigenous, local context to 'post-Fordist' urban entrepreneurialism provides a representation of specific sites of socio-symbolic practices that form a new version of modernity with market-oriented commercial and new modes of claiming. The new middle class that is formed reorients exclusively to a new urban lifestyle, which Seth Schindler (2013) calls 'aestheticization and spectacularization' –relating it to the stylized middle class that has self-created their discrete class, identity and spatialized class politics, which are framed through an aesthetic appeal. The aestheticized component appears to be an important cultural logic in the rise of the new middle class in India that constitutes the wealthy, materially driven and aspirational consumer of (global) cultural signifiers, who can foreground their field of consumption – culturally and economically positioning themselves as part of global capitalism. The emergence of this new social group through their specific practices valorizes their identity through aesthetic self-appreciation, developing its own increasing boundaries. Neoliberal ideologies, foregrounding effective landscapes of lifestyles, further enforce a reconstitution of middle-class practices as an identity category (Anjaria 2009; Pow 2009; Ghertner 2012; Fadaee 2014).

The aestheticized praxis of the new middle class in India is further strongly established by English-language education seeking to cultivate an elitist cultural landscape. Aalok Khandekar (2013) draws evidence of class disparity in terms of the 'cultural leadership' of the newly formed middle class in India that links to his analysis of the post-colonial Nehruvian ideals of 'socialist development' – relating to higher education, coupled with the Nehruvian project of modernist India, that intensified English-language skills and the education system as the epicentre of post-colonial models of development (see also Chatterjee 2004; Fernandes and Heller 2006; Baviskar and Ray 2011; Brosius 2010). This particular educational specificity establishes a cultural ethic emerging in the new middle class in India since the post-independence period, which gradually emphasizes a substantive focus on those privileged social groups who have access to the consumption and affordability of English-education, thus forming hegemonic aspirations, developing their own strategic position and meeting their professional interests. Fernandes and Heller (2006) further note in their analysis how the middle class has gained a firm 'political identity' as a 'class in practice', gaining in importance through India's economic liberalization and globalization, which led to the expansion of private-sector enterprises and 'global processes of outsourcing'. This has enhanced the accessibility and employability of the English-educated middle class in these privatized strategies and technological superiority (Fadaee 2014), leading to India's modernizing aspirations to a brand new rhetoric of growth and development. But it also forms a 'hegemonic bloc' that with its liberalizing tenets threatens the subordinate class, 'the precarious section' – the not-so-rich – leading to an ostensible exclusion or the neoliberal othering of the city's spaces through a strategic framework (Fernandes 2006; Fernandes and Heller 2006).

These social, cultural and economic practices of the newly formed middle class in India echo the Bordieusian notion of 'habitus', which is shaped by the specificities of institutional regimes and lifestyles – articulating par excellence global class-based sentiments (Fadee 2014; Guarin and Knorringa 2014). Their class-position reaffirms a sort of hegemony and hierarchy that structure an increasing salience to power – rigorously practised through the immutable social structure of the historically driven class-formation in itself (Sridharan 2004; Varma 1998, 2004; Corbridge and Harriss 2000). This particular class structure lays claim to the specific class configuration, deploying its self-regulation through the production and reproduction of a certain cultural and economic power, which becomes the constitutive logic of their symbolic identity and representational character (Fernandes 2006). This is to say, what Fernandes (2018: 225) call 'class-in-practice' is a cultural phenomenon that potentially restructures the socio-symbolic practices of the new middle class in India to a logic of relentless identity-based mobilization and an increasing salience of its own material boundaries to form its own identity (Johnstone 2000).

The Indian middle-class identity and its material and symbolic construction relate to a form of 'world class-ness' that further designates the articulation of Asian queer subjects with its characterization of the newly emerging identification and cosmopolitanism, which essentially stylize, fashion and manifest the symbolic imagery of gay identity (Kong 2002). The post-colonial analysis of gay identities likens 'local homosexuality' to 'global gay formation' – proposing a trajectory of the material constellation of identities and categories with an epistemological framework of how capitalist expansion, the neoliberal economic market, trade, and so on, become the material forces enhancing dynamic interactions – with new cosmopolitan traits of class, consumption, pleasure, fantasies and a subject position internalizing the stereotype of 'global gay' identity (King 2007).

'LAKMÉ FASHION WEEK': THE BOMBAY FASHION INDUSTRY

Besides the gay space of the BAS, the other gay scenes in Bombay are linked to various beauty practices and certain embodiments of femininity – characterizing other shades of gay culture associated with fashion and the Bollywood film industry. This section of the chapter especially relates to Tom Boellstorff's (2005) scholarship on gay identities in Indonesia which illustrate the metaphor of an 'archipelago' that signifies the concept of unity and solidarity within differences. Based on this idea, Boellstorff asserts the various ways gay identities are represented yet keep a sense of unity of sexual representation. In relation to this, 'archipelago' connotes multiple viewpoints. Boellstorff notes that multiple gay and non-heterosexual desires and identities are formed in the same political borderland and yet maintain a sense of unified representation of 'gay' identity. The author further states that his concept of the 'archipelagic self' is about same-sex marriage and relationships among Indonesian gay men which are very similar to the cultural practices among Western gay identities. Thus, the differences in geography and people are overcome by shared values of identity, sexual practices and relationships.

In relation to this, the politics of the 'gay archipelago' could be related to the various gay identities and their representation in Bombay. These identities are negotiated in respect of individual choice and the different social, material and cultural consumptions that ultimately build their sense of 'self'.

Fashion is an important element in constructing everyday identities in Bombay. Kuldeep, my friend who is a make-up artist in Bollywood, maintains that the culture of fashion in Bombay always seeks something 'new'. He points out that people in Bombay want to wear those kinds of clothes and to fashion themselves in ways that do not follow a specific trend. They want to dress in a way that becomes a mark of difference. Self-fashioning becomes a kind of trend in itself.

Kuldeep is the official make-up artist in the Lakmé Fashion Week (LFW). The LFW takes place at the Bombay Stadium, near the Oberoi Hotel located by the seaside in the affluent Marine Drive area. It is the most prestigious fashion show in India, and the country's prominent fashion designers unveil their latest designs and promote them on the catwalk; male and female models from India and the West wear these designs. The event is held in March and October every year. The seven days of the show end with a grand finale where the best fashion designer of the season is selected.

A close association with Kuldeep allowed me to get acquainted with her other make-up artist friends and fashion designers. On the days of the LFW, I had the access to the green room, which allowed me to witness and understand the interpersonal relationships of various actors in the fashion industry. Ritu, a junior make-up artist, who works as one of Kuldeep's assistants, guided me to the green room with a gate pass. As I was waiting for Ritu near the main entrance to the auditorium, I saw famous male and female Bollywood actors arriving for the grand finale. Cameramen and newspaper journalists ran forward, taking photographs and trying to interview them, and they posed candidly in front of the cameras. Their presence at the show was in support of their fashion-designer friends. It was Sabyasachi night (Sabyasachi is an eminent Indian fashion designer, best known for bridal wear and embroidered apparel), and the models and make-up artists were busy. The green room resembled a cruise-ship corridor – a long passage with a door at each end and several suite rooms where the models changed their clothes. Inside each cubicle, there was a large mirror covering one wall. The mirrors were surrounded by high powered lights to assist the models to dress, do their make-up and get ready for the show.

During my visits to Kuldeep's house, I became friendly with Sophie, Berry and Rahul. They are sociable individuals, and most importantly, I liked their openness and honesty about expressing their sexual identity. Sophie and Berry use feminine make-up and jewellery. They wear jeans and feminine tops and a scarf around their neck. They have long hair falling to their shoulders. Berry prefers to tie a ribbon across her hair, but Sophie knots hers. Rahul wears male clothes and identifies as a masculine (gay) man; the three are good friends. In Kuldeep's house, I noticed that they were friendly with each other, and I overheard them speaking about the BAS, 'Gay Bombay', boyfriends and shopping, and even sharing stories about their sexual intimacies.

Berry talked about the sociable environment in the film industry, saying that in Bollywood neither homosexuality nor any sort of alternative sexual choices is problematic. While he agreed that there is a lack of explicit queer identities in Indian films, he rationalized this by saying that cinema is made as a form of entertainment for the common population, and Indian audiences would not accept homosexuality; such cinema would essentially end up less profitable and fetch little revenue. He explained that there are many gay directors and film artists in the Bollywood film industry who are not open to the public about their sexual identity.

During the LFW, Kuldeep had assigned two make-up artists to assist each model. There were fifteen models in the show and five different sessions, each with its respective collection of attire and corresponding make-up. Each session was presented by an individual fashion designer launching his or her creations on the ramp. The pressure on the models and the make-up artists was immense. The models finished each session on the ramp and ran to the green room to change their clothes and make-up for the next one.

Berry and Sophie were dressed in similar attire, wearing earrings and necklaces and behaving effeminately. They introduced me to other make-up artists in the green room. Some of their colleagues were gay-identified men and close friends. While working, everyone was talking to each other, including the male and female models; many of them were talking about the gay culture in Bombay, about their male partners, and so on. Their conversations were unrestricted, and the open discussions made me feel that the environment in the green room was gay-friendly; it had a certain comfort that allowed free talk and conversation. The female models did not hesitate to undo their dresses in front of the make-up artists, which surprised me given that displaying certain parts of the body is a matter of public shame in Indian society. The gay make-up artists were addressing the female models as 'baby', 'darling' and 'sweetheart'. The relationship between the models and the make-up artists was friendly; it projected professionalism on the one hand, and respect for each other's gender and identity, on the other. It highlighted a sense of how gender was conflated on lines of effeminacy, or being effeminate; the female and the feminine merged in a sociable environment and professional space – the fashion show. The female models and the (gay) make-up artists shared an emotional space of gender-affability, where the feminine or effeminacy becomes a part of the embodied self. These gendered characteristics superseded the importance of biology or the phallus – the inner gendered desire manifested the true self, in the context of which the models and make-up artists shared a very friendly relationship.

After the show, I had a chance to meet and talk with the make-up artists. Berry, Sophie, Kat and Pam became quite friendly and responsive and were happy to engage in conversation. Some of them identified as effeminate gay men and some not. With Berry and Sophie, for example, their denial of manhood lies in their feminine practices of beautification and certain body transformations, and the emotional association with their male partners as the feminine or the submissive counterpart in the relationship. I discussed some of these themes with Berry.

Me: Are you guys always so public about the beautification of your body? Do you always apply nail polish, and do you always wear ornaments?

Berry: Ahonaa, the way you are seeing me now, I am always the same in public. In my locality where I live, everybody knows me. My identity is not in the closet. My parents know me; I live with my boyfriend.

Me: Does your boyfriend consider you as a boyfriend? What gender term does he use?

Berry: My boyfriend considers me as 'baby' and 'darling' and 'doll' (smiling shyly). He of course does not consider me as his boyfriend. And, in considering my gender, he turns to the Hindi way of calling me 'uski' (hers) instead of putting it in English, although we always converse in English otherwise. He can never see me as a man, but neither does he call me 'she'.

Me: Is he comfortable with your male/female identity?

Berry: Ahonaa, he is very comfortable. If at all we travel in public, I sometimes realize that people are looking at me in a strange way. But it does not bother him. For the sake of my comfort and not to put him to shame, I have undergone laser therapy on my face. It definitely helps me to pass as a woman. But, you should know, Ahonaa, that one does not have to be 'woman' in every sense to 'feel' a woman. I am happy with my genitals; a penis does not bother me at all, so fair enough (smiling).

I also spoke to Sophie:

Me: Sophie, your name sounds pretty feminine; is it your formal name?

Sophie: Yes, it is. My Catholic background has helped me to take this name. I am happy that my passport records my name as 'Sophie', but my gender is ticked as 'male'.

Me: Apart from the visible marks of feminine dress and appearance, in what other ways do you beautify yourself?

Sophie: Ahonaa, you can see my long hair. I hope you appreciate it, because I do have long, shiny and beautiful hair. I always apply a herbal hair pack made of tea leaves, crushed banana, henna and other herbs for my hair. For my skin, I never use soap. I apply only herbal products. I take good care of my hair and skin.

Me: How do you relate your beauty to the beautification of the female models in the fashion shows?

Sophie: I feel I am one of them. When I see the (female) models walk on the ramp, I feel I am walking as a female. Beautifying them, making them look gorgeous is my job. When the audience look at them in awe, I feel I am being looked at and appreciated. I feel so happy.

Me: Do you have a boyfriend? How do they respond to you?

Sophie: I am hesitant about my gender identity. I consider myself a woman. Whenever I have sex with my boyfriend, I always try to hide it [penis] between my legs. It really bothers me. But [it] only matters during sex and not at other times. Me: Have you thought of doing anything about that?

Sophie: No, I am happy with it, really happy otherwise. I hate hair on my face. So I had laser hair-removal sessions at a skin care clinic.

The stories shed light on a form of queer identity in Bombay that projects the trajectory of a type of embodied femininity and self-representation. Within the larger project of 'fashion' in an urban metropolis, these forms of identities with feminine traits, behaviour and beautification, draw evidence of inner desires expressed in the way these make-up artists fashion themselves. As such, it can be said that the fashion industry reflects the modernization of queer identities – their body generates a new sense of agency that constitutes the material conditions of style. This means the stylization of queer bodies demonstrates a deep desire to consume and embody those new orders of (non-)surgical fashion, enabling individuals to express their aspirations and selves with a specific sense of style. Graeme Reid (2003) conveys the profound implication of the embodiment of fashion as part of gay lifestyles, demonstrating the particular significance of the interrelationship of economic capitalism and culture, that reinforces the aspirations and desires of modern consumer society (Gilman 1998; Orlie 2002; Lundberg 2010). Pun Ngai provides a greater insight into the relationship between capital and identity, highlighting the power of capital in the globalizing modernity as crucial in the creation of a form of 'political technology' – capital involves 'regulatory targets' to create heterogeneity and fluid identity projects with new forms of lived experiences and representations (Ngai 2005: 109). Thus, the consumption of beauty therapies by these queer identities in Bollywood and the fashion industry promises a new order of fashion with attributes of freedom indiscernible in their corporeal construction; their being as 'becoming' involves the blending and 'deterritorialization' of the gendered space of a man or a woman. Instead, capitalism and cosmopolitan culture conflate to a solid grounding of 'local' structures or an inherent sense of representation, interlocking in a symbolic–material association of the body, space and identity (Boellstorff 2007).

Further, their identity, in a way, does not fit well with either traditional notions of homosexuality or transgenderism or the modern understanding of 'gender passing' or transsexuality. Instead, it builds a meaning of (non-)locality of the reified bodily signifier of a queer identity, where their inventiveness relies on their very own sense of fantasy, desire and 'becoming'. Moreover, their identity occupies a discursive space of a continual symbolic image of queer sexuality that is a particular site for the production of modernity in Bombay. In other words, these specific identities fragment and transgress the solid grounding of both traditionalism and the Western notions of gender(ed) hierarchy, essentially formulating a centralized manoeuvring of identity categories. Instead, their identity proposes an aesthetic nonchalant habitus of the bodily metaphor and mobility, wherein embodiment of beauty and fashion is the flexible response to the sharp ethno-politics of corporeal and personal liberation.

Voodoo

After the fashion show, the team of make-up artists decided to visit a nearby restaurant for dinner. Kuldeep was happy with the hard work of her assistants, and according to the fashion designers, the show was immensely successful. Sophie and Berry planned to visit Voodoo, a nightclub, for dance and recreation. Voodoo was not far from the fashion show venue.

Sophie explained that Voodoo was the first gay club in India. It was established in the mid-1990s. She added that gay-identified men from other cities also visit the club; they socialize among themselves and form sexual and emotional partnerships there. According to her, the club does not categorically claim to be only for gay people, but it is an unspoken and widely believed gay space for club goers in Bombay.

During the visit, Sophie spoke about the subtle expression of gay identities, sexual intimacies and relationships in the club. Inside the club, people were amicable – either dancing, consuming alcohol, chatting or sitting in groups. Sometimes, there is police scrutiny; they are aware of the club as a place for gay socialization. The club maintains secrecy about its activities due to homophobia and the stigma attached to homosexuality in India.

Sophie also said that Voodoo is the first gay nightclub in India. As we walked towards the dance floor, it was initially quiet, visitors were few and soft music was playing in the background. The club is located in an affluent part of South Bombay. The entrance to the club does not shout 'club' unlike other nightclubs in Bombay. Usually, nightclubs in the city are very appealing from the outside, decorated with twinkling bulbs and attractive signboards. The entrance to Voodoo is a small wooden door; there is no board outside with the club's name on it. A man sits at a table at the entrance selling tickets.

Gradually, visitors started arriving as it approached midnight. They were both male and female. The women looked young and were dressed in tight jeans and tops. Some of their tops were short and tight-fitting. It seemed to me that these women deliberately chose to wear such clothes to highlight their breasts. They also applied loud and intense make-up – bright red lipstick with lip gloss on top. They wore eyeshadow and eyeliner to highlight their eyes and glittering jewellery – earrings and necklaces – which together created a flamboyant effect. Their unusual clothes and exaggerated make-up suggested that these female visitors had a particular purpose in visiting the club. On closer observation, I noticed their gradual intimacy with men who were also visitors to the club. They sat on men's laps and smiled enticingly at other men. By doing this and flaunting their long hair and pouting their glossy lips, they sought to draw attention to themselves.

Time passed and the dance floor filled up. A few men were standing at the side, leaning against the wall. There was something strange about the way they were standing – they all seemed to be touching the wall with their right hand. Sophie hinted at the sexual overtones of their postures, indicating that they are seeking male partners. If a man is successful in getting a partner at the club by his gestures and eye contact, then both of them leave the place and continue their conversation outside. Contact was developed through bodily postures and behaviours – the means of establishing male-to-male relationships at the club. It was expressive yet elusive; the sexual undertones at the club were highly discrete, and yet the fact that it was a space for gay recreation was highly evident from the behaviours and mannerisms of the visitors, relating to their confidence in and knowingness of the space and their actions.

The neighbourhood where Voodoo is located is populated by army hostels and the residences of Bombay-based defence officials. The visitors too had the stereotypical look of army personnel – strongly built men with crew-cut hair and an assertive way of walking. They did not necessarily resemble gay-identified men but were into homosexual activities. Sophie confirmed that the club is the best possible location for gay men to meet partners for sexual intimacy. But, unlike the gay club culture in the West, which is open and frank, Voodoo highlighted a space of gay recreation and fantasies known only by word of mouth. She further added that the club washroom is a space for quick sexual intimacies, but the usual practice is for partners who meet each other to leave the club together. I also recall how Sophie had spoken about the gradual emergence of a homosocial environment in Bombay. According to her, recent times have witnessed the gradual emergence of gay clubs and pubs in Bombay. Gay identity is opening up rapidly in India, and the demand for club and pub culture is also increasing.

Sophie often visits these clubs and parties with her friends. Besides Voodoo, she visits Dharma and Banana Nights which are more to her taste as they are more contemporary and urbane. She described the visitors to these clubs, who identify as gay men. They wear modern trendy clothes – branded jeans and t-shirts. But the recent upsurge of gay clubs in Bombay adds to the class-based consumption of recreation and socialization, in keeping with the idea of mostly the upper middle class and upper economic strata of the city's population visiting these clubs. Unlike Voodoo, which has a history of subtle gay club culture, the recent 'gay nights', or clubbing for gay men, are organized with gradual visibility and even acceptance of same-sex sexualities and culture. Clubs like Dharma and Banana Nights project an open and comfortable gay atmosphere where men are free to talk and behave as they wish. Being 'gay' has become a 'style' and 'fashion' in the urban culture in Bombay, but amidst upper-class society. The gay club highlights the dramatic display of clothes, fashion and style, where English is the medium of communication, and consuming expensive drinks symbolizes their style. Furthermore, it evidences 'boyfriend culture' as these gay men visit clubs mostly with their boyfriends, giving the impression of partnership and evoking a sense of a very common practice of gay-identified men in upper-class society.

A nightclub like Voodoo evokes a subtle representation of gay identities, where gay men are not open about their orientation. The club also signifies a 'pick-up joint' for gay men to meet sexual partners. On the other hand, Banana Club and Dharma signify gay cosmopolitanism where gay men visit with unconcealed identities. Sophie also talked about the various strands of gay identities that she has seen in these clubs. Paul Boyce suggests that the gay club culture in the city of Calcutta projects class-based male-to-male sexualities, giving the impression of being upper middle class, wealthy and Westernized. Boyce also adds that these male-to-male sexual identities, which revolve around notions of 'sexual orientation', are invasive. Rather, in his analysis, homoerotic practices and the interconnectedness of the homo-hetero(sexual) articulation that commonly navigates as well as evades gay spatial construction are in evidence in nascent gay spaces. Voodoo epitomizes an image of homoerotic sociability similar to Boyce's interpretation of a gay bar in Calcutta (Boyce 2007), generating a sense of masculinity and gay culture – alternative modes of non-exclusivity of gay identification where macho men are in search of homoerotic practices in the concealed gay spaces of the city. The machismo culture of the potent (army) men in the gay scene of Bombay gives expression to the identity, interconnectedness and practices of a straight-gay paradigm that navigates the dominant familial life and the heterosexual boundaries, employing gay cultural and erotic practices (Boyce 2007; Misgav and Johnston 2014).

Further, in this analysis, the body metaphor of masculine images in club culture creates an explicit idea of a hyper-masculine image and an expression of erotic friendship clad in the 'leather' gear of a specific cultural imagery of a man. Mark Graham (1998) in his study of the gay leather culture in Stockholm recounts evidence of leather bodies as a site of homoerotic representation. Graham contends that these bodies appear to have a heterosexual identification, which renders invisible the cultural nodes for the understanding of gay-ness (see also Shugart 2008). Yet, while this invisibility is unquestionable, as an 'adorned' body which does not 'meet' the category, it projects a libidinous site in the context of gay sociability. Similarly, the gay eroticism in Voodoo emphasizes a new form of appropriation and of gay eroticized masculinity that eventually draws the importance of spatiality of the community's interaction as a form of gay space. Their particular appearance, behaviour and clothing essentially chart the boundary; the performativity and images reveal a driving force of maleness and desirable bodies that are devoted to masculine enthusiasts and an erotic appropriation in gay territory.

Further to this argument, is Jeffrey Weeks' (1985: 191–193) articulation of gay lifestyles that are oriented to the social, political and economic conditions of popular society: crafting an analysis of the significance of modernity and the cosmopolitan urban experience of consumption. The emerging 'new cosmopolitanism', which Mary J. Kehily and Anoop Nayak (2008) refer to, evokes the importance of the cosmopolitan form of belonging in a postmodern lifestyle that is socially constructed with the interplay of emotions, space and spatiality – the 'club' represents the hybridization of the public–private space where new identities are configured with new encounters that are intimately connected to emotional space (Cattan and Vanolo 2014). The spatialized mobility in the era of neoliberalism builds a curious hybrid urbanity of non-Western cities into a globally significant multicultural and international imagery of hyper consumption; gay nightlife evokes an emerging sense of cosmopolitanism that links a specific form of class to a new political economy of self-representation with putative consumer choices of aesthetics, desirability and the cultural image of body (Graham 1998; Shugart 2008; Benedicto 2008).

Banana Club and Dharma in Bombay render the metaphor of the racialization of gay culture in the non-Western perspective, patterning the consumption of a particular class and identity category with the formation of agency and subject construction. The clubs characterize the emerging urbanity within the city's space, with more expansive symbolic representations of the practices evolved with the trajectory of the agency's interplay with space and spatial construction (Burns and Davies 2009). The new spaces created with the development of urbanization point to the shifting emphasis on the politics of capital as linked to space – representing how the spatial location of capital, production and consumption structures the relations of agency in the spatial context (Low 2016). In other words, the gay club culture postulates an exemplary feature of modern urban life that emulates the dynamics of an elitist style, captivating the imagination of new urban space with the phenomena of socio-spatial units that sexualize style, status and power. These identities importing the more expansive, emerging consumer agency allow their embodiment and performances as 'presentable' through the perspective of how the body is displayed. The notion of the homogenization of consumption reduces national or local cultural differences but embodies capital-driven intercultural traits that reify the gay urban elites (Dossal 2007; Burns and Davies 2009; Ashcroft 2011).

Svati P. Shah (2015) contends that 'queer liberalism' in India charts the framework of the nation's economic potential that allows the marking of a new era, thinking of a 'geopolitical' and economic power that eventually leads to the supremacy and control of social norms and identity categories. Shah's further contention on 'queer liberalism' emphasizes bourgeois-centric private spaces and a framework that epitomizes sexual politics in the culture of neoliberalism – an economic power that hegemonizes gay sociality, commercializing sexual and erotic life, entertainment and the privilege of only the elite to construct a sense of belonging to a postmodern Western cultural form. This further adds to Bobby Benedicto's (2008) notion of 'gay globality' that posits the cultural appropriation of American culture with a racialized trait and cultural fetishism of 'White privilege' thus imposing a gayness to a pattern of consumption and aiming to generate a stereotypical display of identity and self-construction. Further, non-Western homoerotic culture extends a critical role to the tacit nexus of identity and capital, thus framing the discourse of how globalization extends queering as a form of capitalist subjects. 'Trendy clothes', 'boyfriend culture' and trajectories of fashion and style among gay youths in contemporary Bombay reflect what Helene Shugart (2008) terms the 'metrosexual moment', tracing the commercial constellation of identity formation through the self-fashioning of the body and adornment that builds an objectification and identification of the logic of organized homosociality (that is, club culture). Configuring these factors, feminized patterns of behaviour mark an erasure of a necessary premise to establish a 'strategic civility' that is ostensive to the explicit acknowledgement and reinforcement of sexuality, performance and the tacit formation of a class-based urban subculture.

'QUEER AZADI': THE BOMBAY GAY PRIDE

The principal slogan of Bombay's gay pride parade was 'queer *azadi*', or 'queer freedom'. [5] The parade took place on 16 August 2008. According to activists, this date was scheduled to coincide with Indian independence from the British Raj, highlighting the fact that political independence has failed to bring the real essence of independence to certain Indian subjects. Organizers wanted to showcase to the Indian public that Indian homosexuals are facing the same absence of freedom – a sense of being colonized in the shackles of the government, the culture and the people, that impedes the expression of their inherent sense of being and identity. Bombay gay activists stated that India is still influenced by colonial laws that criminalize homosexuality.[6] Much like India under the British Raj, their reasoning was that the gay community has still not received its independence. On that note, the activists sought to symbolically claim sovereignty and freedom for homosexuals, demanding citizenship and human rights. The rally began at the Azad Maidan in South Bombay, contributing to the historical and political context of the demonstration. The Maidan is symbolic of India's struggle for independence against the British Raj. On that day, the Maidan again had a similar political connotation as it admitted the gay rights rally to Bombay city.

The rally was scheduled to start at 2 p.m. Activists, gay groups and CBOs joined the protest. Besides local groups in the rally, there were international non-governmental organizations (INGOs) represented as well, as were Western gay activists and friends and families of the LGBT community. In addition, it was attended by a few celebrities from Bombay such as Bollywood actors, film directors and fashion designers. Like gay pride rallies worldwide, the Bombay rally also used the rainbow flag as a universal sign of solidarity. The participants were waving their flags in order to establish solidarity and unity along lines of their sexual differences. Rally participants also wore badges and carried signs with quotes, such as 'Gay rights are human rights', 'Phek do phek do, 377 phek do' (Abandon it, abandon it, abandon 377), 'We are queer, we are here', and 'I am not gay, but my best friend is; I am here to support'. Most of the participants were dressed in symbolic costumes.[7] Among them there were supporters collectively saying, 'I am proud to be gay', while others exclaimed, 'Lesbian rights are human rights'. The *hijra* community carried banners in English and Hindi: 'Hijre insaan hain; unke adhikar insaan ke adhikaar hain' (*Hijra*s are human beings; their rights are human rights).

Members of all cultures and subcultures attended the rally: *kothi*s, *hijra*s, gay men, bisexuals and lesbians. It showed the diversity of class within this culture. The participants were rich, poor and middle class, evident from their dress, mannerisms and behaviour. Various Bombay-based academic institutes participated in the rally, adding a note of gravity to the rights-based movement. But there was no particular mode of expressing the politics of identity (in the form of rage or otherwise), as articulated by the multiplicities of sexual identities in the rally. For instance, the *hijra*s strikingly brought their *dholak*s (indigenous drums) that they use during *badhai* (blessing ceremonies); they played their *dholak*s as a form of resistance and danced in rhythm. In the same rally, the gay and the lesbian community were busy chanting slogans. The rally exemplified a social movement that mobilized the participants with a sense of unity, despite the differences in terms of their class and representation – a collective motive to establish their sense of identity with a political purpose. The Bombay police considered it necessary to keep a close eye on the rally and protect participants. The activists also remarked that there could have been obstruction and interference from Hindu and Muslim religious fundamentalists whom the LGBT community regards as a cause for concern. Deepak, a young activist, asserted that police protection was indispensable.

The Indian media covered the event, while rally participants walked along the roads of southern Bombay. The intensity of the media coverage was immense. There were photographers everywhere – in the streets, standing on cars and on rooftops. Activists reported that 2,000 people participated. There were children on the roadsides and young adults from nearby slums who started walking with the gathering, not knowing its significance. The rally ended at the Chowpatty beach; activists delivered speeches. They remarked that this year was significant. There was a great possibility that the Delhi High Court was going to decriminalize homosexuality, which would affect the entire country. This encouraged the crowd to shout louder and stronger: 'Phek do, phek do, 377 phek do' (Abandon it, abandon it, abandon 377). The parade seemed to be a form of resistance and also a culture of representation – the ways in which the queer population of Bombay, who in the everyday are unable to express their sexuality and identity, are able to be open and expressive as they walk in the rally and be what they desire to. The slogans seemed to add an impetus to the rally, coupled with the element of fun – expressing themselves and the feeling of solidarity and confession to a larger audience seemed to create delirium and ecstasy (Figure 7.1).

The pride rally in Bombay is in line with Kath Browne's (2007) depiction of the geographies of emotions that are constituted in a particular space, bringing into context the performative dimensions of space, those practices that evidence the political understanding of social relations. The pride rally reveals the spatial politics of the intersection of queer sexualities in heterosexual spaces, highlighting the significance of spatialities (Halberstam 2003, 2005). It cuts beyond the public–private realm and disrupts the heterosexualization of public spaces. It further brings in the complex conceptualization and the discursive importance of 'politics' and 'pleasure' that place the material geographies of queer marginalization in a specific spatial context. That is to say, the hegemony of heterosexualized spaces is subverted, as 'street' plays present transgressive possibilities of the centrality of emotions, expressions, fun, politics and hedonism (Broad 2002; Brighenti 2007). Kath Browne's (2007) further assertion of the parade as a 'collective walk' and a performative practice relates to carnivalesque playfulness and the fluidity of sexuality, which is evident from the various carnivalesque displays in the parade (see also Monro 2005).

Figure 7.1   'Queer Azadi' – the Bombay gay pride parade in 2008. Geeta (left), Leela (middle) and a *hijra* named Mumtaz (right) holding the 'Queer Azadi' banner.

Source: Photograph by the author.

In the context of Bombay, 'Queer Azadi', the playing of *dholak*s and gay men cross-dressing in colourful flamboyant feminine clothes, long wigs and loud make-up present certain non-heterosexual displays, evoking a site of disruption that they project through a form of playfulness. The sounds of *dholak*s and the visual metaphor of the flamboyant gay men mark the ambiguity of the playful celebration in the busy streets of Bombay. Again, the celebratory cultural atmosphere that navigates through heterosexualized spaces conveys a certain sexual expression, lending a particular meaning and role to the parade. This further evokes how the pride march represents a mechanism of claiming citizenship rights. This sort of political claiming is reframed through the spatial dynamics of the territorial locale of urban spaces, opening up the tacit interconnectedness of space as 'political'. James Holston and Arjun Appadurai's celebrated scholarship on 'cities and citizenship' evokes the fundamental meaning of citizenship as claiming the ideological tenets of participation and universality, further signifying the performance of its citizens, giving centrality to sovereign power in the territorial location of streets and public spaces (Appadurai and Holston 1999: 9–12). The authors point to the relationship between people and cities as political – its spaces signify the different relationship of local, national and global processes, evoking a politics of democracy. This further entails a meaning of the hybridity of class, race or other forms of difference, bringing in the ideology of universal equality (Holston and Appadurai 1999).

The gay parade in Bombay builds a structure of certain global cultural processes of citizenship framing an organized social practice via the mechanism of the march. This sort of practice forms evidence of identity politics, wherein differences bring in the culture of solidarity and challenge the basic principles of 'liberal citizenship', thereby reconstituting a social movement based on democracy, mobilization and empowerment (Bertone 2013; Cappellato and Mangarella 2014; Ammaturo 2016).

Their chant for *azadi* (freedom) further adds to the conditions of their lifestyles and the everyday politics of life – *azadi* forms the foundation of their claiming of sexual citizenry, urging for a cultural transformation that aims to destabilize homophobic processes and to redefine sexual rights. It further adds to a political agenda of integrating marginalized communities, in a way claiming a national identity in the process. The march further reflects a profound morphology of the radical membership of local, national and global forces of queer identities and alliances that constitute citizenship with transnational forces and yet expand and erode the rules and meanings of local and national practices, conflating the streets and the city's spaces as territories of a political movement.

Conclusion

This chapter offers an insight into the new consumer culture and the new ways in which cosmopolitanism has been portrayed in Bombay, displaying a complex melange of seemingly diverse queer identities and their everyday experiences. Taking into account the broader political economy of cosmopolitanism, the chapter sketches class-based phenomena as offering a structure of knowledge with a particular sociocultural norm that obeys a particular form of urban lifestyle, a specific type of consumption and the desire to be 'cosmopolitan', constituting a complex interplay of sexual and bodily imageries and ways of representation within various strands of male-to-male sexualities in Bombay. Bobby Benedicto (2008) attempts to deliver the idea of 'capitalist imperialism' as a Western formulation that also reflects in the gay culture in the non-West: 'a growing homogenization of consumption' formulating a political economy of 'global culture' in terms of experiences and the homogenization of the identity category, simply based on the consumers' cultural context. The desires and aspirations of the cosmopolitan gay culture in the city's spaces are caught up within the power matrices of class. Benedicto's further assertion, borrowing from Homi Bhabha's interpretation of race, proposes an understanding of a class-based subject encounter with 'White stereotypical race-ness': internalizing the subject position of class hierarchy and superiority of First-World White privilege in the cultural and everyday dynamics among a limited section of the Third World that primarily articulates a fierce sense of difference (see also Bhabha 1998).

NOTES

1   The description of the Bombay Alternative Sexualities (BAS) is based on my extensive ethnography of an urban gay group or association of middle-class and upper-middle-class gay men in the city. MAS is the pseudonym of the actual organization. Naming it MAS closely relates to their ideology of seeking to develop strong community sentiments and solidarity, joining hand-in-hand with like-minded people who not only identify their sexual orientation as gay but also support and understand 'alternative' sexualities. MAS's main aim is to create a space, both intellectual and emotional, where various 'alternative' issues of sexuality and sexual being are discussed to bring a sense of dignity to all.

2   Rohan's physical appearance is described to illustrate by contrast the stereotype of modern gay identity in Bombay; the dominant social view of the homosexual male in India is effeminate and submissive. Moreover, the gradual ethnographic reading in this chapter highlights how gay identity in Bombay is widely related to the same stereotypical Western perception of the homosexual. This sexual identification adds to the different meanings of masculinity and male sexual identity based on the cosmopolitan social climate of Bombay.

3   The 'Saturday meeting' that Rohan mentioned is their monthly meeting held every second Saturday of the month.

4   Jagjit Singh was a famous Indian classical singer renowned for his *ghazal*s. He is often called the 'king of *ghazal*s'. *Ghazal*s are lyrical poems set to music, a popular genre in the Indian subcontinent and the Middle East; the songs are slow and rhythmic, and the lyrics have deep philosophical meanings.

5   The principal slogan of the Bombay's gay pride parade was 'Queer Azadi'. *Azadi* is an Urdu word (also used in Hindi) which means freedom and emancipation.

6   In 2009, the Delhi High Court ruled Section 377, which was a colonial law, as 'anti sodomy' Act. This law indirectly referred to same-sex acts and relationships between two consenting adults as illegal. But under Article 21 of the Indian Constitution, Section 377 violates the right to privacy and personal liberty. Four judgment benches were setup in 2009 with several rounds of back-and-forth for nearly two decades, when Naz Foundation Trust, New Delhi, filed a petition to the Delhi High Court to decriminalize Section 377 in the early 1990s.

Subsequently, in 2009, the Delhi High Court ruled that Section 377 cannot be used to punish sex between two consenting adults.

7   Emblematic costumes relate to a sense of 'colour' signifying gay parades. This further constitutes a symbol of celebration – a celebration of sexual otherness. 'Colour' also represents a global unification of gay identities, linked to a global protest for a particular political cause.

BIBLIOGRAPHY

Allen, K. R., and D. H. Demo. 1995. 'The Families of Lesbians and Gay Men: A New Frontier in Family Research'. *Journal of Marriage and Family* 57(1): 111–127.

Ammaturo, F. R. 2015. 'The "Pink Agenda": Questioning and Challenging European Homonationalist Sexual Citizenship'. *Sociology* 49(6): 1151–1166.

———. 2016. 'Spaces of Pride: A Visual Ethnography of Gay Pride Parades in Italy and the United Kingdom'. *Social Movement Studies* 15(1): 19–40.

Anjaria, J. S. 2009. 'Guardians of the Bourgeois City: Citizenship, Public Space, and Middle-class Activism in Mumbai'. *City and Community* 8(4): 391–406.

Appadurai, A. 1996. *Modernity at Large: Cultural Dimensions of Globalization.* Minneapolis: University of Minnesota Press.

———. 2001. 'Deep Democracy: Urban Governmentality and the Horizon of Politics'. *Environment and Urbanization* 13(2): 23–44.

Appadurai, A. and J. Holston. 1999. 'Cities and Citizenship', In *Cities and Citizenship*, edited by J. Holston, 1–16. Durham, NC: Duke University Press.

Ashcroft, B. 2011. 'Urbanism, Mobility and Bombay: Reading the Postcolonial City'. *Journal of Postcolonial Writing* 47(5): 497–509.

Banerjee-Guha, S. 2002. 'Shifting Cities: Urban Restructuring in Mumbai'. *Economic and Political Weekly* 37(2): 121–128.

———. 2009. 'Neoliberalising the "Urban": New Geographies of Power and Injustice in Indian Cities'. *Economic and Political Weekly* 44(22): 95–107.

Baviskar, A., and R. Ray (eds.). 2011. *Elite and Everyman: The Cultural Politics of the Indian Middle-classes.* New York and London: Routledge.

Beck, U. 2002. 'The Cosmopolitan Society and Its Enemies'. *Theory, Culture and Society* 19 (1–2): 17–44.

Bell, D., and J. Binnie. 2004. 'Authenticating Queer Spaces: Citizenship, Urbanism and Governance'. *Urban Studies* 41(9): 1807–1820.

Benedicto, B. 2008. 'Desiring Sameness: Globalization, Agency, and the Filipino Gay Imaginary'. *Journal of Homosexuality* 55(2): 274–311.

Bertone, C. 2013. 'Citizenship Across Generations: Struggles Around Heteronormativities'. *Citizenship Studies* 17(8): 985–999.

Bhabha, H. 1998. 'Anxiety in the Midst of Difference'. *POLAR: Political and Legal Anthropology Review* 21(1): 123–137.

Binnie, J., J. Holloway, S. Millington and C. Young (eds.). 2016. *Cosmopolitan Urbanism*. London and New York: Routledge.

Boellstorff, T. 2005. *The Gay Archipelago: Sexuality and Nation in Indonesia*. Princeton: Princeton University Press.

———. 2007. 'Queer Studies in the House of Anthropology'. *Annual Review of Anthropology* 36: 17–35.

Bose, B., and S. Bhattacharyya (eds.). 2007. *The Phobic and the Erotic*. New Delhi: Seagull Publications.

Boyce, P. 2007. 'Conceiving Kothis: Role, Agency and Anthropology in the Construction of Male-to-Male Sexualities in India'. *Medical Anthropology* 26 (2): 175–203.

Brewis, J., and G. Jack. 2010. 'Consuming Chavs: The Ambiguous Politics of Gay Chauvinism'. *Sociology* 42(2): 251–268.

Brickell, C. 2000. 'Heroes and Invaders: Gay and Lesbian Pride Parades and the Public/Private Distinction in New Zealand Media Accounts'. *Gender, Place and Culture* 7(2): 163–178.

Brighenti, A. 2007. 'Visibility: A Category for the Social Sciences'. *Current Sociology* 55(3): 323–342.

Broad, L. K. 2002. 'Social Movement Selves'. *Sociological Perspectives* 45(3): 255–290.

Broad L. K., S. L. Crawley and L. Foley. 2004. '"Doing Real Family Values": The Interpretive Practice of Families in the GLBT Movement'. *Sociological Quarterly* 45(3): 509–527.

Brosius, C. 2010. *India's Middle Class: New Forms of Urban Leisure, Consumption and Prosperity*. New Delhi: Routledge.

Browne, K. 2007. 'A Party with Politics? (Re)making LGBTQ Pride Spaces in Dublin and Brighton'. *Social and Cultural Geography* 8(1): 63–87.

Burns, K., and C. Davies. 2009. 'Producing Cosmopolitan Sexual Citizens on the L Word'. *Journal of Lesbian Studies* 13(2): 174–188.

Cappellato, V., and T. Mangarella. 2014. 'Sexual Citizenship in Private and Public Space: Parents of Gay Men and Lesbians Discuss their Experiences of Pride Parades'. *Journal of GLBT Family Studies* 10(1–2): 211–230.

Cattan, N., and A. Vanolo. 2014. 'Gay and Lesbian Emotional Geographies of Clubbing: Reflections from Paris to Turin'. *Gender, Place and Culture* 21(9): 1158–1175.

Chatterjee, P. 2004. *The Politics of the Governed: Reflections on Popular Politics in Most of the World*. New York: Columbia University Press.

Corbridge, S., and J. Harriss. 2000. *Reinventing India: Liberalization, Hindu Nationalism and Popular Democracy*. Cambridge: Polity Press.

Dossal, M. 2007. 'Locality, Power and Identity in Bombay City'. *Economic and Political Weekly* 42(52): 38–41.

Fadaee, S. 2014. 'India's New Middle Class and the Critical Activist Milieu'. *Journal of Developing Society* 30(4): 441–457.

Fernandes, L. 2006. *India's New Middle Class: Democratic Politics in an Era of Economic Reform*. Minneapolis: University of Minnesota Press.

——— (ed.). 2018. 'Conceptualizing the Post-Liberalization State'. In *Feminists Rethink the Neoliberal State: Inequality, Exclusion, and Change*, edited by L. Fernandes, 1–31. New York: New York University Press.

Fernandes, L., and P. Heller. 2006. 'Hegemonic Aspirations: New Middle Class Politics and India's Democracy in Comparative Perspective'. *Critical Asian Studies* 38(4): 495–522.

Field, T. L., and G. Mattson. 2016. 'Parenting Transgender Children in PFLAG'. *Journal of GLBT Family Studies* 12(5): 1–17.

Ghertner, D. A. 2012. 'Nuisance Talk and the Propriety of Property: Middle Class Discourses of a Slum-free Delhi'. *Antipode* 44(4): 1161–1187.

Gilman, S. 1998. *Making the Body Beautiful: A Cultural History of Aesthetic Surgery*. Princeton: Princeton University Press.

Goodman, D., and R. Robinson. 2013. *The New Rich in Asia: Mobile Phones, McDonald's and Middle Class Revolution*. New York and London: Routledge.

———. 2009. 'Neoliberal Subjectivity, Enterprise Culture and New Workplaces: Organised Retail and Shopping Malls in India'. *Economic and Political Weekly*. 44(22): 45–54.

Graham, M. 1998. 'Identity, Place and Erotic Community Within Gay Leather Culture in Stockholm'. *Journal of Homosexuality* 35(3–4): 163–183.

Guarin, A., and P. Knorringa. 2014. 'New Middle-class Consumers in Rising Powers: Responsible Consumption and Private Standards'. *Oxford Development Studies* 42(2): 151–171.

Gupta, C. 2001. *Sexuality, Obscenity and Community: Women, Muslims and the Hindu Public in Colonial India*. New Delhi: Permanent Black.

———. 2002. '(Im)Possible Love and Sexual Pleasure in Late-Colonial North India'. *Modern Asian Studies* 36(1): 195–221.

Halberstam, J. 2003. 'What's That Smell? Queer Temporalities and Subcultural Lives'. *International Journal of Cultural Studies* 6(3): 313–334.

———. 2005. *In a Queer Time and Place: Transgender Bodies, Subcultural Lives*. New York: New York University Press.

Hansen, T. B. 2001. *Wages of Violence: Naming and Identity in Postcolonial Bombay*. Princeton: Princeton University Press.

Harvey, D. 2005. *A Brief History of Neoliberalism*. Oxford and New York: Oxford University Press.

Inda J. X., and R. Rosaldo (eds.). 2002. *The Anthropology of Globalization: A Reader*. Malden, MA: Blackwell.

Johnstone, B. 2000. 'The Individual Voice in Language'. *Annual Review of Anthropology* 29: 405–424.

Kehily, M. J., and A. Nayak. 2008. 'Global Femininities: Consumption, Culture and the Significance of Place'. *Discourse Studies in the Cultural Politics of Education* 29(3): 325–342.

Khandekar, A. 2013. 'Education Abroad: Engineering, Privatization, and the New Middle Class in Neoliberalizing India'. *Engineering Studies* 5(3): 179–198.

King, K. R. 2007. 'Global Gay Formations and Local Homosexualities'. In *A Companion to Postcolonial Studies*, edited by H. Schwarz and S. Ray, 508–519. Hoboken, NJ: John Wiley and Sons.

Kong, S. T. 2002. 'The Seduction of the Golden Boy: The Body Politics of Hong Kong Gay Men'. *Body and Society* 8(1): 29–40.

Leahy, M. 2013. 'Ulrich Beck's Cosmopolitanisation Thesis: A Philosophical Critique'. *Australian Journal of Political Science* 48(2): 152–163.

Low, M. 2016. *The Sociology of Space: Materiality, Social Structures and Action*. New York: Palgrave Macmillan.

Lundberg, A. 2010. 'Journeying Between Desire and Anthropology: A Story in Suspense'. *Australian Journal of Anthropology* 11(1): 24–41.

Misgav, C., and L. Johnston. 2014. 'Dirty Dancing: The (Non)Fluid Embodied Geographies of a Queer Nightclub in Tel Aviv'. *Social and Cultural Geography* 15(7): 730–746.

Monro, S. 2005. *Gender Politics: Citizenship, Activism and Sexual Diversity*. London: Pluto Press.

Mythen, G. 2013. 'Ulrich Beck, Cosmopolitanism and the Individualization of Religion'. *Theory, Culture and Society* 30(3): 114–127.

Ngai, P. 2005. *Made in China: Women Factory Workers in a Global Workplace*. Durham, NC, and London: Duke University Press.

Orlie. M. A. 2002. 'The Desire for Freedom and the Consumption of Politics'. *Philosophy of Social Criticism* 28(4): 395–417.

Patterson, C. J. 2000. 'Family Relationships of Lesbians and Gay Men'. *Journal of Marriage and Family* 62(4): 1052–1069.

Peck, J. 2011. 'Neoliberal Suburbanism: Frontier Space'. *Urban Geography* 32(6): 884–919.

Pow, C-P. 2009. 'Neoliberalism and the Aestheticization of New Middle-class Landscapes'. *Antipode* 41(2): 371–390.

Rantanen, T. 2005. *The Media and Globalization*. London and New Delhi: SAGE Publications.

Reid, G. 2003. '"It Is Just a Fashion!" Linking Homosexuality and "modernity" in South Africa'. *Etnofoor* 16(2): 7–25.

Schindler, S. 2013. 'The Making of 'World Class' Delhi: Relations Between Street Hawkers and the New Middle Class'. *Antipode* 46(2): 557–573.

Shah, S. P. 2015. 'Queering Critiques of Neoliberalism in India: Urbanism and Inequality in the Era of Transnational "LGBTQ" Rights'. *Antipode* 47(3): 635–651.

Shugart, H. 2008. 'Managing Masculinities: The Metrosexual Movement'. *Communication and Critical/Cultural Studies* 5(3): 280–300.

Sinha, M. 1995. *Colonial Masculinities: The 'Manly Englishman' and the 'Effeminate Bengali' in the Late Nineteenth Century*. Manchester: Manchester University Press.

Sridharan, E. 2004. 'The Growth and Sectoral Composition of India's Middle Class: Its Impact on the Politics of Economic Liberalization'. *India Review* 3(4): 405–428.

Tan, C. K. K. 2015. 'Spaces of Pride: A Visual Ethnography of Gay Pride Parades in Italy and the United Kingdom'. *Social Movement Studies* 15(1): 1–22.

Varma, R. 1998. 'Uncivil Lines: Engendering Citizenship in the Postcolonial City'. *NWSA Journal* 10(2): 32–55.

———. 2004. 'Provincializing the Global City: From Bombay to Mumbai'. *Social Text* 22(11): 65–89.

Vicziany, M., and J. Bapat. 2009. 'Mumbadevi and the Other Mother Goddesses in Mumbai'. *Modern Asian Studies* 43(2): 511–541.

Weeks, J. 1985. *Sexuality and Its Discontents: Meanings, Myths, and Modern Sexualities*. London: Routledge.

8

Postscript

In light of the discussion thus far, the book echoes Martin Heidegger's mediation on the essence of modern technology, presenting a reflection on the concept of bio-power and biopolitics. Heidegger's posthumously published *Beiträge zur Philosophie* (*Contributions to Philosophy*, 1999), written between 1936 and 1938, suggests a critique of the metaphysics of modernity. Heidegger's discussion on machination, or 'machenschaft', refers to 'making' (*poesis*, *techne*), which further relates to the concept of 'being' as 'makeable', or more precisely, self-making. Heidegger's modernity is inclined to *machenschaft*, or in other words, objectification and subjectification of beings, submitting to the illusive attempt at technological nihilism. This quest for understanding human life further allows the establishment of the study of the subculture – involving a new conception of knowledge, practice and 'truth'. Foregrounding this ordering of life, modern self-empowering subjectivity, or Michel Foucault's regulation of the life of the population that constitutes 'bio-power', is immanent within the history of Western political rationality (Sinnerbrink 2005; see also Joronen 2012). However, Giorgio Agamben rejects Foucault's historical analysis of bio-political governmentality, arguing instead that bio-power exercised over 'bare life' discloses the 'inner truth'. But in examining this connection of bio-power and totalitarianism, Agamben seeks to analyse the fundamental political problem of modernity that understands the intimate relationship between 'sovereign power' and 'bare life'. For Agamben, the norm in modern political rationality has exposed the 'sovereign violence' to the biological existence and 'political control' of one's life (Lechte 2013: 58; Oksala 2010).

So, in this work, rather a critique, I try to uphold the 'sovereign model of power' that re-inscribes bio-power within the crucial logic of bio-politics and the development of modern capitalism. In other words, 'politicization' manifests a critical account of the neoliberal governmentality of the body's control and bio-political affinities that are grounded in the dynamics of corporeal life.[1] I also seek to delineate the ontological position of one's own desire. Understanding the nexus of desire and the bio-political management of life is the symbiosis between the nihilism of 'machination' as appropriated by Heideggerian direction and the realization of living beings in the metaphysics of the subjective consciousness as the site of social subjection. Guattari and Negri (1990: 14–16), deterritorialize the productive composition of a machine as 'the machinic liberation of desire' – a site for revolutionary transformation. Therefore, 'desire' is the coordination of multiple causes as emerging in a complexity that captures and crystallizes a set of signifiers (Guattari 1992: 38).

In doing so, the book transposes the interaction between the multiplicity of forces that determine the meaning and complexity of universalized sexual representations.[2] In other words, the object of desire is a constructed image, or performativity, that builds on a symbolic transcendental signifier. That is to say, these displacing representations are a liberation of the form of a desiring body that participates in machinic functioning. 'In becoming', desire occupies a 'feeling' that constitutes an affectual aspect of subjective interiority – desire dissipates the ordinary and individuates an entity in itself. In this piece of work, 'desire' involves the constitution of multiple affective interplays in 'becoming' – indicating the possibility of sexual multiplicities. The lived corporeality acquires subjective fascination in expressing the trajectories of subjectivity: the feminine or female. Thus, 'becoming' is the spectacular 'outside'; the significant 'outside' characterizes the deterritorialization of implicit sexual presuppositions, which are bounded by language and law. Further, this conjunction of deterritorialization connects a polymorphous representation of the body's exterior, as well as interior.[3]

Again, the management of desire and its affectual imperative resists authoritative bio-political embodiments, criss-crossing the sovereign interventions in individuals' life-engineering and their gendered self. Within this framework, an immanent position of transcendence points to the revolutionary materialist interpretation of the self. From a Freudian–Lacanian psychoanalytic metapsychology, such transcendence relates to the ontogenetic emergence of 'the being' – situating it within a symbolic order. The redefinition mediates an integrated organic foundation which is more than material subjectivity, advancing re-ontologized appearances that operate between self-consciousness, spatiotemporal experience and reflective acquaintance (Perelló and Biglieri 2012; Gilford 2016). At this juncture, material transcendence is non-articulable, signifying open possibilities of multiple reflexive autonomous subjectivities. In this light, what it presents is the emergence of an exceptional moment of 'becoming' – feminine or to-be-woman – that runs into the transitory capacities of cultural embodiments, seamlessly constituted in riddles and conflicts.

The plurality of values and the particular type of political engagement that ensure both individuals and collectives are regarded as sovereign gender(ed) citizens, must be acknowledged. Hence, the democratic public life and personal space in cosmopolitan Bombay lay emphasis on diversity and difference – resonating with the social expression of 'difference' through multiple, yet interconnected narratives of sexual subcultures. Drawing attention to otherwise silent and marginalized voices within contemporary cosmopolitan Bombay enriches the debate on truly critical frames of reference that disavow the rhetoric of modernity. This task of re-inscribing the order to disrupt the totalitarian impulse of the global design of Western modernity as well as emancipatory ideals that justify imperialism – the underlined representations – strongly bases an anti-essentialist standpoint which recognizes gendered experiences differently with reference to class, race, sexuality, identity, space, faith and location. The recognition of these intersectionalities means addressing the complex interplay of dialogic spaces anchored within the desiring horizons of emotions. Quite significantly, Leshkowich and Jones (2003) refer to 'homogenized heterogeneity' that appropriates the 'difference' and transforms the contours of cosmopolitan fantasies as suggested by consumerist ideology. The fantasies again are regulated by a class structure. That is to say, this study identifies the intense and ambivalent desires embedded in practices of cosmopolitan consumption – its materiality reinstates an aesthetic engagement, inciting the commodifying logic of capitalism.[4]

Also, the book attempts to undo the already-given narratives and to break free from harbouring aesthetic and affective dimensions of sexual otherness in the city spaces of Bombay. Conceiving the aesthetic and emotional reflections of these subcultures – the articulation of varied festivities, as well as their participation in and embodiment of varied public cultures – frames a pivotal analysis of their sociability and critical potential. Further, the etymological meaning of aesthetics sees an emerging configuration of translocal deterritorialized ensembles based on embodied localism as well as internationalism.

The book therefore expresses a discursive mode of sexual subjectivity; the materiality of the body foregrounds a new bio-political regulation that could potentially influence de-subjectification for a new kind of self-fashioning. What could also be related here is Foucault's (1981) delineation of bio-power and the management of the population. Foucault's classical governmentality includes the exercise of discipline over bodies – an 'anatomo-politics' or biopolitical regulation of a population, or self-formation through 'ethical care of the self' (Foucault 1981: 139; see also Scott 1990; Bartky 1997). But Dean's (1994) governmentality for the self-formation of subjects relates to political subjectification created by 'political' reasons. Therefore, what is meant by 'governmentality' here is a technical attempt to render aspects of conduct that further reinforce its rationale with specific and differentiated norms. In other words, governmentality is enmeshed with a complex matrix of rationalities and practices that seeks to embody technologies of perceptibility and subjecthood (Elden 2005). Thus, the embodied project as appropriated is a piece of work that fosters the efficacy of different modes of corporeal ordering (governmentality) through new regulatory and disciplinary mechanisms.

Staples (1997) talks about the 'new economy of discipline' of the body, trying to draw on the new techniques delineated by the technological space. The modern totalizing aspect of technology accounts for increasing 'disciplinary consciousness' by mindful 'watching' (Mathiesen 2010; see also Elmer 2003; Simon 2004). In other words, the perceptible lens is focused on an increasing surveillance – analysing how bodies undergo surveillance through technological networks that governmentality builds for bio-political vigilance, on the trajectories of technology-led inclusion and exclusion. Moreover, the technology is embodied; human subjects are consumed within the new sociality of a new situation of control. This socio-technical environment remarks the efficacy of the surveilling assemblage – the technological fetishism in the modern world implies constructed interpretations of categories and cultures (Ball 2009; Donaldson and Wood 2004; Graham and Wood 2006). The main argument that I want to put forward is to establish the importance of surveillance. '[S]urveillance is the determination of particular spaces and relationships to those spaces through categorization, boundary maintenance, observation and enforcement' (Elden 2007). Therefore, 'surveillance' reinvigorates an exclusionary model; a mode of social ordering of how gendered representations self-actualize and self-order the spatiotemporal specificities of the self. 'Technological embodiment' is thus a new exclusionary model that establishes a sign, a value, a subject, effacing local particularities. Technological governmentality reinstates a transcendentalist view of pre-given history – a new logic of multiple gendered representations, desires and aspirations that further informs a state of autonomous liberated subjects.

In this book, the discursive dispersion is in line with the renunciation of the identity category of subjects as a unitary, closed entity, hence building the possibility of pluralist recognition. The multiplicity of gendered representations and plurality of relations cannot be considered as a single gendered category. Within the new frontiers of consumer culture in contemporary Bombay, 'cosmopolitanism' thus realized is the multiplicity of social relations that embraces differentiation within the dimensions of the discursive construction of 'people'. 'People', as Laclau (2005: 85) argues, is an 'absent fullness', the plurality of subject positions that emerges as a transition from popular subjectivity. This book thus navigates the symbolic framework of 'gendering', a process of constant 'becoming'. 'People' for Laclau is the 'game of differential and equivalential articulation' so as to say differentiality is the characteristic discourse addressing the discursivity or the space of non-totality (Laclau 2005: 89).

'Gendering' in this book is an increasing emancipation of the order of a fixed gendered signifier. The transition, or the embodiments that it charts, builds experiences that are mediated through different modes of symbolization. A political logic to this heterogeneity is the moment of how gender is performed differently. This performative unevenness is the emerging rupture of an existing gendered order and, also, a space of un-ordering where there is radical discontinuity and an element of negation of any hegemonic project of gendered articulation. This reminds me of Antonio Gramsci's anti-essentialist approach to grasp the multiplicities of struggles against varied dominations (Jackson 2017). A political expression of this is what Chantal Mouffe (2018: 5) calls the 'anti-establishment movement'. Evoking such thought here tries to situate 'the values' of the manifold struggles against subordination that resonate with the aspirations of many. In common ground to the defence of equality is reaffirming an extension of democratic values that could also emerge within the democratic demands of a consumerist–capitalist space.

In the conjuncture of this totalizing moment, I certainly uphold the 'representative' character of the non-totality. In so doing, I render the moment of the constitution of 'people' and 'plurality' as the essence of representation. Again, the political moment of this plurality is 'the act': the foundation of the newness of what it establishes; a new order that marks the locus of the proliferation of the dialectics of differences. Essentially, what we see in this book is the logical subversion of a particular context or situatedness of a particular gendered order. Gender and gendering as evoked is a space of clear inconsistence. In other words, I uphold instances of these unstable and disparate essences that constitute the radical gendering essence. The assertion of such unevenness is the moment of transcendence – seemingly, no element is strongly overdetermined by the historical order of gender-corporeality. This moment of subversion that I want to establish from identarian politics to representational politics is a process of serious non-centrality of the material representation of gender. The premise of this considers a political war on singularity seen as open to contingent variations.

Conceptualizing these multiplicities, the book considers a constant process of corporeal negotiation that tries to build an agnostic space with dispersed embodying possibilities. Drawing on Mouffe's (2000) paradigm, this indicates the aesthetics of the 'political making' that is incongruent with the dominant consensus. Therefore, this representational critical juncture of the multiplicities of gendered bodies in Bombay installs an image and character of non-naming, revolutionized, desired imagery – creating a condition of self-inscription of total rupture from the existing order. 'Becoming' is thus the realization of self-engagement with the state and its representational institutions that characterizes the bio-political production conditioning the democracy of heterogeneity. Generating this cooperation is the development of cognitive capitalism.

Conceiving these plural engagements through manifold representations is a new egalitarian form of life in a cosmopolitan space. Instancing this further is the affective discursivity and the negotiation of belonging that construct the social. As Baruch Spinoza (Gatens 2000; Newland 2018: 8–10) shows, an act of transcendence through 'affect' is premised on the notion of thought rather than on the notion of materiality. And 'the thought' is allegiance to the creation of 'value' – a democratic individuality that acknowledges the different modes of allegiance to a passionate spur of desire, leading to specific action. Thus, the book ends saying that 'affect' and 'desire' connect the experiences evoked here, making us perceive new possibilities. Creating these conditions of radicalization is the key symbolic marker envisaging new frontiers of freedom and social justice.

DEATH AND THE SUNRISE

I end the book with the narrative of the death of a *hijra* for two reasons. First, it emphasizes the importance of 'desire' for every *hijra* who craves conjugal love from their *panthi*. Second, it is extremely rare for anyone, least of all an ethnographer, to be permitted to witness the death of a *hijra*. Therefore, this final narrative provides a rare and exclusive insight into a private matter.

'Silk Mummi guzar geye!' (Silk Mummi has died!) Silk Mummi, an elderly *hijra* in Malvani slum, passed away due to illness. The popular belief among the *hijras* was that she died because she had been suffering from an illness for a long time. Some *hijras* like Sruti, Madhu and others in the Sakhiyani office, who are community workers, said that she died because of HIV/AIDS. Dr Patil in the slum, and other doctors in government hospitals, confirmed that her health condition was poor and there was little chance of her recovering. Sruti further stated that she herself had taken the initiative to accompany Silk Mummi to hospitals for check-ups; sometimes she made her food and reminded her to take her medicine on time. Sruti did whatever she could to ensure that Silk Mummi stayed well.

I had visited Silk Mummi's house several times with Sruti. She was hospitable and always offered us tea and biscuits. Once she told me about her life, how she had come to Bombay as a young child, how she was abused and beaten by the owner of the roadside tea stall where she worked. After she joined the *hijra* community, she became *chela* (disciple) to one of the *gurus* (head of a *hijra* house), and after a year of her affiliation with the *hijra* community, she underwent castration; ever since then, she had stayed in Malvani slum. When she spoke about her love and emotions, her eyes filled with tears. She told us about her love for a man when she was a young *hijra*. Silk Mummi lived with the man for five years. She said that they used to live as *pati–patni* (husband–wife) – she cooked for him, washed his clothes, took care of household expenses, bought him gifts, and so on. In the end, however, the man took advantage of her; he deceived her by taking all her jewellery, money and other valuables. He left Silk Mummi and married a woman. Silk Mummi added that the man had once promised her that someday he would marry her, observing Hindu marriage rituals. While telling this story, she became more emotional and confessed that the man had once put *sindur* (vermilion) on her forehead: the Hindu symbol for a married woman. 'We are married in the eyes of God,' Silk Mummi confessed in a tearful voice.

A few days before her death, Silk Mummi had high fever; her body was covered in a rash, and she had spots on her face. During that time, Sruti regularly visited Silk Mummi to look after her. She was also taken care of by her neighbours who cooked food for her and took it to her home. Then Silk Mummi died. The news spread across Malvani slum. It was a Wednesday afternoon when I was visiting the Sakhiyani office. When I received the news about her death, I rushed towards her home and saw that *hijra*s had gathered around her shabby, one-room house, near the deep drain of the slum. Sruti said that the last rites would be observed following Islamic rituals. Silk Mummi changed her religion to Islam after she joined the *hijra* community. This process of converting to Islam is common among the *hijra*s as they believe that Islam, as a religion, is far more embracing of *hijra* identities than the Hindu religion and gives them respect.

The *maulana* (Muslim priest) arrived at her house. Sruti and other *hijra*s bathed the deceased for the last time. They then dressed her in a red *sari*, and put glass bangles on her arms, lipstick on her mouth and various ornaments on her body – necklaces and nose rings and, in fact, everything – to beautify her. It is a common belief among the *hijra*s that their death signifies the end of a sorrowful life and that the dead person should leave her home dressed as an Indian 'bride'. They hold the notion that after someone has died, it is time to start rejoicing and celebrating, because they believe in rebirth and that the new life will be full of happiness for the deceased. Dressing as a bride also symbolizes 'eternal marriage'. After she was dressed, the *maulana* and the other *hijra*s recited Islamic prayers in the presence of her body.

Silk Mummi had said that her final wish was that her *marad* (man) put *sindur* on her forehead. She had expressed this desire to her neighbours when she realized that she would not survive for long. At some stage, Silk Mummi had shown Mehru, her neighbour, where the man lived in the slum. Mehru asked some of the *hijra*s to accompany her to call the man. As they went in to his house, they found that he was ailing in bed. They told him about Silk Mummi's death. They requested him earnestly to fulfil her last wishes and pleaded with him to go with them. The man agreed, but because he was unwell, the *hijra*s hired a cycle-rickshaw (a public, two-seater form of transport, drawn by a bicycle) and brought him to Silk Mummi's house. On the way, they bought *sindur* from a shop.

The man walked with a stick and sat beside Silk Mummi. He took a pinch of *sindur* in his hand and put it on her forehead. Then he held her hand, cried intensely and asked for forgiveness, saying, 'Mujhe maaf kar deye, Silk, agar ho sakey to' (Forgive me, Silk, if possible). He wept so bitterly that the *hijra*s had to pull him back to allow the *maulana* and his (male) assistants to take the body to the burial ground.

The *maulana* said that the last rites would be performed considering her as a 'man'. All *hijra*s are buried in the same manner. He rationalized that as *hijra*s are born biologically male, they should be buried as males. They took her body to the nearest burial ground close to Aksa beach, which is not far from Malvani slum. *Janaza* (specific Islamic rites) was followed and *salah*s (prayers) were recited. As they walked, they chanted Islamic prayers: 'Inna Lillahi Wa Inna Ilayhi Raji'un' (Indeed to Allah We Belong and to Allah We Shall Return). The *hijra*s joined the funeral procession. Some of them were in tears while they walked, and some expressed their sorrow by saying' 'Woh bahut achhi thi' (She was [a] very good [person]).

After the burial, they sat on the beach for some time. It was dawn, and they could see a vendor selling tea at the corner of the road that ran alongside the beach. The *hijra*s bought themselves cups of tea. (At that time of day, the *chaiwala* [tea vendor] usually had fishermen as customers). The sun started to appear on the horizon in the east; reddish-yellow rays gradually spread across the entire sky. It was beautiful to watch the fishermen going out to sea in their boats for the day's catch. Women arrived from the nearby slums and hurriedly set up their vegetable stalls for the morning market. The *hijra*s walked back to Malvani slum. They were fatigued and drowsy from the funeral ceremony, but still performed their dress rituals and adorned themselves with jewellery and make-up for their relevant 'work' of the day – *badhai* (blessing), *mangti* (begging) and *pan* (prostitution).

NOTES

1   The consumption of modern technology and body modification is further related to the politics of 'perception' or visualization by which society perceives the newly formed body. This conception is based on how the body is presented and visualized, thus giving a 'cultural' meaning to its embodiment. As Anne Balsamo recalls, the body is perceived by society as a set of social standards based on looks, appearance, dress, performance, gendered expressions, and so on (Balsamo 1999: 13). This argument flows throughout the book, showcasing the fact that body dispositions are enhanced by public visibility and, in doing so, create the impression of its gendering.

2   To sum up, the period of globalization and the different ways of cultural and material consumption bring to the fore new ideas of the opportunities and technologies available by means of which gender liminal persons have re-represented themselves. Their sense of identification is enmeshed within the interlinkage between globalized culture and resources and the politics of consumption, establishing new senses of identities. At the same time, however, the reconfiguration of the new set of identities is linked to the old ways of their representation but a cosmopolitan remapping and emergence of universal styles of re-representation and cultural belonging. To emphasize further, the consumption of technology as part of the embodiment project by which these identities reconstitute their bodies illustrates an explicit sense of representation that intersects social class and cultural differences. My ethnography as illustrated talks about acts of subversion and new ways of representation – evoking perceptibility, embodiment, sustenance and occupation, interpersonal relationships, and the changing pattern of solidarities and movement. The elements of cosmopolitanism and the high degree of urbanization in Bombay evoke features of globalized modernity with new traits of communication, production, consumption and other political and cultural strategies that ultimately shape the contemporary non-normative sexual identities in the city.

3   Chris Shilling states that human bodies are always in a process of 'becoming', in the context of how bodies change and transform in bodily appearance (Shilling 2003: 6). This idea of 'becoming' indicates the construction of the body in relation to modernity and the consumption of material goods. Shilling argues that the body, in modern society, is influenced by a consumer-based culture and the market mechanism of commodity production. The mutable body reflects the constitution of new selves and identities through access to specialized medicines, surgical technologies, beauty therapies and other transformation

devices and procedures. As my ethnography shows, in Bombay, these processes of transformation are also linked to a form of 'sexed embodiment' – gender reassignment surgery (GRS) and hormonal therapy – in an endeavour to build a new gender identity.

4   There are interrelationships between space, gender and identity in the context of globalized modernity, while identities are in a constant process of movement (Ong and Peletz 1995: 9; Adkins 2002). These processes are related to the fluid flow of ideas, knowledge, culture and languages from one place to the other. In this context, the production of newly formed bodies is part of the cultural manifestation of modernity and emphasizes the link to a global, capitalist, political economy (Mills 1999). This trait of modernity is also seen in the 'locale' (a particular location in the Global South) that is further shaped by local and global characteristics to produce a discrete, cultural construction. As Nancy Duncan states, the cosmopolitan sophistication of a non-Western space is based on 'global localism', where, due to postcolonialism and economic urbanism, the space delivers its unique cultural trait that showcases 'global' as well as 'local' characteristics (Duncan 1996: 5).

BIBLIOGRAPHY

Adkins, L. 2002. *Revisions: Gender and Sexuality in Late Modernity*. Maidenhead, UK: Open University Press.

Ball, K. 2009. 'Exposure: Exploring the Subject of Surveillance'. *Information, Communication and Society* 12(5): 639–657.

Balsamo, A. 1999. *Technologies of the Gendered Body: Reading Cyborg Women*. Durham, NC, and London: Duke University Press.

Bartky, S. L. 1997. 'Foucault, Femininity, and the Modernization of Patriarchal Power', In *Feminist Theory Reader: Local and Global Perspectives* (5th edition), edited by C. Mccann, S-K. Kim and E. Ergun, 25–45. London and New York: Routledge.

Dean, M. 1994. '"A Social Structure of Many Souls": Moral Regulations, Government, and Self-Formation'. *Canadian Journal of Sociology* 19(2): 145–168.

Donaldson, A., and D. Wood. 2004. 'Surveilling Strange Materialities: Categorization in the Evolving Geographies of FMD Biosecurity'. *Environment and Planning D: Society and Space* 22(3): 373–391.

Duncan, N. (ed.). 1996. *Body Space: Destabilizing Geographies of Gender and Sexuality*. London and New York: Routledge.

Elden, S. 2005. 'The Problem of Confession: The Productive Failure of Foucault's "History of Sexuality"'. *Journal for Cultural Research* 9(1): 23–41.

———. 2007. 'Governmentality, Calculation, Territory'. *Environment and Planning D: Society and Space* 25(3): 562–580.

Elmer, G. 2003. 'A Diagram of Panoptic Surveillance'. *New Media and Society* 5(2): 231–247.

Foucault, M. 1981. 'History of Systems of Thought, 1979'. *Philosophy and Social Criticism* 8(3): 353–359.

Gatens, M. 2000. 'Feminism as "Password": Re-thinking the "Possible" with Spinoza and Deleuze'. *Hypatia* 15(2): 59–75.

Gilford, P. 2016. *Love, Desire and Transcendence in French Literature: Deciphering Eros.* London and New York: Routledge.

Graham, S., and D. Wood. 2006. 'Digitizing Surveillance: Categorization, Space, Inequality'. In *Surveillance, Crime and Social Control*, edited by C. Norris and D. Wilson, 537–558. London and New York: Routledge.

Guattari, F. 1992. *Chaosmosis: An Ethico-Aesthetic Paradigm.* Translated by Paul Bains and Julian Pefanis. Bloomington and Indianapolis: Indiana University Press.

Guattari, F., and A. Negri. 1991. *Communists like Us: New Spaces of Liberty, New Lines of Alliance.* Translated by M. Ryan. New York: Semiotext(e).

Heidegger, M. 2012 (1999). *Beiträge zur Philosophie (Contributions to Philosophy).* Translated by P. Emad and K. May. Bloomington: Indiana University Press.

Jackson, R. P. 2017. 'Antonio Gramsci: Persons, Subjectivity, and the Political'. In *Subjectivity and the Political*, edited by G. Rae and E. Ingala, 561–591. London and New York: Routledge.

Joronen, M. 2012. 'Heidegger on the History of Machination: Oblivion of Being as Degradation of Wonder'. *Critical Horizons* 13(3): 351–376.

Laclau, E. 2005. *On Populist Reason.* London and New York: Verso.

Lechte, J. 2013. *Agamben and the Politics of Human Rights: Statelessness, Images, Violence.* Edinburgh: Edinburgh University Press.

Leshkowich, A. M., and C. Jones. 2003. 'What Happens when Asian Chic Becomes Chic in Asia?' *Fashion Theory: The Journal of Dress Body and Culture* 7(3–4): 281–299.

Mathiesen, T. 2010. 'The Viewer Society: Michel Foucault's "Panopticon" Revisited'. In *Crime and Media: A Reader*, edited by Chris Greer, 506–521. London and New York: Routledge.

Mills, M. B. 1999. *Thai Women in the Global Labour Force: Consuming Desires and Contested Selves.* New Brunswick, NJ: Rutgers University Press.

Mouffe, C. 2000. *The Democratic Paradox.* London and New York: Verso.

———. 2018. *For a Left Populism.* London and New York: Verso.

Newlands, S. 2000. *Reconceiving Spinoza.* Oxford: Oxford University Press.

Oksala, J. 2010. 'Violence and the Biopolitics of Modernity'. *Foucault Studies* 10: 23–43.

Ong, A., and M. G. Peletz (eds.). 1995. *Bewitching Women, Pious Men: Gender and Body Politics in Southeast Asia*. Berkley and London: University of California Press.

Perelló, G. and P. Biglieri. 2012. 'On the Debate Around Immanence and Transcendence'. *Cultural Studies* 26(2–3): 319–329.

Scott, C. 1990. *The Question of Ethics: Nietzsche, Foucault, Heidegger*. Bloomington: Indiana University Press.

Shilling, C. 2003. *The Body and Social Theory*. London: SAGE Publications.

Simon, B. 2004. *Identity in Modern Society: A Social Psychological Perspective*. Malden, MA: Blackwell.

Sinnerbrink, R. 2005. 'From *Machenschaft* to Biopolitics: A Genealogical Critique of Biopower'. *Critical Horizons* 6(1): 239–265.

Staples, W. G. 1997. 'Foucault and Political Reason: Liberalism, Neo-liberalism, and Rationalities of Government by Andrew Barry, Thomas Osborne, Nikolas Rose (Review)'. *Contemporary Sociology* 26(5): 598–599.

Glossary

aadmi	man
abbu	father
Afghani *kurta*–pajama	two-part dress often stitched and worn by men in Afghanistan
ariyaal chissa	very handsome, a slang in *hijra* language
as-salamu aleykum	Islamic way of greeting
autorickshaw	three-wheeler passenger carrier
azadi	independence
baba	father or fatherly figure
badhai	blessings
beta	son
bhahar gaon	foreign land
bhai	brother; protector
bharatiya sanskar	Indian values or ethics
burkha	outer garment worn by Muslim women covering the entire body, with a veil over the face and a net eyepiece to see through
chaadar	holy cloth
chaadar chadhana	offering a piece of holy cloth
chaiwala	tea seller
chela	disciple, follower
chocolate	condom or contraceptive in *hijra* language
customar	customer, referred to clients for sex work

dargah	Islamic religious place for worship
dargah bazaar	shopping area around a *dargah*
dera	secluded place often used for unlawful activities
desi daru	country liquor
dhaba	low-budget eatery, highway-side eating place in South Asia
dhamni	breasts in *hijra* language
dhanda	occupation; sex work, begging or offering blessings in *hijra* language
Dilli	Delhi
dholak	drum
dudh	milk; breastmilk in *hijra* language
dupatta	scarf or stole worn by women in South Asia
gaand	buttocks
galli	lane
gandu	a derogative term for one who does not have a penile erection
ghagra-choli	a skirt (*ghagra*) worn with a blouse (*choli*) and a scarf or stole (*dupatta*)
gori	police in *hijra* language
hafta	week; slang for the protection money collected periodically by gangsters and corrupt policemen
Haji Malang	a mausoleum in the Kalyan district, near the city of Bombay
harami	bastard
harmones	hormones
hijra rewal	*hijra* language
jalsa	gathering for music and dance
jarat	the third day after the day of burial of a *hijra*
kabarsthan	graveyard
kachhe jhupri	temporary shanty houses
Kamatipura	sex-work zone or red-light district in Bombay
kameez	long knee-length shirt
kanun	law
khadim	Islamic religious priest
khel	game
khel khel mein	in play
khomat	oral sex in *hijra* language
kothi	effeminate homosexual man usually belonging to a lower economic section of society

maidan	field
mangti	begging in *hijra* language
marad	man
masti	fun
maulana	Islamic religious priest
mehfil	gathering; informal meet involving music and dance
mohalla	locality
namaz	the act of offering prayers in Islam
nayak	head of a *hijra* clan
nirvan	castration in *hijra* language
pan	sex work in *hijra* language
panthi	boyfriend, client or lover in *hijra* language
pati	husband
pati–patni	husband–wife
patni	wife
Phek	to throw
qawwali	Islamic songs and rhymes
raasta	path
saaxy	sexy, pronounced *saaxy* by *hijra*s and *kothi*s
sachi aurat	real woman
salwar kameez	a South Asian dress, comprising a long tunic, with usually half or full sleeves, and trousers that can be loose (*salwar*) or fitting (*churidar*)
sampurna	complete
sari	South Asian dress comprising a long, single piece of cloth draped over the body
sharam	shame; embarrassment
sindur	vermilion
Sufi	someone who believes in Sufism, a religious practice within Islam whose goal is to have a direct, personal experience of God
sufiyana	a cultural or devotional environment, known as *tasawwuf* in the Arabic-speaking world, a form of Islamic mysticism that emphasizes introspection and spiritual closeness with God
swaraj	self-governance
thelawala	rickshaw puller
transgenderism	an umbrella term for gender non-conforming individuals

transsexual	a person who has undergone medical treatment, such as surgery, to alter the sex they were assigned at birth
Urs	annual festival at an Islamic religious place
waater	buttock in *hijra* language
waater dhurana	anal intercourse in *hijra* language

Index